## Family, Law, and Inheritance in America

Yvonne Pitts explores inheritance practices by focusing on nineteenth-century testamentary capacity trials in Kentucky in which disinherited family members challenged relatives' wills. These disappointed heirs claimed that their departed relatives lacked the capacity required to write a valid will. These inheritance disputes crisscrossed a variety of legal and cultural terrains, including ordinary people's understandings of what constituted insanity and justice, medical experts' attempts to infuse law with science, and women's claims to independence. Pitts uncovers the contradictions in the body of law that explicitly protected free will while simultaneously reinforcing the primacy of blood in mediating claims to inherited property. By anchoring the study in local communities and the texts of elite jurists, Pitts demonstrates that the term *capacity* was laden with legal meaning and competing communal values about family, race relations, and rationality. These concepts evolved as Kentucky's legal culture mutated as the state transitioned from a conflicted border state with slaves to a developing free-labor, industrializing economy.

Yvonne Pitts is an assistant professor in the department of history at Purdue University. She received a Filson Fellowship at the Filson Historical Society in Louisville, Kentucky, and has been a fellow at the J. Willard Hurst Summer Institute in Legal History at the University of Wisconsin Law School. Dr. Pitts has been published in *The Journal of Women's History*.

## Cambridge Historical Studies in American Law and Society

**Series Editor**
Christopher Tomlins, *University of California, Irvine*

**Previously published in the series:**

David M. Rabban, *Law's History*

Kunal M. Parker, *Common Law, History, and Democracy in America, 1790–1900*

Steven Wilf, *Law's Imagined Republic*

James D. Schmidt, *Industrial Violence and the Legal Origins of Child Labor*

Rebecca M. McLennan, *The Crisis of Imprisonment: Protest, Politics, and the Making of the American Penal State, 1776–1941*

Tony A. Freyer, *Antitrust and Global Capitalism, 1930–2004*

Davison Douglas, *Jim Crow Moves North*

Andrew Wender Cohen, *The Racketeer's Progress*

Michael Willrich, *City of Courts, Socializing Justice in Progressive Era Chicago*

Barbara Young Welke, *Recasting American Liberty: Gender, Law and the Railroad Revolution, 1865–1920*

Michael Vorenberg, *Final Freedom: The Civil War, the Abolition of Slavery, and the Thirteenth Amendment*

Robert J. Steinfeld, *Coercion, Contract, and Free Labor in Nineteenth Century America*

David M. Rabban, *Free Speech in Its Forgotten Years*

Jenny Wahl, *The Bondsman's Burden: An Economic Analysis of the Common Law of Southern Slavery*

Michael Grossberg, *A Judgment for Solomon: The d'Hauteville Case and Legal Experience in the Antebellum South*

# Family, Law, and Inheritance in America

*A Social and Legal History of Nineteenth-Century Kentucky*

YVONNE PITTS
*Purdue University*

CAMBRIDGE
UNIVERSITY PRESS

CAMBRIDGE UNIVERSITY PRESS
Cambridge, New York, Melbourne, Madrid, Cape Town,
Singapore, São Paulo, Delhi, Mexico City

Cambridge University Press
32 Avenue of the Americas, New York, NY 10013-2473, USA

www.cambridge.org
Information on this title: www.cambridge.org/9781107035508



First published 2013

Printed in the United States of America

*A catalog record for this publication is available from the British Library.*

*Library of Congress Cataloging in Publication data*
Pitts, Yvonne.
Family, law, and inheritance in America: a social and legal history of nineteenth-century
Kentucky / Yvonne Pitts, Purdue University.
pages cm. – (Cambridge historical studies in American law and society)
Includes bibliographical references and index.
ISBN 978-1-107-03550-8 (hardback)
1. Inheritance and succession – Kentucky – 19th century.
2. Wills – Kentucky – 19th century. I. Title.
KFK1346.P58 2013
346.76905′209034–dc23 2012044901

ISBN 978-1-107-03550-8 Hardback

*To my family:*

*Those related by blood and those related by affection*

# Contents

# Tables, Figures, and Map

TABLES



FIGURES



MAP

# Acknowledgments

The cultural importance of inherited property first struck me when I was sitting in an airport on my way to a history conference during graduate school. A woman sitting across from me was on the phone, emotionally describing how she had found her late "Granny's crochet hook." She was gently holding this worn crochet hook as though it were a talisman imbued with the spirit and memory of her late grandmother. The hook itself was available in any craft store for a couple dollars. It occurred to me that the hook had taken on immense emotional value as a material symbol of the obviously close relationship she had with her grandmother. Of course, inherited property often has great monetary value and lacks the sentimental attachments of that particular crochet hook. I realized, though, that if I intended to write about the multiple historical meanings of inheritance, I had to look at inheritance practices as conveying more than material wealth. They transmitted all manner of familial affection, angst, and memories. That moment led me to think much more deeply about inheritance, not just as the transfer of wealth, but also as the transmission of a lifetime of emotions, ranging from fervent love to deep enmity.

This project began while I was in a seminar at the University of Iowa School of Law on "Gender and the Law," co-taught by my mentor and dissertation advisor, Linda K. Kerber, and Patricia Cain, who became my second reader on my dissertation. I owe Linda Kerber an enormous debt of gratitude for her insightful guidance, her encouragement, and her support. Linda's scholarship was revelatory for me, but it is her remarkable kindness and generosity to aspiring young scholars I will not forget. Patricia Cain patiently led me through the law of wills, ever reminding me that good legal history demands good legal training. I also wish to thank the other members of my dissertation committee: Allen Steinberg, Leslie Schwalm, and Douglas Baynton. Sarah Hanley and Susan Lawrence read drafts and offered valuable comments. Sharon Romeo and Heather Kopelson offered important insights through a supportive reading group in graduate school. James Mohr was kind enough to read an early version of Chapter 3 and offer comments and insight. Laura Edwards, Barbara Welke, and Diane Miller Sommerville have inspired me through their scholarship and gave valuable comments at early stages of the project at various conferences. I am certain that I never would have made it to the PhD program at the University of Iowa without my first mentor and my dear friend, Sandra VanBurkleo, at Wayne State University. Growing up in a neighborhood on the edge of Detroit where many of us were the first generation to attend college did little to prepare me for the challenges of advanced study in graduate school. When I arrived at Wayne State clad in combat boots and a tie-dyed shirt, Sandra saw something I was unaware I possessed and nurtured it with immense patience. She introduced me to the world of ideas and to legal history. She is a brilliant scholar, a talented artist, and a compassionate and empathic person. My life would have been much different without her influence.

I owe a great debt to many of my wonderful colleagues at Purdue University, especially Caroline Janney. She is a very dear friend, colleague in the best sense of the word, and a rigorous scholar for whom I have great admiration. She read through numerous drafts, pushed me to think about why Kentucky has an important legal history to tell, and has talked me off several ledges, sometimes late at night, always with humor. I also wish to thank Mike Morrison, Alicia Decker, Nancy Gabin, and John Larson, all whom have given me valuable support. I was fortunate enough to have a pre-tenure leave at Purdue University and was awarded a Library Scholars Grant that allowed me valuable research and writing time. Erica Cornelius Smith worked as a research assistant and spent many hours sifting through and scrupulously coding the original wills into a clean dataset, which she then helped me analyze. Her expertise in data analysis has made this project much better.

I have admired the scholarship of Chris Tomlins since I first read it in graduate school, and his work continues to provoke and challenge my thinking. To work with him as the series editor has been an absolutely amazing experience. This project is undoubtedly much better for his comments and direction. I also owe a debt of gratitude to Abby Zorbaugh at Cambridge University Press for her patience and good nature. I have had the good fortune to work with several dedicated archivists. A Filson Fellowship allowed me to access the world-class collections at the Filson Historical Society in Louisville, Kentucky. I did extensive work at the Kentucky Department for Libraries and Archives, assisted by its able staff and archivist Jim Prichard. In 2005, I had the benefit of participating in a wonderful scholarly community at the J. Willard Hurst Summer Institute of Legal Studies at the University of Wisconsin School of Law in Madison, Wisconsin. I also thank the editors at the University of Missouri Press for permission to reprint my substantially revised essay, "'I Desire to Give My Black Family Their Freedom': Manumissions, Inheritance, and Visions of Family in Antebellum Kentucky," which appeared in Angela Boswell and Judith McArthur, eds., (*Women Shaping the South: Creating and Confronting Change* (Columbia: University of Missouri Press, 2006).

There are those too who have influenced this project in immeasurable, invaluable ways, although some of them have no idea what testamentary capacity is or why I have been obsessed with it for so long. Marla Hurst, Lynnette Grays, and Merrie "Maddog" Daniels have supported me through some very difficult moments. My brother, Bill Pitts, sister-in-law Diana Pitts, and their beautiful children, Kayla, Gracie, and Will reminded me to eat lots of ice cream and to go outside. My aunt and uncle, Joe and Pat Pitts, have never wavered in their support. My father Bill Pitts's quiet intelligence and my mother Helen Pitts's unconditional support inspire me still. Without their encouragement and love, I would not have completed this project. My mother did not live to see the end of this project, but she always had more faith than I that it would get done. I miss her terribly still. I met Michelle Rhoades, my partner of more than a decade, at a friend's house in graduate school. Michelle is a talented scholar, a formidable chef, a wonderful raconteur, and I am grateful to share in her love and passion for life. She and our son Robert remind me daily of all the beautiful, magical things in life that cannot be found in a book.

# Introduction

In 1858 at the Trigg County, Kentucky courthouse, William Miller described his deceased sister Jane Miller as "naturally a woman of very strong mind and of more than ordinary intelligence but in her latter years her mind had become greatly weakened by her long continued bodily infirmity."[1] Miller appeared in court because he was involved in a will dispute – a testamentary capacity challenge – over his sister's last wishes concerning her property. Jane Miller had behaved like many other testators (people who wrote wills) in leaving much of her estate to her brother Josiah and his family. She simultaneously deviated from conventional inheritance practices by disinheriting her other siblings and emancipating her slaves. Her disinherited heirs tried to overturn her will, claiming that Jane Miller's weakened mind allowed her chosen beneficiaries to inappropriately influence her decisions. In the language of the law, they claimed that Miller lacked testamentary capacity and wrote her will under the undue influence of her beneficiaries, including the slaves she manumitted. While disputed wills make up a small portion of all wills submitted for probate, these cases reveal a critical juncture where legal conceptions of free will, family, and the limits of the "privateness" of property meet.

In the American legal system, inheritance has traditionally bound families together through property transfers while exposing conflicts over legitimacy, authority, and social and sexual behavior. It reveals the uneasy coexistence of two elements of American social and legal practices in

[1] "Testimony of William H. Miller," Transcript, *Sarah v. Miller* (1864), Case 74, Box 3, Kentucky Court of Appeals Records (hereafter KCAR), Kentucky Department for Libraries and Archives, Frankfort, Kentucky (hereafter KDLA).

the nineteenth century. The first was a much older, deeply rooted preference for shared blood as a conveyor of social identity, legal status, and rights.[2] Traditional inheritance, dating back into the mists of Americans' English past, dispersed wealth through a patriarchal legal structure that favored male descendants over female descendants. Even bastardy and poor laws demonstrated the importance of determining blood relation, if only to deny inheritance rights and assign paternal financial responsibility.[3] The second element was the impulse toward individual autonomy and contractual rights, which began to eclipse the primacy of blood.[4] Testamentary freedom, with its attendant right to disinherit bloodline heirs, had its statutory roots in the sixteenth century and reflected the nascent coherence of the values that would develop into liberal individualism. It allowed responsible individuals to express their sense of morality and familial justice and acknowledged that factors such as affection, retribution, or obligation (to individuals, churches, or other institutions) might impose debts upon testators that blood did not.

In the lives of nineteenth-century Americans who wished to dispose of their property, writing a will was much more than a singular act undertaken in the last years of one's life. Rather, many family members participated in testamentary decision making, all with different motivations and opinions on the moral rectitude of the testator's choices. The result of this process, the will, was – and still is – often subjected to the scrutiny of the community through the probate procedures, legal challenges, and neighborhood gossip networks. The legal challenges to wills on the ground of lack of capacity (testamentary capacity cases) are the subject of this book.

From Shakespeare's King Lear to Doris Duke, each generation has its cautionary tales about inheritance disputes, depicting family relations

[2] For a study that illustrates the importance of blood and legal ties, see Carolyn Earle Billingsley, *Communities of Kinship: Antebellum Families and the Settlement of the Cotton Frontier* (Athens: University of Georgia Press, 2004).

[3] James Ely, Jr., "'There Are Few Subjects in Political Economy of Greater Difficulty': The Poor Laws of the Antebellum South," *American Bar Foundation Research Journal* 10 no. 4 (Autumn 1985): 869–72.

[4] On the importance of blood and legal relations as determinative of rights, see Amy Dru Stanley, *From Bondage to Contract: Wage Labor, Marriage and the Market in the Age of Emancipation* (New York: Cambridge University Press, 1998); Peter Bardaglio, *Reconstructing the Household: Families, Sex and the Law in the Nineteenth Century South* (Chapel Hill: University of North Carolina Press, 1995); Michael Grossberg, *Governing the Hearth: Law and the Family in Nineteenth Century America* (Chapel Hill: University of North Carolina Press, 1985).

gone awry, casts of alienated heirs, designing lawyers, and decedents of questionable sanity. National headlines dramatize the importance of inheritance. Recent examples include the salacious suit over the inheritance left to Hollywood personality Anna Nicole Smith by her elderly oil baron husband, and the dispute over New York philanthropist Brooke Astor's will, replete with accusations of elder abuse, dementia, and forgery. Nineteenth-century Americans breathlessly watched their share of inheritance dramas, like the tawdry, often vicious, public unfolding of disputes over the wills of Cornelius Vanderbilt and Caroline Fillmore, the widow of President Millard Fillmore. During the process of writing wills and dispersing property, inherited property becomes inscribed with cultural and symbolic values that sometimes far exceed its economic value. Whether a thimble collection or a family mansion, these items become symbols of years of family history.

How and why does inherited property, a legal fiction at its core, become laden with social and cultural values that both reflect and inflect our notions of familial order? Intergenerational property transfers link relationships in the intimate familial realm to the public, legal, and economic worlds. According to eighteenth-century English jurist William Blackstone, testamentary freedom made a man "a good citizen," allowed him to punish "heirs disobedient and headstrong," and let testators provide for "the exigence of their families."[5] Whether decedents transferred property through a will, according to intestate laws, or informally among family members, inherited property publicly encoded value judgments about relationships between individuals.

When testators reached their "dead hands" from the grave to continue controlling their property, they did so because they met a legal standard of mental capacity.[6] William Miller's testimony about his sister Jane highlights the tensions and contradictions in this standard. He probably derived his assertion of her "more than ordinary intelligence" from his assumptions about women's innate abilities within a hierarchy of fixed, gendered values. He referred to her perceived mental decline in tandem with her physical deterioration, marking her physical body as an external indicator of her internal mental strength. Other witnesses told stories that spanned forty years, describing Jane Miller's young adulthood

[5] William Blackstone, *Commentaries on the Laws of England, Book the Second* (Oxford: Clarendon Press, 1775), 11–12.

[6] The image of the "dead hand" has been associated with wills and trusts for centuries. See Lawrence M. Friedman, *Dead Hands: A Social History of Wills, Trusts, and Inheritance Law* (Stanford: Stanford University Press, 2009).

and giving their opinions as to how her political and religious beliefs may have influenced her will-making decisions. Neighbors described her strange appearance and erratic behavior, which they believed indicated her mental unsoundness. Others portrayed her as perhaps a bit eccentric, but a pious, intelligent, and morally scrupulous woman. The multiple depictions of the same woman reveal how ordinary people had a range of ideas about mental unsoundness and sanity. They also believed they could pass judgment of the rectitude of testators' wills because these decisions affected people they knew in the local community. Trial witnesses believed they had some propriety over other community members' testamentary decisions, evinced in strongly opinionated testimony and by their willingness to state whether they thought the will was just.

The formal practices of inheritance law – publicly reading and recording wills, determining intestacy division, transferring of the deceased's property to heirs and beneficiaries – shaped how families understood their most intimate relationships. Testamentary capacity trials made public complex issues involving responsibility and obligation within families and local communities. Although the family was often depicted as a bedrock institution, in reality families were fragile, requiring maintenance through legal oversight and social regulation. Inheritance served as one such mechanism. Behind the seemingly strict legal formalism of inheritance law lay all manner of cultural conflict. Although states' laws differed, especially concerning married women's testamentary rights, all states shared a goal of making post-mortem property transfers uniform and predictable. In spite of legislative and judicial efforts to realize these goals, local legal practices also provided opportunities for litigants in will challenges to challenge or even subvert those values the statutes or judiciary sought to strengthen.

Historians have written extensively about inheritance.[7] Social historians have availed themselves of the benefits of probate records, which

[7] Hendrik Hartog, *Someday All of This Will Be Yours: A History of Inheritance and Old Age* (Cambridge: Harvard University Press, 2012). James Mohr, *Doctors and the Law: Medical Jurisprudence in Nineteenth Century America* (New York: Oxford University Press, 1993); James Mohr, "The Paradoxical Advance and Embattled Retreat of the 'Unsound Mind': Evidence of Insanity and the Adjudication of Wills in Nineteenth Century America," *Historical Reflections* 24 no. 3 (1998): 415–35; Susanna Blumenthal, "The Deviance of the Will: Policing the Bounds of Testamentary Freedom in Nineteenth Century America," *Harvard Law Review* 119 (2006): 959–1034. See Bardaglio, *Reconstructing the Household*; Brenda E. Stevenson, *Life in Black and White: Family and Community in the Slave South* (New York: Oxford University Press, 1996); Nancy Bercaw, *Gendered Freedoms: Race, Rights and the Politics of the Household in the Delta,*

county court clerks carefully preserved because they recorded property transactions. Much of the older scholarship on inheritance took quantitative approaches, often applying data from probate records in the service of broader studies on property, family life, and wealth distribution.[8] In the 1980s, women's historians delved into the history of inheritance to help elucidate the slow progression of married women's property laws and the struggles for women's equality.[9] Inheritance law likewise has been central to historians of the South who have explored how antebellum testamentary practices disrupted slavery by exposing the contradictions between recognizing slaves' humanity and their legal definition as property.[10] All of these studies recognize, rightly so, that inheritance is about power.

*1861–1875* (Gainesville: University Press of Florida, 2003); Carole Shammas, *A History of Household Government in America* (Charlottesville: University of Virginia Press, 2002). Most studies deal with wills written in Northern states and counties, and many focus on colonial New England or the Early Republic.

[8] See, for example, Lee J. Alston and Morton Owen Shapiro, "Inheritance across Colonies: Causes and Consequences," *The Journal of Economic History* 44 no. 2 (June 1984): 278; Richard Chused, "Married Women's Property and Inheritance by Widows in Massachusetts: A Study of Wills Probated between 1800 and 1850," *Berkeley Women's Law Journal* 2 (Fall 1986): 42–88; Carole Shammas, Marylynn Salmon, and Michael Dahlin, *Inheritance in America from Colonial Times to the Present* (New Brunswick and London: Rutgers University Press, 1987); David E. Narrett, *Inheritance and Family Life in Colonial New York City* (Ithaca: Cornell University Press, 1992); Mary Louise Fellows, "Wills and Trusts: The Kingdom of the Fathers," *Law and Inequality: A Journal of Theory and Practice* 10 no. 1 (Dec. 1991): 137–62; Suzanne Lebsock, *The Free Women of Petersburg: Status and Culture in a Southern Town, 1784–1860* (New York: W.W. Norton & Co., 1984); Marvin B. Sussman, Judith N. Cates, and David T. Smith, *The Family and Inheritance* (New York: Russell Sage Foundation, 1970); Joan Hoff, *Law, Gender, and Injustice: A Legal History of U.S. Women* (New York: New York University Press, 1991).

[9] Fellows, "Wills and Trusts: The Kingdom of the Fathers"; Chused, "Married Women's Property and Inheritance by Widows in Massachusetts"; Shammas, Salmon, and Dahlin, *Inheritance in America from Colonial Times to the Present*; Marylynn Salmon, *Women and the Law of Property in Early America* (Chapel Hill: University of North Carolina Press, 1986); Lebsock, *The Free Women of Petersburg*.

[10] Arthur F. Howington, "'Not in the Condition of a Horse or an Ox': *Ford v. Ford*, the Law of Testamentary Manumission, and the Tennessee Courts's Recognition of Slave Humanity," *Tennessee Historical Quarterly* 34 no. 3 (1975): 249–65; Adrienne D. Davis, "The Private Law of Race and Sex: An Antebellum Perspective," *Stanford Law Review* 51 (January 1999): 221–88; Yvonne Pitts, "'I Desire to Give My Black Family Their Freedom': Manumissions, Inheritance, and Visions of Family in Antebellum Kentucky," 50 – 73, in Angela Boswell and Judith McArthur, eds., *Women Shaping the South: Creating and Confronting Change*. Columbia: University of Missouri Press, 2006; Bernie D. Jones, *Mixed Race Inheritance in the Antebellum South* (Athens: University of Georgia Press, 2009).

## LEGAL NARRATIVES AND EVIDENCE OF LAW

This study draws on two methodological approaches, each associated with a distinct evidentiary base, each producing a distinct narrative of the nature of legal change in general and the development of testamentary capacity jurisprudence in particular. In the first, historians scrutinize what Robert Gordon has called "mandarin" law, or the texts produced by legal elites, a category that included state high court and federal judges, treatise writers, prominent jurists, law professors, and state and federal lawmakers. These historians analyzed how law shaped political and economic structures, how constitutional doctrine and appellate case developed, and how market capitalism and legal liberalism emerged.[11] Gordon saw virtue in using these texts because they are "among the richest artifacts of legal consciousness" and represent the "most rationalized and elaborated legal products."[12]

This rationalization and elaboration was itself a goal for the early nineteenth-century legal elites. Many jurists believed that law should be, as treatise writer Tapping Reeve was purported to say, a "science ... a regular well-compacted system."[13] In the early days of the American republic, this scientific rationalism, a product of the Enlightenment, when translated into legal practices, provided a powerful tool for protecting the newly articulated rights held by American citizens. It also structured and justified how courts and legislatures assigned rights and legal disabilities through a hierarchy determined by sex, race, and property ownership. If this rationalism in law led to enlightened justice, its shortcomings were made apparent when two areas of law conflicted with each other. One such area was the contradiction between laws that defined slaves as

[11] See, for example, John Phillip Reid, *Rule of Law: The Jurisprudence of Liberty in the Seventeenth and Eighteenth Centuries* (Dekalb: Northern Illinois University Press, 2004); William Novak, "Law, Capitalism, and the Liberal State: The Historical Sociology of James Willard Hurst," *Law and History Review* 18 no. 1 (Spring 2000): 97–146; Morton Horwitz, *The Transformation of American Law, 1780–1860* (Cambridge: Harvard University Press, 1979).

[12] Robert Gordon, "Critical Legal Histories," *Stanford Law Review*, 36 no. 1/2, Critical Legal Studies Symposium (January 1984): 120. Gordon's point in 1984 was that the new critical legal historians would use mandarin texts but also look beyond them to other sources of law.

[13] Timothy Dwight, *Travels in New England and New York* (London: W. Baynes and Son, 1823), 4, 295, quoted in Howard Schweber, "The 'Science' of Legal Science: The Model of the Natural Sciences in Nineteenth-Century American Legal Education," *Law and History Review* 17 no. 3 (Fall 1999): 421.

property in most legal constructions but also as persons in other areas.[14] Inheritance law revealed such a contradiction, which was drawn from competing values at the core of the legal system. It recognized free will *and* moral obligations to others.

Historian Susanna Blumenthal has written a "doctrinal story" of testamentary capacity jurisprudence in which she finds that by the end of the nineteenth century, appellate judges were hesitant or "conservative" in affirming findings of testamentary incapacity, seeking instead to guard expressions of "human autonomy."[15] Jurists became disillusioned with medical experts' increasingly influential trial testimonies and research findings, which were based in a medical determinism that too often found testators insane. The very notion of free will came under assault. After their predecessors revealed the problems with applying efficient legal rules based in medical and legal science, late nineteenth-century mandarin writers came to terms with "apparently perverse wills precisely because of their doubts … and because of the value they placed on the idea of human freedom."[16] This acceptance augured the development of the turn-of-the-century modernism that informed the thinking of legal pragmatists and legal realists. The intellectual history of law need not embrace an overly deterministic evolutionary functionalism in explaining change over time. Jurists ceded the advantages of medical experts' efficiency and scientism to a much messier and less coherent application of legal rules to protect testamentary freedom and the legal concept of free will. As Blumenthal has argued elsewhere, mandarin texts remain a vital, if overlooked, element of the conglomerate sources of law.[17]

Another group of historians shifted the scope from case law and panorama of doctrine to the microcosm of the local. These historians approached law as unfolding daily through gritty confrontations far removed from the rarefied seminar rooms and sedate judicial chambers where elites debated the "rule of law." Historian Ariela Gross has termed this approach "cultural-legal history."[18] These historians show

[14] Ariela Gross, *Double Character: Slavery and Mastery in the Antebellum Southern Courtroom* (Princeton: Princeton University Press, 2000).

[15] Blumenthal, "The Deviance of the Will," 1199.

[16] Ibid., 1034.

[17] Susanna Blumenthal, "Of Mandarins, Legal Consciousness, and the Cultural Turn in US Legal History," *Law and Social Inquiry* 37 no. 1 (Winter 2012): 167–86.

[18] Ariela Gross, "Beyond Black and White: Cultural Approaches to Race and Slavery," *Columbia Law Review* 101 (April 2001): 644. Gross was not the first scholar to advocate using this sort of approach, which drew from the work of law and society historians and critical legal scholars. For a discussion of the roots of this approach, see Hendrik

how outsiders and dependents influenced legal change by focusing on the myriad sites where law happened every day: taverns, streets, brothels, kitchens, slaves' quarters, newspapers, and county courtrooms.[19] Legal history and ordinary people's interactions with law looked much different from this perspective. By viewing trials as competing narratives or performances, these historians laid bare the seemingly irreconcilable social and cultural tensions that often receded into the background in mandarin texts. Law was a way for ordinary people to both claim and destabilize authority, and a lens through which they envisioned their relations to people and objects.[20]

Integrating these two approaches to the doctrinal and the local reveals the moral and legal complexity of inheritance practices and testamentary capacity jurisprudence. From this vantage point, it becomes clear that the legal and social practices of inheritance reverberated through an American society that placed high value on wealth and status acquisition. Laura Edwards has demonstrated the insights this methodological integration yields in *The People and Their Peace: Legal Culture and the Transformation of Inequality in the Post-Revolutionary South*.[21] She unmasks the operation of localized law that was "virtually undetectable" in histories focused on mandarin texts. Edwards reveals the existence

Hartog, "Snakes in Ireland: A Conversation with Willard Hurst," *Law and History Review*, 12 no. 2 (Autumn 1994): 370–90; William E. Forbath, Hendrik Hartog, and Martha Minow, "Legal Histories from Below," *Wisconsin Law Review* (July/August 1985): 759.

19 Scholars employing these new approaches to legal sources include: Steven Wilf, *Law's Imagined Republic: Popular Politics and Criminal Justice in Revolutionary America* (New York: Cambridge University Press, 2010); Gross, *Double Character*; Walter Johnson, *Soul by Soul: Life inside the Antebellum Slave Market* (Cambridge and London: Harvard University Press, 1999); Laura F. Edwards, *Gendered Strife and Confusion: The Political Culture of Reconstruction* (Urbana: University of Illinois Press, 1997); Laura F. Edwards, "Law, Domestic Violence, and the Limits of Patriarchal Authority in the Antebellum South," *The Journal of Southern History* 65 no. 4 (1999): 733–70; Diane Miller Sommerville, *Rape and Race in the Nineteenth Century South* (Chapel Hill: University of North Carolina Press, 2004); Barbara Welke, *Recasting American Liberty: Gender, Race, Law and the Railroad Revolution, 1865–1920* (Cambridge: Cambridge University Press, 2001); Joshua Rothman, *Notorious in the Neighborhood: Sex and Families across the Color Line in Virginia, 1787–1861* (Chapel Hill: University of North Carolina Press, 2003).

20 Some of the most recent and exciting historiographical interventions are discussed in "*Symposium Issue:* 'Law As...' Theory and Method in Legal History," *UC Irvine Law Review* 1 no. 3 (September 2011).

21 Laura F. Edwards, *The People and Their Peace: Legal Culture and the Transformation of Inequality in the Post-Revolutionary South* (Chapel Hill: University of North Carolina Press, 2009).

of idiosyncratic yet powerful legal processes grounded in maintaining "the peace," a set of values that placed communal interests over those of individuals. "The peace" worked through the interdependency of all community members, rather than gaining its legitimacy through values based in a discourse of individual rights. Law was organic but still distributed power through dominant/subordinate relationships such as master/slave and husband/wife. Eventually, state law came to dominate legal narratives after a concerted effort by legislators and jurists to eradicate localized law's influence. Their focus on protecting property rights led them to develop a much more visible body of rationalized state law grounded in individual rights as an antidote to inchoate legal localism. Eventually, this state law prevailed, while legal localism remained hidden as archival echoes of an earlier world view.

This study seeks to build on evidentiary methods elucidated by Edwards and others, which examine mandarin texts as separate from and in contentious conversation with localized law.[22] Law was, as Christopher Tomlins has argued, a "modality of rule" shot through society.[23] Placing local legal texts (defined broadly to include popular, ephemeral, and extralegal sources) alongside and contrapuntally to doctrine and appellate case law reveals new insights into both categories. Although distinct, the boundaries between mandarin and localized law were permeable, each accruing values from the other. Inheritance law had its own version of "the peace," balancing a concern for doing justice to testators' family members and heirs with an equal and eventually dominant preoccupation with protecting the semblance of testators' free will. By the turn of the twentieth century, the legal process of testation had become standardized, with lawyers' and layman's manuals containing elaborate instructions, forms, and warnings about potential legal hazards.[24] This systemization of inheritance law emerged in part because of the persistence of bloodline inheritance as an ideal even as the post–Civil War legal regime embraced a deep commitment to individual rights as the guardians of liberty. Disinheriting bloodline heirs was risky business even for the most resolute testators, and formality and systemization offered some protection.

22 Susanna Blumenthal has written an excellent essay describing this development in "Of Mandarins, Legal Consciousness, and the Cultural Turn in US Legal History."

23 Christopher L. Tomlins, *Law, Labor, and Ideology in the Early American Republic* (New York: Cambridge University Press, 1993), esp. chapter one, 19–34.

24 See, for example, G. A. Gaskell, *Gaskell's Compendium of Forms, Educational, Social, Legal and Commercial* ... (Chicago: Standard Publishing, 1889), which had four versions of wills in which testators could insert the appropriate information.

Even as the formalization demanded by state law eventually triumphed, localized law never completely disappeared.[25] Elements remained, insinuated into legal digests through case law that elaborated on the meaning and application of formalized legal tests for testamentary capacity. Litigants drew on both the formalist law expressed in treatises and appellate court decisions and localized law in will challenges. When necessary, they argued in terms of a strict, formalist legal understanding of capacity to demonstrate that at the moment of writing the will, testators met or failed these established legal tests. At other times, and sometimes in the same cases, litigants advanced their claims by drawing on a much more expansive understanding of capacity grounded in their interpretations of years of familial history. In some areas of testamentary capacity law, localized law ran parallel to and converged, only to separate again from its mandarin counterparts as it developed across time. For example, testators who manumitted or left property to slaves faced allegations of insanity from unhappy heirs in a legal climate that made all manumissions increasingly difficult by mid-century as sectional tensions grew. Still, testators resolutely continued to manumit slaves until the Civil War. This commitment to recognizing African American beneficiaries in spite of legal barriers in state law and possible capacity challenges was followed by white testators' overwhelming repudiation of naming African American beneficiaries after emancipation even though state law no longer made such devises so difficult. In these intervals between localized law and state law, capacity was defined.

Capacity itself was a concept crucial to localized, state, and even constitutional law. It determined how much and under what conditions individuals could participate in their communities and how the American legal system distributed rights. Capacity was and is antecedent to political, social, and legal participation. Almost every debate in American history over the exercise or expansion of legal rights included lengthy discussions about whether a particular group possessed the capacity or rationality to execute the right. Suffrage, property rights, access to education, and jury service for women and African Americans serve as

[25] Edwards makes this point when discussing the nature and presentation of claims made by freed people in the aftermath of the Civil War. Edwards, *The People and Their Peace*, 286–98. In inheritance law, this persistence of localism was ensured less by external legal or constitutional events than by the intractable problems inherent in applying a universal legal standard of capacity.

prominent examples.[26] Individuals' self-sovereignty sprang from their rationality. John Locke wrote in *On Civil Government*, "The freedom … of man, and liberty of acting according to his own will, is grounded on his having reason."[27] This appeal to free will appeared in many cultural incantations. Religious tenets drawn from the Second Great Awakening and even the secular philosophy of Ralph Waldo Emerson, a reaction to the Enlightenment, championed the virtues of free will. The unschooled frontiersman trumpeted by Jacksonian Democrats had "common sense." Throughout the nineteenth century, those desiring expanded rights, particularly African Americans and women, argued that they had the capacity to exercise those rights just as citizens (usually white males) who already exercised those rights did.[28] For at least three centuries, lack of capacity has also been a central plank in arguments to deny rights to individuals or groups.

Focusing on one area of law – testamentary capacity law – brings the contrapuntal dynamic between localized and mandarin law into sharp relief. Testamentary capacity jurisprudence demonstrates that the process of state-level legal systemization happened in fits and starts across the nineteenth century. For example, the evolution of women's testamentary jurisprudence deviated significantly from the overall tenacity of legal localism in mental capacity challenges. Most states mirrored Kentucky in their early statutory codes by defining the capacity to write a will as anyone over age twenty-one and "being of sound mind and not a married woman."[29] These statutes separated legal capacity from mental capacity. While the "sound mind" (mental capacity) requirement derived its early meanings largely through localized law, the jurisprudence surrounding

[26] Linda K. Kerber, *No Constitutional Right to Be Ladies: Women and the Obligations of Citizenship* (New York: Hill and Wang, 1999).

[27] John Locke, *Second Treatise of Government*, C. B. McPherson, ed. (Indianapolis and Cambridge: Hackett Publishing Company, 1980).

[28] Nancy Isenberg, *Sex and Citizenship in Antebellum America* (Chapel Hill: University of North Carolina Press, 1998), 23–5; Jacob Katz Cogan, "Note: The Look Within: Property, Capacity, and Suffrage in Nineteenth-Century America," *Yale Law Journal* 107 (November 1997): 473–98. Political historians have studied capacity as part of consent theory embodied in Enlightenment and Lockean political thought. See Holly Brewer, *By Birth or Consent: Children, Law, & the Anglo-American Revolution in Authority* (Chapel Hill: University of North Carolina Press, 2005); John Dunn, "Consent in the Political Theory of John Locke," *The Historical Journal* 10 no. 2 (1967): 153–82; Jimmy Casas Klausen, "Room Enough: America, Natural Liberty, and Consent in Locke's Second Treatise," *Journal of Politics* 69 no. 3 (2007): 760–9.

[29] 1797 Kentucky Acts, Ch. 180 § 1.

married women's testamentary capacity (legal capacity) was formalized and formulaic early on.

In challenges to a testator's "sound mind" or mental capacity, juries sometimes ignored judges' instructions on the letter of the law. Before rendering opinions, juries and witnesses weighed the claims of disinherited heirs and the beneficiaries, taking an approach at odds with the formal legal focus on individual testators' mental states. Juries returned verdicts inconsistent with existing rules in appellate case law or rejected medical or statutory definitions of mental unsoundness. At the appellate level, judges sometimes deferred to these jury verdicts, creating seemingly erratic case law. Such opinions sometimes cited key community members' local knowledge of the testator as the basis for their ruling. For example, in an 1834 case, the appellate court quickly dispensed with the allegation of Molly Yates's mental unsoundness, noting that the will's draftsman and subscribing witnesses were men of "respectability, intelligence."[30] Through the late nineteenth century, local definitions of mental capacity and insanity continued to infuse the application of state law through its absorption in case law. Legal digests summarizing existing statutory and case law were rife with notes on cases that had created exceptions, elucidated specific circumstances, and offered guidance on how to interpret the "sound mind" requirement.[31] This phenomenon of the infusion of the local into the application state law resulted from what Blumenthal has identified in her study of testamentary capacity and doctrine: the difficulty in applying a technical legal test to ascertain sanity, coupled with the ultimate unknowability of testators' mental states.

The evolution of *legal* capacity, based on the testator's status and situationality, tells the opposite story from that of *mental* capacity. It became systematized, rights based, and inflexible early on at the local and state level. In the statute, "being of sound mind" was followed by "not a married woman," which delineated the legal capacity to write a will. This standard excluded the majority of adult women in the nineteenth century.[32] By virtue of sex, women were aberrant testators. They had to meet a legal standard for capacity dependent on their marital status and

[30] *In re Yates Will*, 32 Ky. 215 (1834).

[31] See, for example, C. S. Morehead and Mason Brown, *A Digest of the Statute Laws of Kentucky, of a Public and Permanent Nature... With References to Judicial Decisions, Vol II* (Frankfort: Albert G. Hodges, 1834). These digests and statutory guides were published regularly throughout the nineteenth century.

[32] Numerous exceptions existed in practice and in law. These are discussed in depth in Chapter 5.

a masculine standard of mental capacity dependent on socially inscribed behavior and appearance. When any woman wrote a will, the two parts of the capacity requirement mutually defined a juridical and social context that inherently cast suspicion on her ability to control property.

Challenges to testators' legal capacity generated scores of trials across the nineteenth century, in part because female testators who wished to evade common law rules drew from a parallel, but no less byzantine system of equity rules. The jurisprudence of legal capacity hewed to formalized rules that were consistently enforced in appellate and local courts in a way jurists never embraced for mental capacity. Under common law, married women's inability to write wills emanated from the doctrine of coverture, which subsumed women under their husbands' legal identity. Kentucky Court of Appeals Judge Boyle echoed eighteenth-century English jurist William Blackstone when he held in 1811 that "In legal contemplation, the very existence of the wife is merged in that of the husband. So completely is she identified with him, that for all civil purposes she is deemed to have no will of her own."[33] Equity, summarized in the maxim *ubi jus ib remedium* ("where there is a right, there must be a remedy"), created provisions under which married women could make wills in specific, limited circumstances, most often by having a separate estate created. Under equity rules, women had testamentary rights not recognized under common law. Testators, disinherited heirs, and beneficiaries made claims drawing on equity and statutory law to establish or refute married women's testamentary capacity.

With so many contradictory claims based in arcane legal technology, uniformity and clear applicability was paramount. Beginning in mid-century, states' legislatures began adding statutes to carve out spaces for married women's testation. For judges and lawyers who argued these cases, determining legal capacity required technical knowledge of case law, statutory changes, and equity law. After that, the issue of capacity was a question of making arguments about whether an individual testator was within those legal boundaries. Mental capacity challenges played out differently but were equally complex, as they required sensitivity to particular local circumstances, a need to reconcile contradictory legal imperatives at the state level, and a willingness to divine the inner workings of testators' minds.

The juridical test for mental capacity was premised on the assumption that testators accepted an obligation to recognize the primacy of shared

[33] *Crostwaight v. Hutchinson*, 5 Ky. 407 (1811).

blood. When disinherited heirs took wills to court claiming that testators were "insane," judges instructed juries to measure testators' mental states against a three-pronged legal test that has remained almost unchanged. To write a valid will, testators needed only (1) to have sufficient capacity to comprehend the extent and condition of their property, (2) to recognize the "natural objects of their bounty," and (3) to have a fixed purpose in mind when dividing their property.[34] This test was deceptively simple. The ability to recognize the "natural objects of his bounty" meant that testators were required to acknowledge their bloodline heirs. Children required recognition. As the Kentucky Court of Appeals judges reasoned in 1856, if the testator "had sufficient capacity to dispose of his estate in a rational manner, he must necessarily have had capacity enough, not only to know his children, but also to understand his obligations to them as a parent."[35] Testators who failed to indicate that they knew the "natural objects of their bounty" risked having their wills overturned. Some testators deliberately left children they wished to exclude from their estate one dollar to fulfill the legal requirement of recognition. Testator Elijah Moore made sure to identify all his children, although he left two daughters who were "in affluance [*sic*] and worth more than us all I will them only one dollar each."[36] Other relationships, including marriage, did not require the same explicit recognition as part of the capacity test.[37] The mental capacity standard melded blood to property. Once testators recognized their heirs, the mental capacity standard was lower than most other legal acts involving property and consent, such as signing a contract. As influential treatise writer Isaac Ray noted in 1838, the mental capacity to write a will did "not require the same degree of intelligence as the administration of property."[38] The standard remained low in terms of its technical interpretation throughout the century. Prominent New York attorney Jacob Shrady's often reprinted 1897 essay on mental unsoundness advocated that if testators had any understanding "at all, and be

[34] See *Den v. Vancleve*, 5 N.J.L. 589 (1819). For a Kentucky version of this test, see *In re Reed's Will*, 41 Ky. 79 (1841), in which the Court of Appeals notes that a testator "had a settled purpose for many years," recognized his children, albeit unequally, and identified all portions of his estate.

[35] *Tudor v. Tudor*, 56 Ky. 383 (1856).

[36] "Will of Elijah Moore" (1885), Harrison County Will Book L, 302–3, Harrison County Court Clerk Records, KDLA.

[37] Testators' wives received a dower share regardless of formal acknowledgment in wills. Widowers under most circumstances received an estate by courtesy.

[38] Isaac Ray, *A Treatise on the Medical Jurisprudence of Insanity* (Boston: Charles C. Little and James Brown, 1838), 130.

not an absolute idiot, totally deprived of reason, he is the lawful disposer of his own property."[39] When applied in local and appellate courts, the testamentary capacity standard became a malleable category open to interpretation, in which "capacity" could be mobilized as a behavioral sanction.

When witnesses testified about testators' capacity to write a will, competing trial narratives emerged, which articulated values about property, familial obligations, and inheritance. Across geography and time, certain images consistently reappeared, such as the worthy, often needy heir unjustly wronged by the insane testator or the profligate child deserving disinheritance. This study locates these images in the legal values that gave them specific form and substance. It documents an ongoing manufacture and implementation of a grammar of capacity. This grammar had its own vocabulary, internal syntax, and consistent structure that imputed meaning into the concept of "capacity." Judges, jurists, and individuals used the grammar of capacity to make distinctions about testamentary privileges when individuals' actions appeared procedurally sound but went beyond the pale of acceptable behavior.

Identifying this grammar of capacity as a coherent, longitudinal element of these disputes makes localized law more visible. Legal actors implemented the grammar of capacity to explain relationships between testators and their families. They articulated normative and prescriptive rules that determined the legal ability to participate fully in inheritance practices. Studying this grammar of capacity goes beyond its discursive value in exposing structures and values in inheritance practices. Testation was part of a legal process in which words made events happen. Writing a will often expressed testators' values, feelings about their families, and their sense of justice. Testator Henry Ackler wrote a will in which he distributed his estate evenly among his children, except for his daughter, who received an additional $170 "for services rendered."[40] Ackler did two things: he recognized and then tangibly rewarded his daughter. Once probated, his words translated into economic gain for his daughter beyond that received by his other children. At the same time, they positively reinforced the narrative of the dutiful child serving her father.

39 Jacob Shrady, "Mental Unsoundness as Affecting Testamentary Capacity," *Medical Review of Reviews* (November 1897): 2.

40 "Will of Henry Ackler" (1853), Harrison County Will Book F, 576, Harrison County Court Clerk Records, KDLA.

This book explores the dialogues between local community members, county judges and juries, local physicians and medical experts, and appellate judges in Kentucky. The Court of Appeals' judges frequently acted as conservative brakes on emerging legislative and medical trends. (The Court of Appeals was Kentucky's highest court in the nineteenth century.) In the late 1860s, for example, the Court of Appeals appeared ready to accept "moral insanity" as a condition that precluded testators from writing valid wills. Poised to grant more weight to medical experts' testimonies in the mid-century, by the mid-1880s this trend reversed itself and the Court of Appeals judges made clear that they determined capacity and would impose a legal and not a medical standard. Broadly, their testamentary capacity jurisprudence over the nineteenth century indicates that they were committed to balancing the political and social imperatives of fostering stable family units against the republican promise guaranteeing white male independence through control over private property and dependents.

For men, the Court of Appeals's reluctance to accept new definitions of insanity or to expand women's capacity worked to protect their property rights. The threat of a mental capacity challenge to deviant wills also created an incentive for male testators to continue testating in patterns bounded by blood and custom. For women, the court's stolid defense of male testamentary privilege and its protection of marital unity meant that women's testamentary wishes were held to a double standard of legal and mental capacity, both positing the universal testator as a white male head of household. Women's sexual behavior, sanctioned as wives or scrutinized as single women, mattered greatly when witnesses and juries evaluated their ability to write a valid will even if they had legal capacity. Occasionally female testators prevailed, particularly when the Court of Appeals expressed skepticism about local juries and witnesses who overtly imposed their own judgments on testators. These cases reveal the localized and state law's competing values. For example, in *Ross v. Weaver* (1881), Robert Heard, a juror, commented that he believed Anne Cooke's estate "ought to go to her relations."[41] Testator Anne Cooke had disinherited her sister in favor of James Ross, her alleged paramour. Clearly, some community members believed that, by virtue of Anne Cooke's immoral conduct, her testamentary choices should be cancelled in favor of those sanctioned by the legislature and community. In this case, the appellate

[41] "Testimony of Robert Heard," in *Ross v. Weaver* (1881), Case 13247, Box 527, KCAR, KDLA.

court upheld Cooke's will and the broader principle of testamentary freedom against the perceived arbitrariness of local juries.

### THE BLOODLINE IDEAL: THE PERSISTENCE OF CONSANGUINITY

The custom of transferring property to legitimate bloodline heirs had precedents dating to the Magna Carta.[42] By 1285, the statute of *De Donis* permitted landholders to secure land to their families in perpetuity by a form of entail, which meant that it could not be transferred outside of the bloodline or away from "heirs of the body." Under English feudal law, primogeniture (inheritance by the eldest son) generally determined the succession of land, ensuring a stable, patriarchal system of property transmission between generations.[43] The legal doctrines of primogeniture and entail allowed the landed elite to retain their economic and political authority across time by keeping large estates intact. The male heads of these powerful families checked royal power because they had the means to challenge the crown through military or political power derived from their landed wealth.[44] Feudal practices made choosing beneficiaries outside of bloodlines very difficult. After the Norman Conquest, much of the common law defining kinship focused on determining inheritance and property rights through bloodline, but only when heirs descended from a marriage recognized in canon law.[45] Legitimacy and bloodline fused to create and define a claim on property. Historians and legal theorists have conducted a long-running debate about the definition of a property right.[46] When does an object, idea, entity, or person become "property" in addition to its physical or conceptual manifestation? Legal realist Morris Cohen defined a property right in 1927 as "a relation not between

[42] Shammas, Salmon, and Dahlin, *Inheritance in America from Colonial Times to the Present*, 42; Sussman, Cates, and Smith, *The Family and Inheritance*, 23.

[43] Mary Murray, *The Law of the Father: Patriarchy in the Transition from Feudalism to Capitalism* (London: Routledge Press, 1995), 58–9.

[44] Holly Brewer, "Entailing Aristocracy in Colonial Virginia: 'Ancient Feudal Restraints' and Revolutionary Reform," *The William and Mary Quarterly* 54 no. 2 (April 1997): 308.

[45] Sam Worby, *Law and Kinship in Thirteenth-Century England* (Woodbridge Royal Historical Society/Boydell Press, 2010), esp. chapter two.

[46] Stuart Banner, *American Property: A History of How, Why, and What We Own* (Cambridge: Harvard University Press, 2011), esp. chapter three; Jane B. Baron, "Property and 'No Property,'" *Houston Law Review* 42 no. 5 (January 2006): 1425–49; Gregory Alexander, "Dead Hand and the Law of Trusts in the Nineteenth Century," *Stanford Law Review* 37 no. 5 (May 1985): 1189–1266.

an owner and a thing, but between the owner and other individuals in reference to things."[47] Inherited property brings into sharp relief the legal complexity of this definition. In order to claim a right to inherited property through lineal descent, one had to establish a relationship to a person (the deceased) in order to possess the relationship to the thing (the inherited object or land).

While land by default followed the paternal bloodline, other legal devices such as *maritagium* and jointure ensured heirs of the wife (her children) would inherit and allowed the future exclusion of her husband's collateral heirs who were related by marriage and not blood.[48] These devices kept property brought to a marriage from the wife's father in her family's bloodline. *Mortmain* (literally the "dead hand") statutes, originally directed against the Catholic Church, further limited testamentary options by prohibiting testators from leaving land to corporations. Property owners had more freedom to will personal property such as livestock, jewelry, and currency to beneficiaries, although the law controlled some of its division under widows' rights (dower claims).[49] Even after property holders took advantage of the doctrine of common recovery developed in the fifteenth century to work around entails, freedom of testation remained caught in legal snarls. In 1540, Parliament passed the Statute of Wills, which granted limited rights of testation to male freeholders against the wishes of Henry VIII, who had pushed through the much more restrictive (and beneficial to the Royal Treasury) Statute of Uses five years earlier.[50] Indeed, inheritance was a hot political issue. In 1543, another parliamentary statute held married women's wills invalid, a legal condition later imported to the United States.[51] The requirement that the testator be of sound mind dates to a 1542 statute that declared invalid the wills of idiots and persons *de non sane*.[52] Of course, these rights had limited applicability, because they were almost exclusively confined to freeholding men. Debates over inheritance persisted; during the end of the sixteenth century, English jurists argued that the freedom

[47] Morris Cohen, "Property and Sovereignty," *Cornell Law Quarterly* 13 (1927): 12.

[48] Joseph Biancalana, *The Fee Tail and Common Recovery in Medieval England* (New York: Cambridge University Press, 2001), 7–8 and chapter three, "Living with Entails," 141–94.

[49] Carole Shammas, "English Inheritance Law and Its Transfer to the Colonies," *American Journal of Legal History* 31 no. 3 (April 1987): 146.

[50] John Malcolm William Beam, *The Decline of English Feudalism, 1215–1540* (Manchester University Press, 1967), 293–4.

[51] Fellows, "Wills and Trusts: The Kingdom of the Fathers," 137, n. 7.

[52] Statute 34 & 35 Henry VIII c. 5 § XIV.

to disinherit family would offer incentive for wives to remain faithful to husbands and children respectful toward fathers. Others argued that testamentary restraints were needed in order to protect surviving family members from pauperism.[53]

Early British North American colonists imported and then adapted inheritance practices to the new economic environments of each region. In the absence of a will, primogeniture remained the legal default in the Southern colonies, while the Northern colonies with the exception of New York and Rhode Island opted for a system of multigeniture or distribution among multiple bloodline heirs.[54] Some testators continued to entail property. Not until after the American Revolution did Southern state legislatures abolish primogeniture and entail, goaded by republicans like Thomas Jefferson who saw them as vestiges of the feudal aristocracy.[55] When lawmakers eliminated restrictions on disinheriting descendants, they made land more easily alienable in an economy rife with land speculators, many of whom were state legislators themselves. These changes did more than allow greater testamentary freedom. Revolutionary leaders framed them as incorporating the new republican ideal of self-sovereign citizens making virtuous choices about their property free from governmental interference. To their advocates, the changes in inheritance law brought together the values of the Revolution: private property, free will, and an enlightened recognition of civic and familial obligations.

By another measure, the practice of testation was deeply antirepublican. Much of the ideological fervor of the Revolution gushed from a rejection of inherited status, most closely associated with the king.[56] As Thomas Paine so colorfully noted, "One of the strongest natural proofs of the folly of hereditary right in Kings, is that nature disapproves it, otherwise she would not so frequently turn it into ridicule, by giving mankind an ass for a lion."[57] Inherited wealth and status, went the criticism, encouraged indolence and corruption. Early nineteenth-century radical

53 Shammas, Salmon, and Dahlin, *Inheritance in America from Colonial Times to the Present*, 26.

54 Alston and Shapiro, "Inheritance across Colonies," 278.

55 John Orth, "After the Revolution: 'Reform' of the Law of Inheritance," *Law and History Review* 10 no. 1 (Spring 1992): 33–44; Brewer, "Entailing Aristocracy in Colonial Virginia," 311.

56 Stanley Katz, "Republicanism and the Law of Inheritance in the American Revolutionary Era," *Michigan Law Review* 76 no. 1 (1977): 1–29.

57 Thomas Paine, *Common Sense* in *Common Sense, The Rights of Man, and Other Essential Writings*, edited with an introduction by Sidney Hook (New York: Penguin Books, 1984), 32–3.

labor reformer Thomas Skidmore argued that familial inheritance must be abolished to achieve real equality of opportunity in a democracy. In *The Rights of Man to Property* (1829), Skidmore railed against the permanent economic privilege conferred to certain groups through inherited property, arguing that wills "originated in wrong and usurpation" only to "curse the world in calamities."[58] He called for state redistribution of estates outside of deceased property owners' families. Almost a century later, in 1918, Progressive reformer Harlan Eugene Read proposed abolishing inheritance through taxes because of the social inequality undeserved wealth fostered.[59] Neither Skidmore's nor Read's radical visions gained much traction; they assaulted the liberalist equation of political independence with private property at the heart of much of the postrevolutionary political thought. Liberty was protected by secured property. The new nation moved toward a general inheritance law that granted male property owners greater testamentary rights over unencumbered land. Inheritance practices, for all their dynamism in the nineteenth century, had changed slowly in previous centuries. One value persisted through the political and legal tumults of the late eighteenth and nineteenth centuries; passing property through familial bloodline was and continued to be a powerful ideal in inheritance practices.

## KENTUCKY HISTORY AS AMERICAN LEGAL HISTORY

This study examines inheritance practices in nineteenth-century Kentucky. Rather than providing a picture of a provincial backwater, Kentucky's legal history represents the trajectory of much of the nation. As settlers pushed westward, Kentucky's legal culture mutated with the shifts from a frontier region, to a border/slave state, to a developing free-labor, industrializing economy.[60] Historians have recently renewed their interest in Kentucky, positioning it as crucial site where the nation's conflicting ideological and cultural loyalties were articulated and fought over. Recent scholarship approaches Kentucky as "America's crossroads," a vast middle

[58] Thomas Skidmore, *The Rights of Man to Property: Being a Proposition to Make It Equal among the Adults of the Present Generation, and to Provide for Its Equal Transmission to Every Individual of Each Succeeding Generation on Arriving at the Age of Maturity* (Ming, 1829), 256–7.

[59] Harlan Eugene Read, *The Abolition of Inheritance* (New York: Macmillan, 1918).

[60] Stephen Aron, *How the West Was Lost: The Transformation of Kentucky from Daniel Boone to Henry Clay* (Baltimore: Johns Hopkins University Press, 1996).

ground or a dynamic borderland between North and South.[61] Writing about Kentucky as a region is not novel. E. Merton Coulter, as long ago as 1926, in *The Civil War and Readjustment in Kentucky*, described Kentucky as a "remarkable intermixture" of Northern and Southern philosophies.[62] Although many of these studies focus on the Civil War and Reconstruction, conflicts within internal border regions have deep historical roots before the war and an extensive legacy after Reconstruction.[63] Approaching Kentucky as part of a liminal legal and cultural ground, both embracing and rejecting legal and cultural values from its Northern and Southern neighbors and struggling to assert its own legal identity, offers an opportunity to reconceptualize more broadly the importance of the region as a space where individuals made explicit their ideological commitments because they were contested. From this vantage, Kentucky and the border states' legal history magnifies and focuses the overall legal development of the nation.

This ambivalence (or pluralism) played out in the Commonwealth in the debates over the advantages of the gradual abolition of slavery during the antebellum period and the subsequent creation of a Confederate Lost Cause memory after the war.[64] Kentuckians lacked the Deep South's axiomatic acceptance of slavery but never embraced free labor as a superior labor system.[65] Historians partially attribute Kentucky's decision to

[61] Aaron Astor, *Rebels on the Border: Civil War, Emancipation and the Reconstruction of Kentucky and Missouri* (Baton Rouge: Louisiana State University Press, 2012), 3; William C. Harris, *Lincoln and the Border States: Preserving the Union* (Lawrence: University Press of Kansas, 2011).

[62] E. Merton Coulter, *The Civil War and Readjustment in Kentucky* (Chapel Hill: University of North Carolina Press, 1926. Reprint: Peter Smith Publishers, 1966), 3.

[63] Jeremy Neely, *The Border between Them: Violence and Reconstruction on the Kansas-Missouri Line* (Columbia: University of Missouri Press, 2008).

[64] Anne Elizabeth Marshall, *Creating a Confederate Kentucky: The Lost Cause and Civil War Memory in a Border State* (Chapel Hill: University of North Carolina Press, 2010; James C. Klotter, *Kentucky Justice, Southern Honor, and American Manhood: Understanding the Life and Death of Richard Reid* (Baton Rouge: Louisiana State Press, 2003); Harold B. Tallant, *Evil Necessity: Slavery and Political Culture in Antebellum Kentucky* (Lexington: University of Kentucky Press, 2003); Barbara Fields, *Slavery and Freedom on the Middle Ground: Maryland during the Nineteenth Century* (Yale University Press, 1985).

[65] For a discussion of race law in Kentucky, see Christopher Waldrep, "The Impact of Race on Law in Kentucky: A Research Note," *Register of the Kentucky Historical Society* 92 no. 2 (1992): 165–82. Historians have debated whether Kentucky was more Southern or Northern in its antebellum outlook. On this subject, see Keith C. Barton, "Good Cooks and Washers: Slave Hiring, Domestic Labor and the Market in Bourbon County, Kentucky," *Journal of American History* 84 no. 2 (1997): 436–60. This study

remain in the Union during the Civil War to an attempt by the proslavery majority to protect Kentucky slavery. Henry Watterson, the postwar editor of the *Louisville Courier-Journal* observed that "Kentucky's head was with the Union and her heart was with the South."[66] As Watterson and, later, historian E. Merton Coulter wryly observed, Kentucky seceded from the Union after the Civil War.[67] After 1866, many Kentuckians continued to share racial attitudes with their Southern counterparts while looking across the Ohio River to the industrializing North as a model for social and economic progress.[68] Rather than dismissing Kentucky because of what some historians have identified as its distinctiveness, Kentucky merits its closer scrutiny because these shifting loyalties reveal the dynamism in which law and culture change over time.

The destruction of slavery shaped changes in Kentucky testation patterns and in how Kentuckians conceptualized the family and the household as overlapping yet distinct entities. Before the Civil War, the most common form of interracial testamentary gifts were manumissions. By freeing a slave, the testator also deprived his or her heirs-at-law of their "rightful inheritance." Occasionally, slaveholders also left property to newly manumitted slaves. These wills received close examination by local communities. During trials disputing these wills, the blood or sexual relationships between the testator and beneficiaries were defended or derided by the litigants. Slaves were part of the household and, to some testators, part of the family.

After the Civil War, interracial testation patterns changed, as did jurists and family members' scrutiny of nonconforming wills. Rather than interracial bequests, one of the foci of postbellum trials became testators' reasons for disinheriting children and wills in which testators willed property to second wives. Few white testators continued to bequeath property to mixed-race beneficiaries. When they did, the testators usually made an explicit connection to service, as when white testator James Young left property to Mary, identified as "col girl," because it was "due her for

views Kentucky as a part of the South, especially in terms of its legal system and race relations.

[66] Henry Watterson, "The South at Christmas," in Arthur Krock, ed., *The Editorials of Henry Watterson, Compiled with an Introduction and Notes by Arthur Krock* (New York: George H. Doran Co., 1923), 21.

[67] Michael A. Flannery, "Kentucky History Revisited: The Role of the Civil War in Shaping Kentucky's Collective Consciousness," *The Filson Club History Quarterly* 71 no. 1 (January 1997): 37 and Coulter, *The Civil War and Readjustment in Kentucky*, 329.

[68] George C. Wright, *Racial Violence in Kentucky, 1865–1940: Lynching, Mob Rule and "Legal Lynchings"* (Baton Rouge: Louisiana State University Press, 1990).

services rendered me in my old age."[69] After the war, the overwhelming majority of testators ignored African American household members in inheritance practices. Court transcripts indicate that several testators' households included African American servants, some of whom testified at trials but received no property. Far more frequently, testators recognized white relatives as caretakers and contributors to the household through testamentary gifts. In *Bush v. Lisle* (1889), testator Frank Lisle left his estate to his sister Manerva, with whom he had lived as he was dying from advanced syphilis. An African American boy who testified at the trial and was hired by Manerva to take care of some of the more odious tasks required by Lisle was not recognized in the will.[70] The scrutiny of testators' wills shifted to focus to how the white family distributed wealth between generations, reflecting a social and legal concern with consolidating property and social status among whites.

Kentucky is also rich ground for studying women's access to property and authority. Formally unreconstructed after the Civil War, Kentucky's legislature did not draft a new constitution until 1890, unlike the other reconstructed Southern states. Most Southern states inserted married women's property rights and liberalized inheritance law in their new Reconstruction constitutions. In Kentucky, however, married women's property and inheritance rights developed piecemeal. Kentucky legislators and jurists had an extended, rich conversation about women's legal and mental capacity, demonstrating how gender ideologies infused arguments about who could control property. As testamentary beneficiaries, women were particularly vulnerable to constraints on legacies in part because Kentucky's restrictive laws closed other avenues through which women could access property. Some testators disinherited or threatened to disinherit daughters who married contrary to their wishes. Testator Conrad Rompf wrote a will in 1885 in which he disinherited his daughter Juliana for conducting an illicit affair. He also believed that she practiced witchcraft.[71] Although inheritance law appeared neutral in terms of

[69] "Will of James Young" (1872), Warren County Will Book 4, 114, Warren County Court Clerk Records, KDLA.

[70] As historian Kimberly Shreck has argued in her examination of testation patterns among a Missouri interracial family, "post-bellum social order could not tolerate or accommodate the persistence of some aspects of antebellum life, especially the conflation of interracial households and families." Kimberly A. Shreck, "Splitting Heirs: Gender, Race and the Properties of Unreconstructed Households," PhD dissertation, University of Missouri–Columbia, 2004, 3.

[71] *Schildnecht v. Rompf's Ex'x*, 4 S.W. 235 (1887).

favoring one sex over the other in ability to inherit, in practice it was not. When sons had to choose between a marital partner or paternal ire and disinheritance, they generally had many more opportunities for acquiring property beyond inheriting it. Disinheriting daughters and making testamentary gifts to wives contingent on their continued widowhood reveal how a body of law seemingly neutral to gender roles in practice reinforced patriarchal authority.

Disinherited heirs-at-law challenged wills for complex reasons. In many cases, they believed a testator's mental disease caused him or her to write a will contrary to long-standing wishes and affections. Other motivations included greed or freedom from conditional legacies that limited their behavior if they wished to claim their inheritance. In *Gordon v. Morrow* (1889), the beneficiaries' attorneys argued that testator Mattie Gordon's aunt had said she was "mad because she had not received as much as she thought she should have received and said she would break the will."[72] Whatever the complex motivations behind these suits, it fell upon the challengers to prove the testator was insane or unduly influenced in order to overturn the will. That the challengers initiated suits believing they would prevail tells us how they used law and understood prevailing social ideas about sanity, morality, and gendered conduct.

Testamentary challenges illuminate a lynchpin in familial relations. Who has the mental ability and the legal authority to select beneficiaries and to transmit material wealth and socioeconomic benefits, including human beings held in bondage? Property holders used promises of inheritance to control heirs' and potential beneficiaries' behavior. Bloodline relatives, caretakers, enslaved people, and children saw inheritance as their just reward or as compensation for care in an era in which state-sponsored social services were primitive or nonexistent. As the lawyers defending Jane Miller's will reminded the court, "No brother but Josiah H Miller offered her a home and gave her protection in her days of poverty and want."[73] Finally, lawmakers sought to assure a stable property law that promoted land alienability and predictable wealth transfers.

Throughout the nineteenth century, anywhere from 20 to 35 percent of the population wrote wills, usually with a testamentary intent that deviated from the intestacy scheme. Without accurate death records by which to compare the number of deaths with the number of estates

[72] "Brief for Appellants," in *Gordon v. Morrow* (1887), Case 19068, Box 813, KCAR, KDLA.

[73] "Apellant's Brief," in *Sarah v. Miller* (1864), Case 74, Box 3, KCAR, KDLA.

probated, it is difficult to compile statistics on the percentages of people who wrote wills and who died intestate within the total population of decedents. Fortunately, nineteenth-century Harrison County Court clerks kept a Decedent Index that noted the method of distribution of all estates that the court oversaw. Between 1795 and 1905, wills controlled 38.3 percent of all estates that went through the court.[74] This number skews higher than national averages for two reasons. First, the estates in the dataset had to be valuable enough to go through probate. Generally, the more valuable the estate, the more likely the property holder would write a will. The dataset excludes estates too small to probate or those in which surviving family informally distributed the decedent's belongings, which if included would raise the number of intestate estates. Second, many Harrison County residents were wealthier than those in other counties because their land was more valuable. Still, this finding conforms roughly with other historians' conclusions that testate decedents constituted about one-third of all decedents during the nineteenth century.[75]

This study incorporates quantitative analysis based on a sample of 483 wills drawn from Warren and Harrison counties dated between 1825 and 1897. This dataset, although small, allows limited generalizations about how people actually distributed their property rather than relying on institutional or legal changes to gauge testamentary changes. Having a baseline view of testamentary practices presents a point of reference from which to interpret challenged wills and the motivations of the testators behind them. This quantitative analysis combines the methods of the older studies on inheritance that yielded important insights into social history with the benefits of qualitative analysis for doing cultural history. The quantitative analysis indicates whether certain behaviors changed or remained static, while the prose of the trial records offers clues as to why.

The wills were coded for characteristics such as spousal treatment, transfers or manumissions of slaves, conditional gifts, and references to impairment. These counties were drawn from two of the most populous and economically important regions in Kentucky. Both of these counties had significant black populations compared to counties in other regions

[74] Harrison County Court Decedents Estate Index, 1795–1905, Harrison County Court Clerk Records, KDLA. This percentage was determined by noting the estates assigned an administrator by the court (most likely intestate estates) and those estates that had an executor (estates distributed by a will).

[75] Shammas, Salmon, and Dahlin, *Inheritance in America from Colonial Times to the Present*, 15–17.

of Kentucky: in 1860, Warren County was 31.9 percent black and Harrison County had a black population of 24.9 percent.[76] This attribute, while not representative of much of the rest of Kentucky, permitted a much more detailed quantitative and qualitative study of inheritance and slavery, covered in Chapter 2. The eastern Appalachian counties have been largely excluded from this study. An informal survey of the county court order books indicates that county courts in this area litigated few testamentary capacity cases and fewer of these cases went to the appellate courts. These counties, perhaps because of their geographical isolation, also have more pronounced cultural differences from the other regions of Kentucky.[77]

Warren County is in the southwestern part of the state. Its county seat, Bowling Green, served as an important regional trading hub for tobacco, livestock, and iron, aided by the proximity of the Barren and Green Rivers. Like the southern tier of Kentucky counties, Warren County residents had extensive trading and economic ties with the lower South and generally identified more closely with their Southern neighbors in Tennessee. In 1845, the Kentucky state auditor valued its land at $5.09/acre, placing it in the middle of land values for Kentucky counties.[78] During the Civil War, a substantial number of Kentuckians in this region rejected the legislature's proclamations of neutrality and, later, its endorsement of the Unionist cause. Bowling Green briefly served as the state's Confederate capital when Sidney Johnston's army occupied the lower quarter of the state in late 1861 until he abandoned it in February 1862.[79] After the Civil War, Warren County continued its prominence as a trading hub due to the Louisville-Nashville railroad line, which ran through Bowling Green after 1859. It also saw the development of a small textile industry.

Harrison County, in the northeastern central Bluegrass region, saw heavy early settlement as land-hungry colonists pushed westward. This region includes the wealthiest counties in Kentucky and the highest urban populations in the cities of Louisville, Lexington, and Frankfort, the state

[76] Marion Brunson Lucas, *A History of Blacks in Kentucky from Slavery to Segregation, 1760–1891* (Lexington: University of Kentucky Press, 2003), xx.

[77] See Richard B. Drake, *A History of Appalachia* (Lexington: University of Kentucky Press, 2003). Drake characterizes Appalachia as a "distinct region" whose residents have a "sense of separateness" (ix).

[78] "Reports Communicated to Both Branches of the Legislature of Kentucky at the December Session, 1845 (Auditor's Report), Legislative Document No. 10," (Frankfort: A.G. Hodges, 1845), 213.

[79] Lowell Harrison, *The Civil War in Kentucky* (Lexington: University Press of Kentucky, 2009).

capital. After the American Revolution, it was the most economically developed area and home to much of the elite, including the politically powerful Clay and Breckinridge families. Harrison County was not one of the wealthiest counties in the Bluegrass region, but its land was valued at $10.89/acre in 1845, a relatively high valuation. Sharing its southern border, Bourbon County had an average land value per acre of $34.50, while nearby northwestern Owen County had a much smaller value of $5.69/acre.[80]

This book is arranged topically. In the extended debates over capacity, themes emerge that would lose clarity in a chronological telling. Although this organization may result in some repetition of the facts of cases discussed in multiple chapters, when these cases reappear, it demonstrates how the litigants invoked multiple stands of the grammar of capacity. A thematic approach also makes clear that testamentary capacity jurisprudence did not develop in a clear linear narrative. Rather, different aspects of testamentary capacity jurisprudence had their own developmental trajectories in tandem with social and legal changes. Chapter 1 begins with a discussion of the social attitudes toward the claims and obligations that inhered in familial relationships, particularly those concerning the transmission of wealth. After focusing on how inheritance law and cultural values mapped out an idealized, prescriptive family, this chapter turns to how ordinary people understood the legal definition of sanity and insanity in testamentary disputes. The second chapter explores cases in which testators manumitted slaves or made interracial gifts. In several cases, testators recognized concubines and acknowledged other illicit relationships while disinheriting legitimate sons, daughters, and relatives. In contests over wills involving slave manumissions, slaves had legal standing as the party defending the will and actively participated in a legal system that overwhelmingly fused skin color to status as property. Testators who emancipated slaves threatened racial hierarchies by converting slaves from property to personhood and by legally recognizing slaves' humanity, sometimes to the exclusion of bloodline kin. Testators and black beneficiaries destabilized dominant ideals that rewarded white, legally legitimate families through social and legal privileges, including the expectation of inheritance. The racially determined laws governing marriage, miscegenation, and legitimacy merged seamlessly with the ostensibly neutral laws of inheritance.

[80] "Reports Communicated to Both Branches of the Legislature of Kentucky at the December Session, 1845," 83.

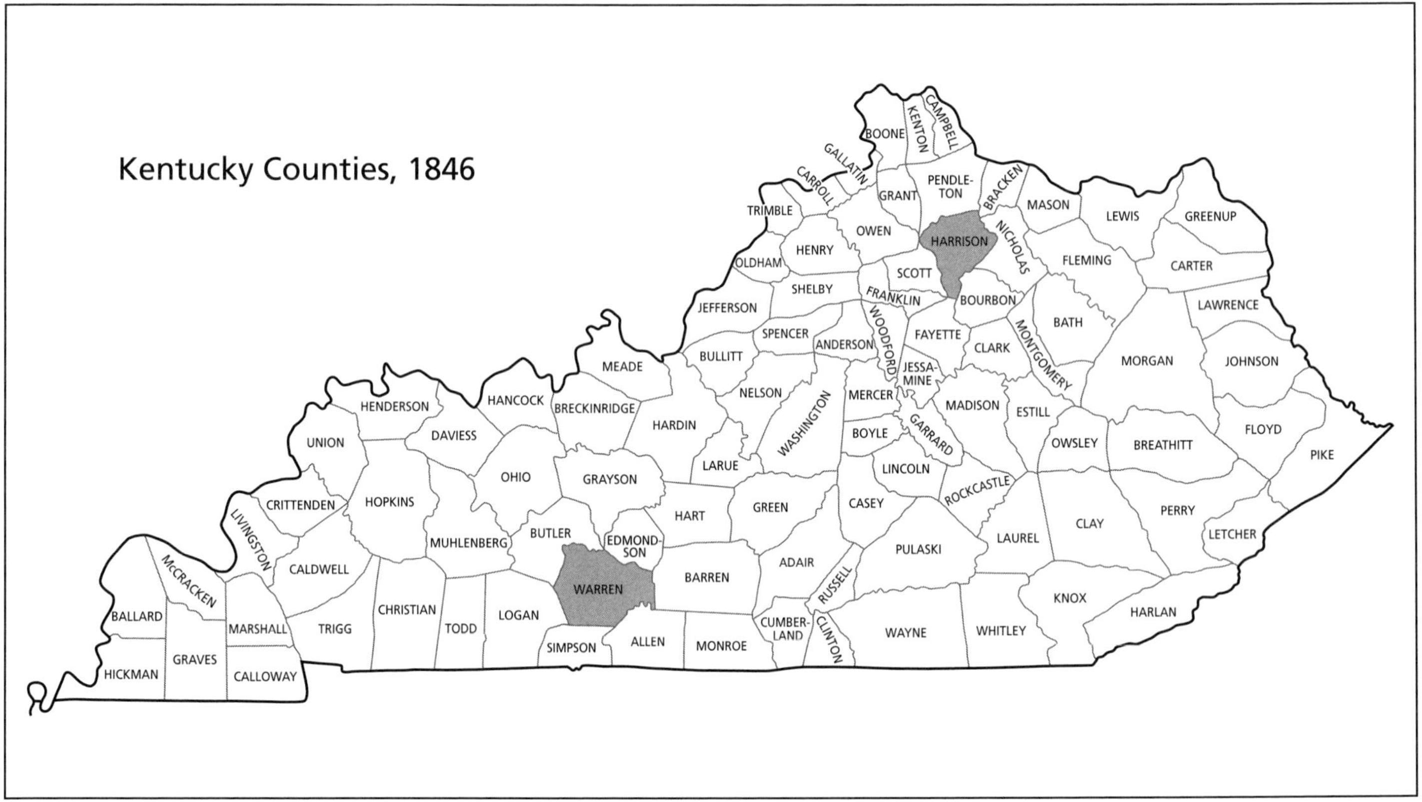


MAP 1.1. Map of Kentucky Counties, 1846 (Harrison and Warren Counties are shaded).

The next chapter explores testamentary capacity jurisprudence from the perspective of medical experts and local physicians. As the nineteenth century progressed, lawyers increasingly turned to expert medical witnesses to explain insanity to juries. Expert testimony brought new forms of knowledge and authority into courtrooms. Insanity as a medical diagnosis was both broader and narrower than judicial definitions of capacity. To medical experts, insanity required a relationship between physical disease and volitional unfreedom that exceeded most jurists' narrow concerns over legal stability and promoting the integrity of the family. For Court of Appeals judges "capacity" meant that testators *appeared* to exercise free will. Making culturally acceptable judgments about their heirs-at-law constituted strong evidence in favor of mental capacity. Dissonance between juridical and medical definitions and expansive medical diagnoses prodded the court to focus on the testator's ability to recognize the "natural" objects of his bounty.

Chapter 4 explores the discussions of physical infirmities and disabilities that suffuse transcripts and case law. Witnesses frequently discussed the physical impairments of testators, linking them to mental unsoundness and moral turpitude. The challengers to testators' wills drew attention to testators' physical deformities and bodily decay to argue that dependent, uncontrollable bodies mirrored uncontrollable minds. The body served as a text to be read through which the state of the testators' intellect and sanity could be ascertained. Lawyers' briefs to the Court of Appeals also described testators using the language of deformity and disability. These reoccurring descriptions emphasize how disability and physical appearance served as legal evidence in determining who had the right to decide the distribution of property.

The final chapter turns to married women's testamentary capacity cases. Women had disposed of property since the Founding in spite of lawmakers' reservations about their ability to write just, responsible wills. Claims that women needed special protection because they lacked rationality appeared in other contexts too, including negligence law, involuntary commitment proceedings, and suffrage debates.[81] The grammar of capacity rather than the language of individual rights mediated women's claims to property. Both categories – capacity and individual rights – rested on

[81] Welke, *Recasting American Liberty*; Hendrik Hartog, "Mrs. Packard on Dependency," *Yale Journal of Law and Humanities* 1 (1988–9): 79–104; Yvonne Pitts, "Disability, Scientific Authority and Women's Political Participation at the Turn of the Twentieth Century United States," *Journal of Women's History* 24 no. 2 (Summer 2012): 37–61.

ideas about women's ability to rationally consent and ultimately to exercise the responsibilities of self-government.[82] In Kentucky, the concern for systemization resulted in narrow, formalized interpretation of women's legal capacity, which had a two-fold effect: it limited women's access to property, which consolidated wealth among white male property holders, and it preserved the legal and social fiction of marital unity under male household authority. Little evidence suggests that female testators or their beneficiaries thought about their inheritance practices as part of broader debates over women's equality, although certainly Kentucky women's rights activists in the later nineteenth century saw property rights as central to their struggle.[83] Instead, transcripts suggest that female testators saw these disputes as deeply personal dramas over familial justice and as high stakes economic battles.

[82] For a discussion on consent and authority, see Brewer, *By Birth or Consent*; Pitts, "Disability, Scientific Authority, and Women's Political Participation at the Turn of the Twentieth Century United States," 37–61.

[83] On the Kentucky's women's rights movement, see Paul E. Fuller, *Laura Clay and the Woman's Rights Movement* (Lexington: University of Kentucky Press, 1975; reprinted 1992); Lynn E. Niedermeier, *Eliza Calvert Hall: Kentucky Author and Suffragist* (Lexington: University of Kentucky Press, 2007).

1

# "Parental Justice"

## *Inheritance and Obligation in Families*

In 1884, a Gallantin County Circuit Court jury heard conflicting testimony describing Samuel Bledsoe. One witness characterized him as a man of "good judgment" while another referred to him as "crippled in his head."[1] No one had petitioned to commit Bledsoe to a lunatic asylum, nor was he claiming insanity as part of a criminal defense. Samuel Bledsoe had died eight months earlier. He had written a will leaving most of his estate to his youngest daughter, Manerva, almost entirely disinheriting his other six adult children. At the trial, Bledsoe's son William claimed his father disinherited him because he disapproved of William's future wife. After he informed his father of his impending marriage, William testified, "He told me if I did marry her he would disinherit me.... He was not competent to make a will so far as can judge after I got big enough to notice."[2] Samuel Bledsoe's excluded children sued to overturn their father's will on the grounds that he lacked the mental capacity to write a valid will and that Manerva had illegally influenced him to favor her. The judge asked a local jury to choose between two narratives: that Bledsoe's will reflected the wishes of a rational, independent property owner or that it captured the ramblings of an incapacitated man doing the bidding of his avaricious daughter.

1 "Testimony of John R. Brown" and "Testimony of BF Furnish," Transcript, *Bledsoe's Ex'x v. Bledsoe* (1886), Case 17095, Box 716, Kentucky Court of Appeals Records (hereafter KCAR), Kentucky Department for Libraries and Archives, Frankfort, Kentucky (hereafter KDLA).

2 "Testimony of William," Transcript, *Bledsoe's Ex'x v. Bledsoe* (1886), Case 17095, Box 716, KCAR, KDLA.

Samuel Bledsoe's will contest translated decades of familial conflict into legal categories designed to facilitate orderly property transmission and conditioned by a preference for bloodline heirs. This case and others like it demonstrate the process by which individuals interpreted decades of discord, perceived injustices, and hurt feelings into conflicting legal narratives in local courtrooms. Themes of obedience and disobedience, greed and altruism, parental honor and filial dishonor appear across time and geography. The first half of this chapter explores how wills functioned as legal instruments *and* as cultural messengers. The second half of this chapter explores how ordinary people understood mental capacity and translated these understandings into the grammar of capacity in courtrooms. Individuals evaluated mental capacity through testators' interactions within their families and communities, their work ethics and business conduct, and their attitudes and behavior toward racial others. These meanings of capacity, constructed in everyday life and overlaid by medical and legal contexts, coalesced in local trials. Nineteenth-century gender and racial ideologies informed how jurists and ordinary people translated behavior into judgments about family and mental capacity, which mediated access to inherited wealth and economic citizenship.

Challenges to wills like *Bledsoe's Executors v. Bledsoe* (1886) reveal how community members negotiated the fault lines in the ideology that used the abstraction of a harmonious family as a metaphor for society and as the embodiment of natural relations between people. At the local level, these cases offered community members and jurors an opportunity to restore justice to wronged family members and negate the benefits undeserving beneficiaries had been acceded by vulnerable testators. Testimonies suggest that to the participants, these trials sometimes had less to do with questions of mental capacity than with arbitrating familial disputes that had perplexed and disrupted communities for years. Trial participants could mobilize the concept of mental capacity to achieve or restore familial and communal justice.

Testators used their wills to enforce punishments, rewards, and obligations. Parents hoped children would obediently supply labor, care, and affection in return for promises of inheritance. Fortunately, most nineteenth-century testators did not use the boiler plate legal language that characterizes almost all wills today. Testators often took great pains to express their intent and the reasons behind their particular gifts, an act of personal vindication made necessary by the legal requirement that they recognize "the natural objects of their bounty." Bledsoe made clear he expected Manerva to take care of her mother when he directed: "it is to be understood that the farm (my farm) is to be managed by Manerva as long as her mother lives for their support."[3] Such language provides tantalizing glimpses into how testators sought to care for loved ones, manage family feuds, and reward or punish relatives from the grave.

Nineteenth-century Kentuckians thought very seriously about the gravity and multiple meanings of writing a will. Discussions of testation were not confined to elderly people in private consultation with lawyers. In 1887, friends, family, and her physician surrounded twenty-five-year-old testator Mattie Gordon when "she was told that she could not recover and had better dispose of her property."[4] Gordon wrote her will on a Thursday and died the following Sunday. As newspapers, medical writings, and personal correspondence demonstrate, epidemics, disease, and accidents were constant companions to every Kentucky family. Lexington resident Susan Yandell wrote to her father of the terrifying virulence of the cholera epidemic of 1833. After assuring her father that she and her family were well, she wrote, "Cholera has visited us in a [more] severe form than most of our physicians expected. In the last 7 or 8 days, from 65 to 75 deaths have occurred from it."[5] Concerns about impending, unpredictable death sparked musings about inheritance. Yandell described a man who "was taken about 2 o'clock & died the same evening. A friend of his ... was laughing & joking about Cholera & sent him word that he would come & write his *will* if he was going to die."[6] For women, childbirth brought a constant reminder of mortality. In 1837, Kentuckian Ellen Green wrote to her husband, Hector, expressing fears about her upcoming delivery. She told Hector that "whether she survives that awful hour, yet rests alone with providence." Green turned to her wishes for her property, telling her husband that she has "enclosed a will made by me some time since," and that if her baby was a girl she wanted "what little dress or Jewelry I have, I wish taken care of for her."[7] These passages reveal the capriciousness of death and how the desire to express testamentary wishes accompanied its contemplation. Inheritance practices

[3] "Will of Samuel Bledsoe," Transcript, *Bledsoe's Ex'x v. Bledsoe* (1886), Case 17095, Box 716, KCAR, KDLA.

[4] "Brief for Appellants," in *Gordon v. Morrow* (1887), Case 19068, Box 813, KCAR, KDLA.

[5] Susan Yandell to David Wendel, June 7, 1833, Mss. A Y 21; FL 12, Yandell Family Papers, Filson Historical Society, Louisville, Kentucky (hereafter FHS).

[6] Ibid.

[7] Ellen Green to Hector Green, August 27, 1837, Mss. G796A, Box 2, FL 14, Green Family Papers, FHS.

were part of daily life; they were not confined to the occasional trial or the public unveiling of a deceased testator's will.

Nor was insanity concealed from public view. Ordinary Americans regularly encountered individuals they considered insane or as lacking mental capacity. The image of the village idiot, a harmless, pitiable figure, appeared in literature and popular culture across Europe and in the United States for centuries. County trial records were sprinkled with "Lunatic Inquests" in which county judges heard testimony and determined "the support, respect and safe keeping of any person who shall be so found to be of unsound mind."[8] Local physicians, neighbors, and family members appeared at these inquests to provide evidence, assume guardianship of "lunatics," or to request court permissions for their support and estate management. These procedures were fodder for gossip networks too. Susan Yandell reported to her mother that Henry Clay's eldest son, Theodore, was "taken to the Lunatic Asylum, three miles from town a few days since. It is generally supposed that his derangement is in a great measure owing to intemperance."[9] Yandell told her mother that Clay "was brought to court and allowed the privilege of summoning witnesses to prove that he was not insane."[10] Mental disease may not have touched all families directly, but mentally unsound individuals visibly inhabited most local communities.

## THE CAPACIOUS FAMILY, WHITE AND BLACK

Family was at the center of inheritance practices. In its narrowest conception, the term *family* referred to relationships established through marriage and blood and conferred with legal legitimacy. Family also served as an anchor for personal identity for Southerners; men were masters and leaders in their households and in public, while women were defined through their roles as wives, mothers, and legal dependents.[11] African American slaves in white households were also legal dependents of the head-of-household. Heads-of-households maintained the order,

[8] 1794 Ky. Acts, Ch. 95 § 1.

[9] Susan Yandell to Sarah Wendel, October 13, 1831, Mss. Y 21; FL 10, Yandell Family Papers, FHS.

[10] Ibid.

[11] Brenda E. Stevenson, *Life in Black and White: Family and Community in the Slave South* (New York: Oxford University Press, 1996), xiii; Carol Bleser, ed., *In Joy and in Sorrow: Women, Family, and Marriage in the Victorian South, 1830–1900* (New York: Oxford University Press, 1991); Nancy Bercaw, ed., *Gender and the Southern Body Politic* (Jackson: University Press of Mississippi, 2000).

through violence if necessary, to control the processes of wealth production in agrarian communities where the household and its land were also workplaces.[12]

Antebellum white Southerners simultaneously understood family as a capacious group within the household and as a narrow unit defined by law and legitimacy.[13] In *The Almoner*, an 1815 journal published in Lexington, one author suggested that "the black part of their family shall be called daily ... to worship along with the white part."[14] When questioned about the health of her neighbor's family in a will challenge, Lucy Ann Magruder testified that the testator's family "never had much sickness ... but they had a good deal of sickness among his black family."[15] Like Magruder, individuals made distinctions between parts of the family, black and white, but they were parts of the whole. The two parts were divided by race and status, creating a vast gulf in lived experience, but not wide enough to exclude slaves from the ideal of the capacious family. Including slaves in the antebellum family was no mere religious prescription. This vision of an organic family had practical and economic rationales beyond a desire to fulfill God's plan. The capacious ideal allowed slave owners to rhetorically elide the violent, coercive nature of slavery behind seeming tolerance and affection.

Testators' wills reflected the ideal of the household head as a benevolent patriarch ruling over all his dependents. This cultural ideal often bowed to the legal reality of slave law in its application. Warren County testator Charles Smith directed that his slave "old Ominda [was] to be at liberty to do as she may wish tho [*sic*] to be under the protection and control" of his son, Benjamin Smith.[16] He also left $100 for the "use & benefit" of Ominda. Smith did not give Ominda legal freedom. His instructions were both paternal and coercive. Ominda remained a slave, while Charles Smith claimed to grant her "liberty" and "protection" under his son's watchful eye. Benjamin Smith would have to support Ominda;

[12] Eugene Genovese, "'Our Family, White and Black': Family and Household in the Southern Slaveholders' Worldview," in Carol Bleser, ed., *In Joy and in Sorrow: Women, Family, and Marriage in the Victorian South, 1830–1900* (New York: Oxford University Press, 1991), 72–3.

[13] Ibid., 69–87.

[14] Anonymous, "An Enquiry Concerning the Duty of Christian Heads of Families Toward their Black Servants," *The Almoner* (Lexington) 1 no. 6 (May 1815): 274.

[15] "Testimony of Lucy Ann Magruder," in Transcript, *Ridgway v. Hall* (1871), Case 4387, KCAR, KDLA.

[16] "Will of Charles Smith" (1847), Warren County Will Book D 239–40, Warren County Court Clerk Records (hereafter WCCC Records), KDLA.

she may have been nearing an age at which her productive labor had little value, and statutory law prevented Smith from manumitting her without financial support. Of course, nothing prevented Benjamin from treating Ominda as he wished. Behind Charles Smith's seeming beneficence, the reality of Benjamin's absolute legal authority would determine the extent of the "liberty to do as she may wish" Ominda would enjoy.

Occasionally, testators acknowledged their mixed-race children. Testator Austin Hubbard left his estate to his enslaved mixed-race daughter, Narcissa. Before Narcissa could inherit the estate, Hubbard stipulated that her inheritance was contingent on "her owner ... let[ting] her go for a moderate price."[17] If her owner refused to agree to a "moderate price," then Hubbard devised Narcissa to his illegitimate white son. Although Hubbard recognized shared blood ties with his enslaved daughter, he predicated his recognition on the economics of slavery. The Court of Appeals sustained Hubbard's will, reinforcing the race-based conflation of a family member with property that structured slave law. The court held that making Narcissa's freedom conditional upon her purchase and subsequent manumission "for a moderate price" was a reasonable attempt to "counteract the cunning and avarice ... among his heirs."[18] Even if white heirs-at-law grudgingly accepted their interracial siblings during testators' lives, recognition of interracial affective or blood ties through inheritance generated contentious disputes.

The Civil War had a profound effect on testamentary practices because it redefined the legal household. Before the war, testamentary freedom potentially subverted legally and morally sanctioned families by recognizing obligations or affections that existed outside the boundaries of race and legitimacy. The aftermath of the Civil War led to the creation of a new property and labor regime based on contract rather than status. After emancipation, African Americans quickly separated themselves from the capacious white families of their masters. African American couples, denied legal marriage as slaves, embraced (and were pushed to embrace by immediate postwar statutes) legal marriage, in part so that black men would assume legal responsibility as the heads of families. In 1898, Kentucky state legislators, as part of the ongoing effort to make inheritance more efficient and uniform, recognized as legitimate children of former slaves who "cohabited with each other as husband and wife" even if they had never married in order to address

[17] *In re Hubbard's Will*, 29 Ky. 58 (1831).
[18] Ibid.

TABLE 1.1. *Interracial Testamentary Dispositions before and after the Thirteenth Amendment*

| | Before 1866 | After 1866 |
|---|---|---|
| All testators | 250 | 232 |
| Interracial dispositions | 18 | 6 |
| Percentage of interracial dispositions among all testators | 7.2% | 2.6% |
| Testate slaveholders | 93 | NA |
| Percentage of interracial dispositions among testate slaveholders | 19.4% | N/A |
| Interracial dispositions outside of household | 1 | N/A |
| Percentage of interracial dispositions outside of household | .4% | N/A |

long-standing problems in defining legal legitimacy among African American families.[19]

The legal recognition of black families severed the legal and rhetorical ties that had included them as dependents in white households. New systems of agricultural labor emerged in which sharecropping African American families negotiated labor contracts with white property owners. Even if white landholders and black sharecroppers shared blood, these ties were rarely acknowledged.[20] Kentucky novelist James Lane Allen lamented the new postwar Kentucky when he wistfully observed that "the preexisting order had indeed rolled away like a scroll." He described labor relations in the new order as "a difficult agreement to effect at all times, because will and word and bond were of no account."[21] These new constructions of family and property virtually eliminated interracial gifts that had occurred (albeit rarely) between white testators and African Americans during the antebellum era.

Table 1.1 shows the patterns in interracial legacies before and after slavery. The post-emancipation legacies are more difficult to identify because black beneficiaries were not identified through reference to their slave status. Still, testators referred to their black beneficiaries as "col'd"

[19] 1898 *Acts of Kentucky*, Ch. 39 § 1.

[20] Jacqueline Jones, "The Political Economy of Sharecropping Families: Blacks and Poor Whites in the Rural South, 1865–1915," in Carol Bleser, ed., *In Joy and in Sorrow: Women, Family, and Marriage in the Victorian South, 1830–1900* (New York: Oxford University Press, 1991), 198.

[21] James Lane Allen, *The Reign of Law: A Tale of the Kentucky Hemp Fields* (New York: The Macmillan Co., 1900), 52–3.

or "of color," a widespread practice and perhaps an effort to clarify their gifts for their executors. The number of post-1866 interracial gifts in Table 1.1 therefore may be a bit lower, but trial records and newspaper reports reinforce the conclusion that they occurred rarely.

As Table 1.1 shows, the capacious vision of family had new limits. The new ideological family that emerged after the Civil War was either white or black. The beneficiaries who triggered a will challenge also changed. No longer could challengers point to the manumitted black beneficiaries as culprits who interceded in the natural familial order. Rather, challengers more closely scrutinized relationships between testators and those on the margins of the legitimate family. When testators chose beneficiaries who were second wives, unmarried sexual partners, or morally dubious, the challengers portrayed those relationships as evidence of mental incapacity. Lawmakers drew from common law tradition when they designed the statutory law of inheritance to consolidate wealth among legally legitimate families. Statutory law discouraged wealth transfers where sexual or blood but illegitimate and morally suspect relationships existed. The legal descriptive "natural" in "natural objects of their bounty" converged with communal beliefs, creating networks of legal rights and obligations between generations of legitimate family members.

## TESTATION: A FAMILY ACT

Intestacy laws, which determined the division of a decedent's estate if he or she died without writing a will, rewarded legitimate bloodline kin. Intestacy statutes theoretically expressed the decedent's likely intent had he or she written a will. In practice, it continued the long tradition of keeping wealth in families, defined through law and blood. During the colonial period, most intestacy statutes followed primogeniture or were adapted to multigeniture. The scheme ranked and rewarded biological and generational relationships, but only those that had the imprimatur legal legitimacy.[22] Legitimacy may have begun with blood but was also adapted by lawmakers to reflect and advance cultural and economic imperatives. In Kentucky, men's illegitimate children could claim a portion of their fathers' estates only if their fathers later married their mothers or "recognized" the children.[23]

[22] Adrienne D. Davis, "The Private Law of Race and Sex: An Antebellum Perspective," *Stanford Law Review* 51 (January 1999): 226–31.

[23] *Revised Statutes of 1852*, Ch. 30 § 6.

Figure 1.1 shows how law in 1834 distributed the estate after the decedent died. Each box indicates the receiving heir(s) if none of the heirs listed above survived. Blood and how much of it flowed in the heirs' veins mattered; the code mandated that when the estate descended to collateral kin, if some of these heirs "be of the whole blood ... and other part of the half blood only, those of the half blood shall inherit only half so much as those of the whole blood."[24] The highlighted boxes in Figure 1.1 show where the law favored a male heir over a female heir. With the exception of the legitimate children who inherited equally, each time the estate moved to a more distant degree of kin, male kin inherited the entire estate before female kin would. Not until 1874 did lawmakers adjust the intestacy pattern so that mothers and fathers inherited equally in the absence of children or grandchildren.[25] Intestacy distribution and the overall structure of nineteenth-century marital and property law concentrated property control in male hands. Even if a female heir inherited, if she was married her husband controlled any property she acquired. He could not sell it but could do just about anything else with it without her permission.

Spouses are conspicuously absent from Figure 1.1. Wives were not heirs to their husbands' estates in an inheritance system designed to keep property in bloodlines rather than pass it through marriage where it could be transferred to heirs unrelated to the wives' deceased husbands. Surviving spouses inherited in fee simple (full title to the estate) only if their husbands or wives had no children and no collateral kin could be located. Wives' claims to their intestate husbands' property were categorized under "Husband and Wife" in Kentucky's statutory code. They were only guaranteed dower, or one-third of the estate for life use, if the marriage had produced children. Widows had control of the dower estate for their maintenance and could not will or convey it.[26] Rather than granting widows financial independence, legislators designed dower laws to prevent impoverished wives from becoming wards of their children or the state. Husbands could make provisions to will dower land after their wives' deaths; in the event of intestacy, the land passed to the heirs-at-law after the widows' deaths.

[24] *A Digest of the Statute Laws of Kentucky* (1834), 562, Title 61 § 13.

[25] 1874 *Acts of Kentucky*, Ch. 31 § 1.

[26] See Marylynn Salmon, *Women and the Law of Property in Early America* (Chapel Hill: University of North Carolina Press, 1986) for a discussion of the legal rights and disabilities of women during the antebellum era; *Revised Statutes of 1852*, Ch. 106 § 4.

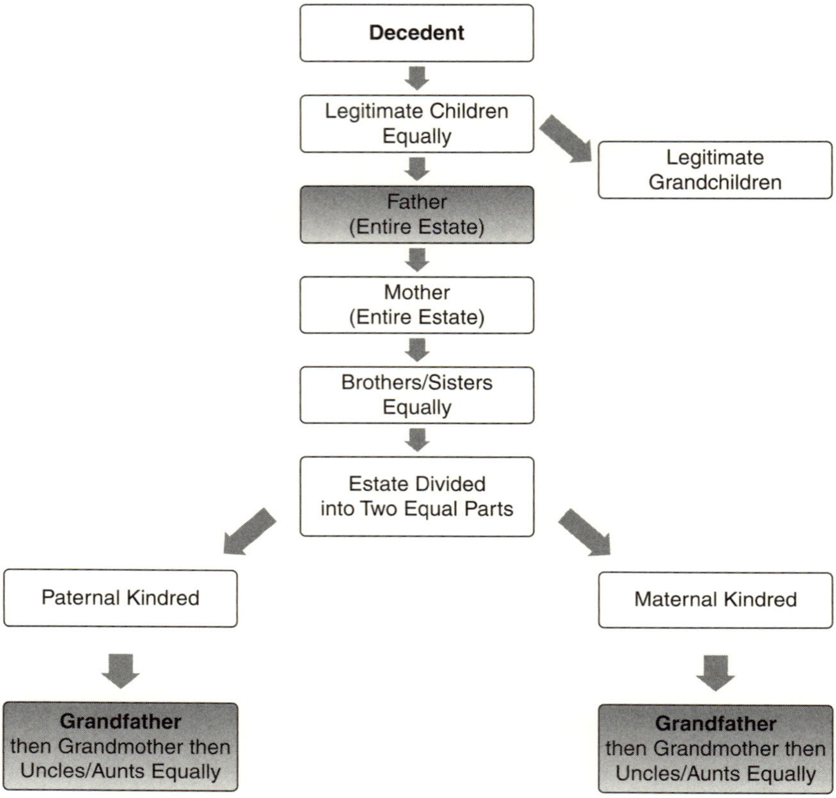


FIGURE 1.1. Intestacy Distribution, 1834.
*Note*: The highlighted boxes show where the law favored paternal descendants until it changed in 1874.
*Source*: *A Digest of the Statute Laws of Kentucky* (1834), 560–2, Title 61 § 1–12.

As opposed to intestacy law's predetermined distribution plan, writing a will emphasized freedom. Wills became legal instruments for both subverting and reinforcing evolving conceptions of reciprocal obligations within families. Some Kentuckians rejected testamentary freedom as unnecessary, catering to the whims of aging testators. Witnesses sometimes claimed that only after the onset of insanity did the testator deviate from convictions that intestacy laws provided a just distribution plan. In the 1873 contest over John P. Wills's will, one witness testified that Wills had said "no man ought to make a will after he was sixty five years old

[and] that he was opposed to making wills. That the law made a good enough will."[27] The Kentucky Court of Appeals took such declarations seriously. In another dispute, after favorably reviewing a jury's verdict overturning William Harrel's will, Justice Robertson noted that Harrel had "declared that the law made the best will.... He also said, not long before his death, that he desired an equal distribution of his estate among his children. In confirmation of that ... he, by extraordinary remonstrances, prevailed on one of his sons to die intestate."[28] These appeals to the virtues of intestate law reflected a belief in the justness of equal distribution among bloodline heirs. The public act of probating and distributing the estate to the heirs-at-law also reinforced the state-sanctioned legal family by rewarding them with wealth.

Through wills, testators made symbolic as well as material statements to their heirs-at-law and beneficiaries. Numerous wills included blessings, good wishes, and expressions of genuine love. John Stove finished his will by bequeathing his "blessing to each of my children and urge them to be loving, patient, and considerate to and with each other and to strive as dutiful children to see the wishes above expressed fully and fairly carried out."[29] These expressions reveal the emotionality of wills, written as testators came to terms with their own mortality and the knowledge that their families' lives would continue without them. Wills gave material effect to affectionate relationships. They anointed favorites and chastised others by expressing testators' feelings through the quantity and quality of gifts. Moreover, these transfers ensured the passage of social and economic status from one generation to another.

Wills, by translating affection into property, blurred distinctions between ostensibly private familial relationships and the public economy. Although wills sometimes redistributed large quantities of wealth, not all testators had large estates.[30] Barzilla Baird's personal estate, which she divided equally between her children and her grandson, sold for $290.85

[27] "Testimony of Benjamin Ellsberry" in Transcript, *Wills v. Lochnane* (1871), Case 5843, Box 229, KCAR, KDLA.

[28] *Harrel v. Harrel*, 62 Ky. 203 (1864).

[29] "Will of John Stove" (1893), Warren County Will Book 5, 99–100, WCCC Records, KDLA.

[30] Carole Shammas, Marylynn Salmon, and Michael Dahlin, *Inheritance in America from Colonial Times to the Present* (New Brunswick and London: Rutgers University Press, 1987), 15–17. Their study estimates that, during the late nineteenth century, wills dictated the distribution of 62 percent of all personal wealth. This included personalty and realty in individual estates in Bucks County, Pennsylvania.

in 1871.[31] Had Baird not written a will, her grandson's share would have been split among his surviving brothers and sisters. Reubin Beck willed his entire estate to his youngest brother, "having a knowledge that there can be but little, think it not worth dividing among my other relatives."[32] Disinherited heirs-at-law went through the trouble of bringing suits to contest wills in estates of all sizes as well. In the 1831 contest over Rachel Higdon's will, which the heirs-at-law pursued to the Court of Appeals, Higdon's estate sold for a total of $202.50.[33] Perhaps these challengers were interested in the monetary value; at the same time, transcripts indicate that many challengers also sought to redeem their reputations after the dishonor or scandal implied by disinheritance.

Testators explained, even justified, their estate divisions to survivors. They often made elaborate declarations of exactly how much property they had given to each heir before their death. These declarations perhaps soothed any imputations of slights but also emphasized that inheritance was a process that began sometimes years before wills were probated. In a will that appeared to disinherit her son, testator Agnes Mayes explained:

> [T]he world may think that I have failed to manifest an affection for my son Daniel Mayes from the fact of my having failed to give him a portion of my property; that such an impression may not exist I now state that I have not been influenced by any want of affection for him, but because in early life he was more liberally provided for by his father.... And in knowledge of the goodness of his heart I know he will acquit his mother of any thing like partiality or a want of filial affection for him. To him and each of my children I bequeath my blessing.[34]

Warren County testator John Jackson noted early in his detailed will that "I would just state that I have already given to my son John S. Jackson all that I intend to give him." He then gave to his son Francis land, "one good horse, one bed and frame," and willed two slaves to

31 "Will of Barzilla Baird" (1871), and "Sale Bill of Personal Estate of Barzilla Baird," 176–7, in Harrison County Will Book J, Harrison County Court Clerk Records (hereafter HCCC Records), KDLA.

32 "Will of Reubin Beck" (1834) Warren County Will Book D (, WCCC Records, KDLA. It is difficult to know the actual size of Beck's estate as he passed property to an heir without a sale. In cases in which the testator mandates a sale, usually probate records include an estate inventory or bill of sale.

33 *In re Higdon*, 29 Ky. 444; "List of the Sale of the Estate of Rachel Higdon," Nelson County Will Book G (1831–1835), Nelson County Court Records, 70–1, KDLA.

34 "Will of Agnes Mayes" (1855), Trigg County Will Book E, 220–1, Trigg County Court Clerk Records, KDLA.

Francis upon the death of his wife. He carefully inserted a clause giving Francis "the privilege of selecting others ... from the rest of my negros" if either named slave died. Francis also received one-fifth of "the crop each year as a remuneration" for "stay[ing] with his mother."[35] In 12.8 percent of the sampled wills, testators included language indicating that one heir had already received part or all of his or her inheritance. Some testators carefully accounted for uneven distribution under the advice of lawyers, aware the capacity test required testators to recognize all of the "natural objects of their bounty." When testators had given an heir their intended inheritance during their lifetime, they sometimes left that heir one dollar. This legal strategy most often did not indicate the testator's ire, although it could. It acknowledged the heir as a "natural object."

When devising property unevenly, testators often mentioned the desire to compensate a beneficiary for care during old age and sickness as part of an informal welfare system. Francis Edwards willed his entire estate to Elijah Bailey, on the condition that "he keep me until my death and if he does not keep me ... whoever takes care of me during my life shall have all of my property at my death."[36] Making testamentary promises contingent on care suggested that testators believed younger generations needed incentives to ensure their good treatment during old age. As C. D. Bradley, a Kentucky attorney observed, writing a will allowed testators

> to reward their children and others who are kind and protectors in sickness and old age and cut off such as neglect their duty they owe to parents and relations. Unhappily unless there was some such motive in addition to the sense of duty, many would suffer & die for want of attention in the midst of plenty.[37]

The notion that heirs required motive beyond duty and affection to care for aging parents contradicted the rhetoric that portrayed families as inclusive, organic units in which ties of affection and responsibility bound generations together. When children lived as dependents in their parents' households, parents had several avenues by which to compel obedience and respect, ranging from good natured cajoling to corporeal punishment. "Parental Authority," an 1846 article in the *Louisville Weekly Journal*, counseled that if fathers taught their sons "submission

[35] "Will of John Jackson" (1841),Warren County Will Book D, 148–9, WCCC Records, KDLA.

[36] "Will of Francis Edwards" (1885), Will Book L, 306, HCCC Records, KDLA.

[37] "Appellant's Brief," in *Sarah v. Miller* (1864) Case 74, Box 3, KCAR, KDLA.

to authority," sons would develop "a habit of filial reverence ... that can never be broken."[38] Once children became adults, however, parents had fewer means of compelling obedience and "filial reverence."

Some testators used conditional promises of material reward to discourage children who might otherwise neglect their parents. Isaac Conrad devised to his son Jackson "the plantation wherein I now live" as long as Jackson "maintain[ed] me and my wife with all things necessary."[39] In an 1872 Georgia will case, Frederick Lamback devised all of his real estate to one son only if he "maintain and support his mother in a manner suitable to her circumstances in life, so long as she shall live." Witnesses testified that in his dying declaration he told his son, "Buddy, don't grieve for me, we have all got to die, take care of your mother."[40] Of course, some children could not afford to provide care for ailing parents without financial assistance. Whether by choice or necessity, some families functioned on two levels: as organic units duty bound by affective ties, and as a collection of individuals pursuing their own economic interests, in which they traded goods or services for wealth.

Table 1.2 shows all wills in which the testator conditioned a gift to the beneficiary on children taking care of an aging relative, usually a surviving parent, but on occasion a disabled sibling or relative. Testators left these sorts of gifts to sons at more than five times the rate they did to daughters among wills that mentioned sons or daughters. This difference reflects marital and legal arrangements. Grown daughters often married and were dependents within their husbands' households. Sons were more likely to establish their own households and have their own familial resources with which to take care of aging relatives. Burdens imposed by the dead hand fell more heavily upon sons' shoulders than daughters'. While sons may have intended to take care of aging parents even without a part of the parental estate, these promises limited their mobility until their surviving parent passed away. In cases in which the surviving parent suffered from physical impairments or chronic disease, this burden could be onerous.

Table 1.3 shows conditional gifts sorted by sex of the testators. Some of the conditional gifts made arrangements if a triggering event occurred. Testator Henrieta Wilson instructed that "In making the above devise of land I suppose that my son E would never marry. If in this I am mistaken

[38] "Parental Authority," *Louisville Weekly Journal*, February 11, 1846.

[39] "Will of Isaac Conrad" (1850), Will Book F, 292, HCCC Records, KDLA.

[40] *Gardner v. Lamback*, 47 Ga. 143 (1872).

TABLE 1.2. *Testamentary Gifts Conditioned on Children Taking Care of a Relative or a Specified Living Arrangement*

| | Conditional Gifts | Number of All Wills Mentioning Son/Daughter | Percent of All Wills Mentioning Son/Daughter (%) | Percent of All Wills in Dataset (n = 483) (%) |
|---|---|---|---|---|
| Conditional gift to a son | 28 | 262 | 10.7 | 5.8 |
| Conditional gift to a daughter | 6 | 312 | 1.9 | 1.2 |

TABLE 1.3. *Testators Making Conditional Testamentary Gifts by Sex*

| | Number of Wills | Percent of Wills |
|---|---|---|
| All testators making conditional gifts | 105 | 21.7% of all wills |
| Male testators making conditional gifts | 95 | 90.5% of wills making conditional bequests |
| Female testators making conditional gifts | 10 | 9.5% of wills making conditional bequests |

and he shall marry and leave lawful children" then she redistributed her estate to include these unexpected grandchildren.[41]

Men made the overwhelming majority of these conditional dispositions because many of them regulated their widows' behavior. William Cox of Trigg County left his wife, Rebeca, control of his real and personal estate during her lifetime or widowhood.[42] This gift granted only "control" and not full ownership. As long as she remained a widow, Rebeca could use the property, but she could not sell or significantly alter it. At her death, or if she chose to remarry, the property would be distributed among his six children. Cox also added a clause concerning his daughter Rutha's choice of a husband, decreeing that if she "marries Nelson More, she is not to have an equal share. I give her Rutha A. Cox five dollars."[43]

41 "Will of Henrieta Wilson" (1870) Harrison County Will Book J, HCCC Records, KDLA.

42 "Will of William Cox" (1855), Trigg County Will Book E, 28, Trigg County Court Clerk Records, KDLA.

43 Ibid.

Testator Willis Arnold hoped to ensure his sons' good behavior and make their upbringing easier on his wife when he directed that "if any of my sons should not come under good selection and be governed by their mother for such children to be bound to some good man as my executor may think proper."[44] Women and children often found that they served their own best interests by obeying male family members' directives.[45] Through these testamentary requirements, testators retained authority over their wives and children's future behavior.

William Cox's authority as a master also continued after his demise. Perhaps doubting his slaves' obedient natures or distrusting his wife's disciplinary ability, he mandated that "if any of the negroes belonging to my estate will not obey their mistres [*sic*] she has the rite [*sic*] to sell said negroes."[46] The persistent threat of sale served as a warning to the enslaved people on the Cox farm that their community remained precarious and was based on their continued ability to meet Rebeca Cox's expectations. William Cox's directions granted Rebeca Cox new authority as a master by allowing her to make a conditional sale of the slaves. At the same time, William Cox created a powerful disincentive toward her remarriage. Cox granted Rebeca the power associated with mastery, while carefully controlling her marital status by linking remarriage to a loss of her financial security. Indeed, testamentary freedom represented enormous power over spouses, family, and slaves.

Testators had a moral imperative to recognize all of their children, especially if they had not proven themselves unworthy through bad behavior. Across states, laws accommodated instances in which testators may not have been aware of legitimate children. In an 1861 Pennsylvania case, the testator wrote a will prior to the birth of another son, who, for obvious reasons, the testator did not name in the will. Basing their decision on common law precedents, the judges declared invalid the entire will and subjected the estate to intestate division. They reasoned: "new moral testamentary duties have accrued to him subsequent to the date of the will such as may be presumed to produce a change of intentions."[47] The judges not only believed the new child deserved inheritance, but they presumed that his birth negated all previous intent. Such obligations attached only to deserving children. Jurists

44 "Will of Willis Arnold" (1835), Warren County Will Book D, WCCC Records, KDLA.

45 Mary Louise Fellows, "Wills and Trusts: The Kingdom of the Fathers," *Law and Inequality: A Journal of Theory and Practice* 10 no. 1 (December 1991): 137–62.

46 "Will of William Cox," 28.

47 *Young's Appeal*, 39 Pa. 115 (1861).

TABLE 1.4. *Wills Disinheriting an Heir*

| | Total Number | Percent of Total Dataset (%) |
|---|---|---|
| Disinherited heirs | 32 | 6.6 |
| Disinherited heirs – received inheritance | 13 | 2.6 |

also took seriously parental authority when testators punished their children for filial disobedience.

The Kentucky Court of Appeals reluctantly accepted disobedience by adult children as a reason for disinheritance. In the 1873 dispute over John P. Wills's will, the court agreed that "He (like men of his temperament sometimes do) doubtless determined that those of his family who would not respect his feelings and wishes should enjoy no part of his estate."[48] Wills had disinherited his granddaughter because she married against his wishes. The court concluded that Wills remained consistent and rational, explaining that "His regard for all the members of his family who yielded to him that degree of obedience and respect to which he conceived himself entitled" justified his will. Disobedience, even by adult children, challenged the ordered relations upon which family reputation and paternal honor were built. Fathers expected respect from their children, and in return passed on the family wealth and status to their worthy children (Table 1.4).

Courts had little tolerance for defiant children in testamentary disputes. In an 1874 Georgia case, a testator threatened to disinherit his son if he married the woman to whom he was engaged. The son and his sister surreptitiously made an agreement to split the estate regardless of the will. When the will was probated and the agreement discovered, the Georgia Supreme Court justice responded angrily to the siblings' attempt to usurp paternal authority. Quoting Joseph Story's *Commentaries on Equity Jurisprudence*, the Georgia Supreme Court affirmed that "The law has a high regard for parental authority, and will give effect to nothing which tends to encourage disobedience to it." The decision rejected the secret sibling agreement, "finding it disagreeable to the public policy of a nation, and especially of a Christian nation," and upheld the will.[49]

[48] *Wills v. Locknane*, 6 Ky. Op. 632 (1873).
[49] *Mercier v. Mercier*, 50 Ga. 546 (1874), quoting Judge Story at 554.

The reasons for which parents disinherited disobedient sons and daughters differed according to parents' gendered expectations of behavior. Testators sometimes deprived daughters who asserted marital independence of property as a means of punishment. Bannister Taylor made his reasons for disinheriting his daughter clear by devising:

> My daughter Martha, without my knowledge, has ... become the wife of an unprincipled scoundrel by the name of James Minor, and as a mark of my disapprobation of her disobedience and disrespect to her parents ... I so order and direct that neither my said daughter, Martha, and the said James Minor shall ever receive or enjoy any part or portion of my estate.[50]

Martha Minor had challenged Taylor's parental authority by eloping with James Minor. Taylor used one of the few weapons he had; he made a public declaration of her insubordination and punished her by disinheriting her. Taylor's will makes clear that Martha angered him for two reasons: her disobedience and her "disrespect to her parents." Although testators also disinherited sons for their marital choices, adult daughters' primary filial responsibility was to marry well, whereas parents had differing expectations for sons as economic producers and heads-of-households.

In addition to making clear disapproval of matrimonial partners, testators disinherited sons who had abandoned their parents, disagreed with them, or dishonored them in business dealings. One study finds similar reasons in Massachusetts will cases.[51] Fathers often expected sons to become economically productive household members while respecting paternal authority. Benjamin Hewitt wrote a will explicitly to disinherit his son Anderson, who "was going to kock [*sic*] me in the head & Kill me because I wanted him to pay me for the land that he ... lived on."[52] In 1880, John Hays disinherited his son Henry, who "left the parental care of me when underage" and divided his estate equally among his remaining children.[53] Similarly, in the Bledsoe case, witnesses testified that Samuel Bledsoe's son William had been disrespectful and threatened violence over a wagon both men used for their farming business. When

[50] *Taylor v. Minor* 13 Ky. Op. 450 (1885).

[51] Glendyne R. Wergland, "Women, Men, Property, and Inheritance: Gendered Testamentary Customs in Western Massachusetts, 1800–1860. Or, Diligent Wives, Dutiful Daughters, Prodigal Sons, Westward Migration, Reciprocity, and Rewards for Virtue, Considered" (January 1, 2001), PhD dissertation, University of Massachusetts, 2001.

[52] "Will of Benjamin Hewitt," Warren County Will Book 5, 70, WCCC Records, KDLA.

[53] "Will of John Hays" (1880), Warren County Will Book 4, 283–5, WCCC Records, KDLA.

children acted contrary to parental wishes, testation became a tool in the limited arsenal of aging parents to assure respect, care, and obedience.[54]

Wills and the disputes over them reveal an economy of caretaking and obligation in families. In cases in which some siblings were rewarded while others were excluded, the favored beneficiaries often claimed that even at great hardship to themselves, they labored above and beyond the call of duty to provide the testator with care or comfort in the absence of their errant brothers and/or sisters. Manerva Bledsoe testified that, although she was frequently sick, "I did the principal part of home work" after her siblings married and left her with her ailing parents.[55] Conversely, when disinherited heirs brought grievances against unequal testamentary distributions to court, they argued that their own behavior did not deserve disinheritance. In the Bledsoe will dispute, one witness testified that Bledsoe had little reason to disinherit William, who had "always treated him [Samuel Bledsoe] with respect like a child should treat a parent."[56] Rather, as William Bledsoe argued, his father wrote an irrational, unjust will because of mental unsoundness and Manerva's inducements. Parents and jurists expected children to demonstrate natural filial reverence, and in turn children would reap the rewards of inheriting family wealth. Testamentary conflicts unmasked long-standing, simmering tensions in families.

## CAPACITY AND INCAPACITY IN TESTATION

The great importance of testamentary practices to individual families also made them important to their local communities. Most people were aware of will challenges. Published legal advice guides warned about them and offered strategies on avoiding them. Testators knew unhappy heirs could challenge their wills; as testator Moses Kimbrough pleaded in his 1872 will, "I hope no one will try to *Brake* [*sic*] or trouble with this deed in any manner shape or form for I think this is a just will."[57]

[54] For a longer treatment of this aspect of testation, see Hendrig Hartog, *Someday All of This Will Be Yours: A History of Inheritance and Old Age* (Cambridge: Harvard University Press, 2012).

[55] "Testimony of Manerva Bledsoe," Transcript, *Bledsoe's Ex'x v. Bledsoe* (1886), Case 17095, Box 716, KCAR, KDLA.

[56] "Testimony of John Williamson," in Transcript, *Bledsoe's Ex'x v. Bledsoe* (1886), KCAR, KDLA.

[57] "Will of Moses Kimbrough" (1873), Harrison County Will Book J, 261, HCCC Records, KDLA.

Local and national newspapers consistently published articles detailing will disputes, complete with commentary extolling the justice served or denied through inheritance practices. *The New York Times* enthusiastically printed reports of every rumor and every motion in the capacity challenge to railroad magnate Cornelius Vanderbilt's will for the two years it dragged on in New York's Surrogate Court.[58] Even as *The New York Times* described every twitch by witnesses, one editorial writer commented disdainfully that the "worst feature of the Vanderbilt will case has been its vulgarity."[59]

Newspaper editors did not just report on will disputes. They interpreted them in the context of the political and social conflicts of the time. The *Times* noted that an expert testifying about mania and delusions of grandeur at the Vanderbilt trial made a "backhanded slap" at Samuel Tilden, the controversial defeated candidate in the election of 1876.[60] When a jury sustained wealthy Georgia farmer David Dickson's testamentary gifts to his illegitimate mixed-race daughter in 1884, the African American newspaper the *New York Freeman* proclaimed a "Righteous Verdict" and provided details of the trial over the "extraordinary will."[61] In 1865, the *Milwaukee Daily Sentinel* approvingly noted that James C. Johnson, a wealthy landholder in North Carolina, had disinherited his brothers because they "identified themselves with the rebel cause."[62] The nascent psychiatric community also carried coverage of the subsequent testamentary capacity trial over Johnson's will because of the controversial testimony of Dr. William Hammond.[63] Across the country, papers including Washington, DC's *National Intelligencer* and San Francisco's *Daily Evening Bulletin* carried stories ranging from a couple lines to several columns on will disputes, usually with editorializing on the justness of the will. The popular press treated will disputes as events open to public commentary and worthy of public interest.

[58] For example, in "The Vanderbilt Will: A Report It Is to Be Contested by Cornelius Vanderbilt," *The New York Times*, February 20, 1877, the author reported: "rumors ... have become common report at one of the leading hotels."

[59] "The Great Will Case," *The New York Times*, March 6, 1879.

[60] "An Expert on Insanity," *The New York Times*, February 27, 1879.

[61] "A Righteous Verdict: David Dickson's Will Giving His Property to a Former Slave Woman Sustained," *New York Freeman*, November 28, 1885.

[62] *Milwaukee Daily Sentinel*, May 24, 1865.

[63] William A. Hammond, M.D., "Opinion Relative to the Testamentary Capacity of the late James C. Johnson, of Chowan County, North Carolina," *Insanity in Its Medico-Legal Relations* (New York: Voorhis and Co., second edition, 1875), 5.

Throughout the nineteenth century, one aspect of the grammar of capacity remained constant even as social and cultural contexts changed. Dependency, either mental or legal, disqualified a person from exercising testamentary freedom. In *Shropshire v. Reno* (1830), the court contended that "*Femes covert* [married women], minors under prescribed ages, persons of unsound minds, are not, therefore, permitted to make wills, because it is deemed safer that the property of such persons should be distributed by the law, than by any ostensible act of themselves."[64] The groups the court cited as lacking legal capacity were dependents either of a male head-of-household or of the state. Lawyers and witnesses consistently narrated stories in which testators lost independence and became physically and mentally dependent on others. In the *Shropshire* case, the Court of Appeals noted that testator Walter Shropshire was "childish and flighty," and "complained in a puerile manner." These descriptions emasculated and infantalized Shropshire. The court rhetorically stripped him of his manly independence by portraying him as an ineffective, whining child. Children's dependency denied them of free will, as did their underdeveloped intellects. As Louisville physician Dr. Charles Caldwell noted in an address titled "Mental Cultivation," "No study of an *abstract nature* should ever be assigned to pupils, while under their twelfth or fourteenth year ... they are incompetent to do it."[65] When witnesses and court judges described testators as childish, they implied that the previously independent, manly testator had regressed into a state of incompetent dependency.

Lawmakers generally assumed that white men as a group possessed the independence and free will to make reasoned decisions concerning their households and dependents. As historian Elaine Frantz Parsons observes, one meaning of manhood "was a certain form of willpower. Independence and strength of will were highly gendered qualities, yet nineteenth century Americans considered the possession of free will as a precondition of full personhood for both men and women."[66] Despite tremendous class differences during the antebellum era, a precarious

[64] *Shropshire v. Reno*, 28 Ky. 91 (1830).

[65] Charles M. Caldwell, "A Succinct View of the Influence of Mental Cultivation on the Destinies of Louisville, An Introductory Lecture Delivered at the Opening of the Louisville Medical Institute," *Louisville Journal of Medicine and Surgery* (1838): 1.

[66] Elaine Frantz Parsons, *Manhood Lost: Fallen Drunkards and Redeeming Women in the Nineteenth Century United States* (Baltimore: Johns Hopkins University Press, 2003), 12.

ideological unity grounded in liberty and independence connected almost all white men.[67] Even as this unity across social classes broke down during and after the Civil War, the idea that whiteness represented independence and rationality did not disappear; instead it gained strength as a tenet of scientific racism. After the Civil War, white politicians used the rhetoric of capacity to disparage black politicians and women as unfit for rational, independent political decision making. If the just testator was a white, independent man executing his final act of justice, then the unsound testator had lost his ability to govern and became weak, dissipated, and dependent.

With women's wills, challenges played out differently. Assertions of independence, either sexual or political, could be evidence of incapacity. In 1862, widow Eliza B. Atkinson left her estate to her caretaker and his family, with whom she had lived during her final illness. She disinherited her deceased husband's children from his first marriage. The Court of Appeals, in overturning her will, concluded that Atkinson was "wrecked in intellect," caused by a "disease peculiar to her sex." The court cited Atkinson's predilection toward "dress[ing] in gaudy colors as any of the young ladies ... ma[king] love to young men and conduct[ing] herself in such an unbecoming and frequently indecent manner."[68] The judges and many witnesses believed Atkinson was insane. As evidence, they compared her behavior to an ideal determined by sex and age and used gendered language to describe her transgressions from rational behavior that marked her incapacity to distribute property. Although gender ideology morphed over time, its influence on testamentary rights remained. In one case still cited in contemporary case law books, an 1947 New Jersey court overturned Louisa Strittmater's will because of "her insane delusions about the male ... that led her to leave her estate to the National Women's Party."[69]

Prevailing racial ideology also shaped how witnesses assessed mental capacity. In the Bledsoe trial, Bledsoe's longtime neighbor, Thomas Baker, testified, "I don't think he had the capacity to make a will ... he

[67] See Stephanie McCurry, *Masters of Small Worlds: Yeoman Households, Gender Relations, and the Political Culture of the Antebellum South Carolina Low Country* (New York: Oxford University Press, 1995), 6; J. William Harris, *Plain Folk and Gentry in a Slave Society: White Liberty and Black Slavery in Augusta's Hinterlands* (Wesleyan University Press, 1985), 6.

[68] *Pecantet v. Grayson*, 60 Ky. Op. 80 (1872). See Chapter 5 for a fuller discussion of *Pecantet v. Grayson*.

[69] *In re Strittmater*, 140 NJ Eq. 94 (1947).

thought the rebels and rebel sympathizers even to the women and children ought to be hung and he would head a band of negroes to help do it."[70] In Kentucky, white-on-black extralegal violence became common after legal emancipation, with ninety-three lynchings occurring between 1867 and 1871.[71] Headlines in local and national papers consistently carried reports of alleged African American barbarity met by extralegal justice. The suggestion of violently unleashing extralegal violence on white rebel sympathizers led Baker to conclude Bledsoe lacked mental capacity. Furthermore, Baker recalled Bledsoe's conviction that female rebel sympathizers should be hanged. This invocation of lynching had far more sinister connotations to the maintenance of the post–Civil War racial order. White vigilantes sometimes justified lynching through moral outrage at allegations that black men raped white women.[72] When Bledsoe suggested that blacks should hang white female sympathizers, he rejected a world view in which sane white men justified extralegal violence as protection for white women. Other witnesses alluded to Bledsoe's unconventional views as "extreme and fanatical in religion and politics."[73] Had Bledsoe made the same statements about retribution by whites on blacks and declared himself a supporter of black subordination, those facts most likely would have been unremarkable.

The testator's own moral failings often led to a finding of incapacity. Throughout the nineteenth century, challengers impugned testators' ability to exercise free will by alleging that testators ceded free will to alcoholic dependency. The Court of Appeals viewed chronic drunkenness with great suspicion; in *Allison's Devisees v. Allison's Heirs* (1838), the court compared intemperance with the incapacity of a child, describing the testator as "very intemperate; and when in his cups ... exhibited marks of imbecility and childishness."[74] Men who drank excessively lost their manly independence, made clear by their neglect of familial and social responsibilities. Even if a usually intemperate testator was sober at the moment he wrote the will, many people believed his addiction to drink had eroded the mental faculties responsible for making moral decisions. Reverend

[70] "Testimony of Thomas Baker," *Bledsoe's Ex'x v. Bledsoe* (1883) Case 17095, Box 716, KCAR, KDLA.

[71] George C. Wright, *Racial Violence in Kentucky, 1865–1940: Lynching, Mob Rule and "Legal Lynchings"* (Baton Rouge: Louisiana State University Press, 1990).

[72] "Lynch Law in Kentucky: Negro Outrages White Girl and is Hung by a Mob," *The Chicago Tribune*, August 28, 1870.

[73] "Testimony of Hugh Montgomery," in Transcript, *Bledsoe's Ex'x v. Bledsoe* (1886), KCAR, KDLA.

[74] *Allison's Devisees v. Allison's Heirs*, 37 Ky. 90 (1838).

Joseph Ramsey, testifying in the 1871 *Wills v. Lochnane* dispute, called the testator an "intemperate man," concluding "the natural tendency of ardent spirits is to impair the mind and to destroy the moral honor."[75] In such cases, testators' own internal weaknesses caused a descent into immorality, alcoholic dependency, and mental incapacity.

Challengers often coupled charges of mental incapacity with undue influence. In undue influence cases, disinherited family members alleged that one of the testator's beneficiaries directed the testator toward making "unnatural" bequests.[76] In some instances, testators unevenly distributed their estates, favoring one beneficiary over other heirs. In other cases, testators disinherited the "natural object of their bounty" for a beneficiary outside of the bloodline such as a slave, illicit lover, or distant and wayward relative. In 1883, the Court of Appeals defined undue influence as "Influence obtained by flattery, importunity, threats, superiority of will, mind, or character ... which would give dominion over the will of the testator to such an extent as to destroy *free* agency ... the law condemns as undue."[77] To the courts, the acquiescence of the property-owning testator's free will to another person's wishes represented a state of mental dependency.

## UNDUE INFLUENCE AND FAMILIAL INTERLOPERS

During the antebellum era, the wills of testators who manumitted slaves were particularly vulnerable to allegations of mental incapacity and undue influence. Sane testators had legal right to manumit slaves. Many community members, however, viewed manumissions with skepticism, questioning the testator's sanity and always alert to treachery by slaves. Testator George Weir directed his executor to hire out his slaves for two years, and then manumit and give them the proceeds of their labor.[78] His

[75] "Testimony of Joseph Ramsey," Transcript, *Wills v. Lochnane* (1873), Case 5843, Box 229, KCAR, KDLA.

[76] Ray D. Madoff, "Unmasking Undue Influence," *Minnesota Law Review* 81 (1997): 571; Julia Cowan Spear, "Undue Influence in Louisiana: What It Was, What It Is, What It Might Be," *Loyola Law Review* 43 (Fall 1997): 443; Brian Alan Ross, "Undue Influence and Gender Iniquity," *Women's Rights Law Reporter* 19 (Fall 1997): 102; Joseph W. deFuria, Jr., "Testamentary Gifts Resulting from Meretricious Relationships: Undue Influence or Natural Beneficence?" *Notre Dame Law Review* 64 (1989): 200–21; Veena K. Murthy, "Undue Influence and Gender Stereotypes: Legal Doctrine or Indoctrination?" *Cardozo Women's Law Journal* 4 (1997): 105–35.

[77] *Wise v. Foote*, 81 Ky. 10 (1883).

[78] *In re Weir's Will*, 39 Ky. 434 (1840).

heirs contested the will, pointing to the manumissions. After concluding that the other provisions in Weir's will reflected a sane mind, the judges admitted that "whether any morbid delusion, amounting to insanity ... influenced him to emancipate his slaves is the only question about which we have felt any difficulty." They concluded with some distaste, "whatever may be the effect of the emancipation of his slaves, he had the right to liberate them."[79] While the bench disapproved of "letting loose, in the bosom of a slave community, a degraded cast of manumitted negroes," it recognized the theoretical right of sane men to manumit slave property. By marshalling images of mentally unsound testators victimized by mendacious slaves, disinherited heirs-at-law played off community fears of empowered slaves controlling testators to gain freedom. Overturning the will, they argued, would rectify such affronts to the system of slavery and to themselves as the unjustly disinherited legitimate family.

The grammar of capacity, shaped by racial ideology, provided ready tropes to discredit emancipatory wills without threatening all rational white men's independence. The Court of Appeals maintained an interest in overseeing the jurisprudence governing manumissions, reflecting the confluence of social and legal concern for the maintenance of the racial order. The grammar of capacity offered an opportunity to regulate emancipatory wills in a manner that the law governing manumissions did not. Labeling testators who emancipated slaves as mentally unsound excluded them from the polity of rational, free-willed white men. Simultaneously, it reaffirmed the image of the strong, independent patriarch who naturalized racial hierarchy by passing property and slaves to white family members.

The nature of undue influence allegations changed dramatically after the Civil War. The figure of the interloper who unduly influenced the testator to disinherit his children changed. After the destruction of slavery, Kentuckians, along with the rest of the South, began to reconstruct a social and familial order in which previously, slaves, at least rhetorically, belonged to the idealized, organic family. White Kentuckians struggled to regenerate a social hierarchy that would order the family while retaining white supremacy. Challengers no longer accused a treacherous racial other of influencing weakened testators. After 1864, testators rarely made interracial gifts, although interracial relationships, sexual and otherwise, continued.[80] Disinherited heirs identified new interlopers, often individuals

[79] Ibid.

[80] Martha Hodes, *White Women, Black Men: Illicit Sex in the Nineteenth Century South* (New Haven: Yale University Press, 1997).

who had legal but not blood ties to the testator. In cases where a male testator had remarried after the death of his first wife, challengers often pointed to the testator's second wife. According to the challengers, the second wife turned the testator's affections against his children by his first wife and deprived these legitimate children of their rightful inheritance. In *Broaddus' Devisees v. Broaddus' Heirs* (1874), George W. Broaddus left his estate to his second wife, Cynthia, for her life, after which it would descend evenly to their five children. He disinherited his children from his first marriage, noting that "I have heretofore given money and property as much of my estate as I feel able to give them."[81] Witnesses testified that Broaddus never would have disinherited his first set of children without Cynthia Broaddus's manipulation while he was ill.

The challengers' lawyers depicted George Broaddus as an infirm victim held hostage to his second wife's pernicious influences. They claimed that when a testator's first wife died, "her husband will not ... forget her children ... unless made to do so. It is unnatural." They depicted Cynthia Broaddus, the second wife, as an object of lust rather than affection, contending that she was "stout, vigorous & luscious. He was a man of strong passions & was doubtless hunting such a woman." They eliminated companionate love and affection toward Cynthia as an impetus for her inheritance. The disinherited heirs then explained how Cynthia Broaddus deprived their father of independence and free will, claiming that she "teased and vexed him ... that his will was broken down ... and he at last did that which when he was strong and free he declared he would never do."[82] The brief contrasted the second wife as a vampish pretender against the claims by the deserving children of the hardworking first wife. They claimed that Broaddus's first wife "by prudence, industry & economy assisted him in making his fortune."[83] The second wife contributed nothing to the economic prosperity of the family and served merely as a sexual outlet for George Broaddus. In this way, the challengers framed the idea of legitimate heirship around the premise that second wives and stepmothers were not a part of the nuclear family worthy of inheritance.

By emphasizing that Cynthia Broaddus did not belong to the original family, the challengers attempted to convince the jury that she deliberately

[81] "Will of G.W. Broaddus," in Brief for Appellants, *Broaddus' Devisees v. Broaddus' Heirs* (1874), Case 6767, Box 266, KCAR, KDLA.

[82] "Brief for Heirs & C," *Broaddus' Devisees v. Broaddus' Heirs* (1874), Case 6767, Box 266, KCAR, KDLA.

[83] Ibid.

interceded to destroy the natural affections between a father and his children. She prevailed by making her husband mentally and physically dependent on her. The jury and the challengers made clear to the community that heirs-at-law must be vigilant about dangerous influences within the boundaries of legal legitimacy. *Broaddus' Devisees v. Broaddus' Heirs* (1874) suggests that the postbellum white family was a fragile unit that required legal and communal monitoring to ensure the orderly transmission of wealth and status.

The focus of undue influence cases turned from antebellum relationships between slaves and testators toward a postbellum concern with shoring up the nuclear white family after the dissolution of slavery. Once slaves were excluded from white households, the legitimate, recognized family became bound by shared race, rather than juxtaposed against an enslaved racial other. Instead of slaves, second wives who inherited became a category of suspect dependents, especially when children resulted from the second marriage. Disinherited heirs rarely accused first wives of exercising undue influence. They were part of the natural familial order, and shared blood ties with the testators' children. Second wives, often younger than first wives, appeared in the family later, did not share blood with the testators' first set of children, and had the potential to bear more heirs. In cases of manumitted slaves or second wives, these heirs interceded between testators and their children, with tenuous claims as deserving beneficiaries. Disinherited heirs-at-law argued against their worthiness to inherit. They employed the culturally constructed grammar of capacity to challenge the testators' freedom to will property.

In *Zimlich v. Zimlich* (1890), Joseph Zimlich left his second wife, Elizabeth Zimlich, part of his estate and almost wholly excluded two sons, Mike and Andrew, from his first marriage.[84] Like Cynthia Broaddus's stepchildren, the disinherited Zimlich sons portrayed their stepmother, Elizabeth Zimlich, as a conniver trying to steal the rightful inheritance of the sons. The contestants' lawyers alleged that Joseph Zimlich "became offended … at the plaintiffs which ripened into a settled aversion, and his last wife … widened the breach with a view to produce a will in favor of herself and her children."[85] To emphasize Joseph Zimlich's dependent mental state, the contestants and their witnesses stripped

[84] *Zimlich v. Zimlich*, 90 Ky 657 (1890) and Kentucky Court of Appeals Records, *Zimlich v. Zimlich* 90 Ky 657, Case 20314, Box 874, Transcript, Volume 1.

[85] "Plaintiff's Instructions to the Jury," in *Zimlich v. Zimlich* (1887), Jefferson County Court of Common Pleas Files, Case 28025, Box 339.

Joseph Zimlich of masculine rationality by referring to him as "a mere child."[86] Elizabeth Zimlich's attorneys countered the images of her as a wily predator with a narrative that portrayed her as the archetypal middle-class Victorian goodwife. They constructed her as "affectionately performing the marital duty of a dutiful wife, of loving and cherishing her husband until death do them part."[87] They presented the sons as examples of filial duty gone awry, noting that they disobeyed Joseph Zimlich and "deserted and abandoned their father in his old age."[88] The notion that the testator held social obligations to those who remained loyal to him suffused the transcripts as a justification for his seemingly aberrant testamentary actions.

The Court of Appeals agreed with this rationale, noting in its decision that while Elizabeth Zimlich may have influenced her husband, she "had the kind of influence over him that a good wife usually has over a kind and considerate husband."[89] By appearing to adhere to the late nineteenth-century gendered role of a dutiful wife, Elizabeth Zimlich reinforced the prevailing gender ideology. Although the local jury may not have approved of her or of Joseph Zimlich's will, the Court of Appeals found no grounds to overturn the will. Elizabeth Zimlich's behavior, as presented by local witnesses, attested to her worthiness as a beneficiary. By choosing beneficiaries considered worthy, Joseph Zimlich appeared rational and wise. His will withstood the legal and social tests of rationality used to monitor family and property.

Disinherited heirs used the idea that familial affection flowed naturally to children to frame one form of insanity, an "unnatural aversion," as the opposite of undue influence. In undue influence cases, the challengers usually claimed that the beneficiary manipulated the testator's affection for his or her benefit. Disinherited heirs-at-law often framed the reason for their omission as an "unnatural aversion" in which the testator harbored an unnatural, irrational dislike or odium toward them. The challenger argued that an insane delusion caused the testator to ostracize a family member for whom he had previously held natural affections. Treatise writer Isaac Redfield noted, "Where a man is insane in respect to his nearest relations and the disposition of his estate, he is incapable

[86] "Brief for Appellees," in *Zimlich v. Zimlich* (1890), Case 20314, Box 874, KCAR, KDLA.

[87] Ibid.

[88] "Brief for Appellants," *Zimlich v. Zimlich* (1890), Case 20314, Box 874, KCAR, KDLA.

[89] *Zimlich v. Zimlich*, 90 Ky 657 (1890).

of making a will."[90] Alleging insanity toward the nearest relation used the cultural power of the idea that devising to one's children was natural. In the *Bledsoe* case, for example, the challengers claimed that Samuel Bledsoe held an unnatural aversion toward his son William; at the same time they accused Manerva Bledsoe of exercising undue influence. Dr. S. B. Robinson testified, "There is insane aversion where a parent takes an aversion to a child without cause. It is an evidence of insanity."[91] These trials involved scrutiny of the testator's behavior as well as that of the disinherited heirs and beneficiaries. Witnesses testified as to whether the heir-at-law's conduct reasonably justified disinheritance or if the heir was indeed the object of the testator's insane aversion.

Courtroom debates over the existence of an unnatural aversion sometimes arose when disinherited heirs asserted sexual independence against the testator's wishes. If the will's beneficiaries argued that the disinherited heir lost all claim to inheritance due to disobedience, the testator's dislike was justified and rational. When the beneficiaries alleged that the disinherited heir dishonored the testator by exercising sexual independence, they emphasized the right of fathers to control their children's marital decisions and determine the line of descent for the family's wealth. Conversely, the disinherited heir usually contended that the testator developed an unnatural aversion toward him or her and entertained imaginary delusions about their sexual proclivities.

When Bannister Taylor disinherited his daughter Martha for marrying J. C. Minor, she disputed the will, claiming that her father harbored an "insane aversion" against her and her husband. This case demonstrated the fault lines in the ideology of family. Taylor disinherited his daughter, an act considered unnatural according to law and custom. Martha Minor, however, had asserted female sexual independence and dishonored her father by eloping. The Marion County Circuit Court jury overturned the will, and the Court of Appeals affirmed that decision, noting in part it believed Taylor had little reason to disapprove of James Minor. Taylor's aspersions were unfounded. They concluded Minor was "of excellent character" and Taylor's reasons for excluding his daughter

90 Isaac Redfield, *The Law of Wills, Embracing the Making and Construction of Wills; The Jurisprudence of Insanity; The Effect of Extrinsic Evidence; The Creation and Construction of Trusts, So Far As Applicable to Wills, with Forms and Instructions for Preparing Wills Part I*, second edition (Boston: Little Brown and Co., 1866), 72.

91 "Testimony of SB Robinson," Transcript, *Bledsoe's Ex'x v. Bledsoe* (1886), Case 17095, Box 716, KCAR, KDLA.

"could only have been conceived by a disordered mind."[92] The court believed Bannister Taylor was insane because he failed to recognize James Minor as a man of respectable and honorable character. The jury chose to limit the testator's independence by declaring him delusionary. It upheld the transmission of property to legitimate children, rather than endorse Taylor's wishes. The jury also implicitly sanctioned Martha Minor's decision to elope, perhaps only because the all-white male jury agreed that her husband's character was honorable.

British philosopher Edmund Burke observed, "The power of perpetuating our property in families is one of the most valuable and interesting circumstances ... which tends the most to the perpetuation of society itself."[93] Family cannot be understood apart from how transferring private property and material possessions served as a mechanism for controlling family members and their behavior. Testators used wills to express complex emotions. Property became more than property – inheritance fetishized property into an expression of affection or odium by testators toward their beneficiaries and heirs-at-law. Exploring the cultural and legal values that influenced testation practices reinforces historians' views that family and property were the foundation of social relations throughout the nineteenth century, even as state law and appellate court decisions reinforced the liberal ideal of the autonomous individual. Analyzing testation practices, particularly disinheritance patterns, allows a broader, previously unexplored look into how familial boundaries of inclusiveness and exclusiveness were drawn. While bloodline proximity was a powerful determinant of inheritance, the ideals of reciprocity, economic concerns, and the preservation of the testator's reputation mattered as well.

Families and communities debated the merits and rationality of testators' perceptions of their heirs-at-law and beneficiaries. Disinherited heirs litigated to acquire property and to restore reputations damaged by the messages encoded in testators' wills. Although legally, any property-owning man who knew his relations and his property and had a fixed purpose in devising it could choose his beneficiaries, testators' families, courts, and local communities subjected wills to far more scrutiny. The legal test for testamentary capacity served as a starting point for public and private debates over testamentary distribution of property.

[92] *Taylor v. Minor*, 12 Ky. Op.450 (1885).

[93] Edmund Burke, *Reflections on the French Revolution and Other Essays* (New York: EP Dutton & Co., 1910), 49, quoted in Marvin B. Sussman, Judith N. Cates, and David T. Smith, *The Family and Inheritance* (New York: Russell Sage Foundation, 1970), 4.

In challenging a will, disinherited heirs challenged the testator's power over property by manipulating the grammar of capacity and rationality by publicly presenting alternative depictions of the most intimate familial relations in testamentary capacity trials. When challengers employed images of irrational and delusional testators, the will's proponents countered with images of justice and honor avenged, reconstituting the language of testamentary capacity to reaffirm and strengthen the nuclear family and the hierarchy that ordered it.

Challengers relied upon several powerful archetypes of mental unsoundness in courtroom narratives. These archetypes had in common the image of the mentally unsound testator losing his independence to physical and mental dependency. The challengers used the grammar of capacity by depicting a testator as becoming dependent on an imaginary delusion, another person's will, or alcohol to influence property distribution. This theme of independence lost played powerfully with juries and audiences who understood masculinity, authority, and whiteness as inseparable from the ability to independently exercise free will. The ability to exercise free will was conditioned by prevailing racial and gender ideologies. Just as racial and gender ideologies informed how communities understood the capacity of testators, they also informed how witnesses testified about the conduct of the heirs. Heirs had responsibilities to their families. In trials, beneficiaries emphasized the importance of these roles and the necessity of punishing offenders who ignored them through the deprivation of the familial estate.

# 2

# "My Black Family"

## *Manumission and Freedom in Inheritance Disputes*

This chapter explores testamentary challenges involving manumissions and interracial gifts. In *Sarah v. Miller* (1864), the case that opened the introduction, testator Jane Miller emancipated her slaves valued at over sixteen thousand dollars.[1] When her brothers Isaac and William discovered she had destroyed her valuable property and their inheritance by the manumissions, they initiated a legal suit to void the will. The Miller brothers claimed their sister was of unsound mind when she wrote her will and under the illegal, nefarious influence of her slaves who manipulated her into freeing them. Two Trigg County juries and numerous witnesses agreed with the brothers; Jane Miller was indeed insane. They based their conclusions on testimony that noted her "remarkable aversion to male society" and her self-imposed isolation from the white community, choosing instead to live near her slaves. Like other will challenges involving manumissions, the challengers concocted a potent evidentiary stew of racial and gender transgressions for the two local juries. In these will challenges, the added dimensions of breaching racial codes created distinct legal and moral conundrums which went to the center of the legal apparatus supporting the institution of slavery. As one of the few areas that allowed slaves active engagement with the law, testamentary manumissions mark an important area of enslaved people's struggle for freedom as they became legal parties in their quest to move from commodified wealth to personhood.

[1] "Appraisement of Jane Miller's Estate," Trigg County Will Book E (1855–1861), Trigg County Court Records, Kentucky Department for Libraries and Archives, Frankfort, Kentucky (hereafter KDLA).

As litigants in testamentary capacity cases, African Americans actively used this body of law to contest their bondage and publicly voice their dissatisfaction with slavery. In Jane Miller's will contest, all twenty-five African Americans who had been her slaves appeared in Trigg County Court and declared their intent to emigrate to Liberia, as required by the will for their emancipation. In doing so, they sent a clear message to the white population of Trigg County: they preferred freedom to bondage even if it meant severe dislocation.[2] Their act explicitly questioned the ideology that promoted the benign nature of slavery and the reality of the capacious family.

Perhaps surprising, the Kentucky Court of Appeals disagreed with the two Trigg County juries and upheld Jane Miller's will. For Jane Miller's slave Sarah and her family, the plaintiffs in the case, the victory was pyrrhic; by the time the Court of Appeals upheld the will in 1864, they had spent six years after Jane Miller's death in slavery.[3] On closer inspection, the Court of Appeals' conclusion reveals the delicate equilibrium these cases demanded jurists negotiate: balancing the legal imperative of maintaining the sanctity of private property rights against the possibilities of racial disorder these wills provoked through recognizing slaves' humanity and creating free, property-owning black residents.

In numerous antebellum will cases throughout Kentucky and the South, testators freed slaves or recognized concubines and other illicit relationships while ignoring legally legitimate sons, daughters, and relatives. Kentuckians, however, unlike their counterparts in the rest of the South, carried on a vibrant, long-running debate over the virtues of slavery and free labor. Until about 1850, Kentucky had spirited antislavery societies dedicated to promoting colonization and slave manumissions through wills as means to gradual emancipation. This antislavery impulse did not preclude a commitment to black inferiority; instead, it reflected a belief that slavery adversely affected white morality and degraded white labor. Lemuel Porter, a physician in Warren County during the mid-nineteenth century, expressed ambivalence about slavery as a drag on Kentucky's industrial potential. Porter lamented that real estate prices would not rise quickly because only "manufacturers can permanently improve a town. These we cannot expect to grow up here in the heart

[2] Transcript, *Sarah v. Miller* (1864), Kentucky Court of Appeals Records (hereafter KCAR), KDLA.

[3] "Testimony of William H. Miller," Transcript, *Sarah v. Miller* (1864), Case 74, Box 3, KCAR, KDLA; *Sarah v. Miller*, 62 Ky. 259 (1864).

of a slave state where labor is so high & scarce."[4] In the late 1840s, Kentucky legislators held a combative constitutional convention in which antislavery advocates who wanted a path to gradual abolition sparred against proslavery supporters who demanded more protection for slave property. Ultimately, the proslavery forces prevailed and the new 1852 constitution and reworked statutes made the process of emancipation much more difficult and expensive. Until then, many slave owners and non-slave owners viewed slavery as an evil necessary to control the black population; after 1850, most Kentuckians joined their Southern counterparts to proclaim slavery a positive good.[5] All of these political machinations affected ordinary people's testamentary practices. Manumitting slaves through wills became more difficult after the new state constitution required freed slaves to move outside Kentucky borders as a condition of manumission.

When testators emancipated slaves or made dispositions to African American beneficiaries, they converted enslaved people from property to personhood and legally affirmed slaves' humanity. In cases in which testators devised to mixed-race bloodline relatives or conjugal partners, these beneficiaries defended their right to inherit; they insisted on alternative visions of families and struggled for recognition of legally unsanctioned, socially disreputable relationships. Table 2.1 shows the frequency across time in which testators manumitted slaves. At any point in the antebellum period, manumissions occurred regularly, even as Kentucky's laws governing manumission and free blacks became more restrictive after 1850.

The racial regime in Kentucky, like other slave states, depended on affirming the naturalness of the master/slave relationship. Testamentary capacity cases reflect common concerns about the implications of emancipation. When testators disregarded the conflation of blackness with property, they disturbed what one historian has called the "harmonious social relations" of the slave economy.[6] Table 2.2 indicates that the Court

[4] Diary of Lemuel C. Porter, April 5 and 6, 1859, Mss. BI / B763, Filson Historical Society, Louisville, Kentucky (hereafter FHS).

[5] Harold B. Tallant, *Evil Necessity: Slavery and Political Culture in Antebellum Kentucky* (Lexington: University of Kentucky Press, 2003); and Steven Channing, *Kentucky: A Bicentennial History* (New York: W.W. Norton & Co., 1977).

[6] See Adrienne D. Davis, "The Private Law of Race and Sex: An Antebellum Perspective," *Stanford Law Review* 51 (January 1999): 221–88; Peter Bardaglio, *Reconstructing the Household: Families, Sex and the Law in the Nineteenth Century South* (Chapel Hill

TABLE 2.1. *Testamentary Manumissions by Decade, 1818–1869*

| Wills Written by Decade | | Number of Wills | Conditional or Immediate Manumission? Yes | No | % of Slaveholding Wills w/a Manumission |
|---|---|---|---|---|---|
| 1818–1829 | Slaveholder | 10 | 1 | 9 | 10 |
| | Not a slaveholder | 31 | N/A | | |
| 1830–1839 | Slaveholder | 14 | 2 | 12 | 14.2 |
| | Not a slaveholder | 28 | N/A | | |
| 1840–1849 | Slaveholder | 21 | 6 | 15 | 28.5 |
| | Not a slaveholder | 33 | N/A | | |
| 1850–1859 | Slaveholder | 24 | 9 | 15 | 37.5 |
| | Not a slaveholder | 35 | N/A | | |
| 1860–1869 | Slaveholder | 24 | 1 | 23 | 2.4 |
| | Not a slaveholder | 33 | N/A | | |
| Total | Slaveholder | 93 | 19 | 74 | 20.4 |
| 1818–1869 | Not a slaveholder | 160 | N/A | | |

of Appeals heard a higher percentage of cases involving emancipatory wills than the overall percentage of emancipatory wills in the Warren and Harrison County will database. The court probably heard more of these cases partially because they tended to involve more complex estate division. These cases also relied on a contested, often contradictory area of slave and inheritance law that was all but impossible to apply mechanically to county level disputes, requiring the highest court to determine outcomes.

When disinherited heirs challenged emancipatory wills, they created an opportunity for trial participants to reaffirm those harmonious racial relations based on black subordination. By disputing the sanity of these testators, juries and communities sought to strip them of rationality, allowing the anomalous wills to be explained away while supporting traditional patterns of testation as the workings of a rational mind. These cases raised broader issues involving the legal and communal regulation of the process through which the household was culturally and

and London: University of North Carolina Press, 1995), xi; and Mark V. Tushnet, *The American Law of Slavery, 1810–1860: Considerations of Humanity and Interest* (Princeton: Princeton University Press, 1981), 188.

TABLE 2.2. *Challenged Wills Involving Manumissions at the Court of Appeals*

| | Probated Wills with Slave Property from Warren and Henderson County Dataset (%) | Testamentary Capacity Challenges Taken by the Court of Appeals involving Slave Property (%) |
|---|---|---|
| Wills with manumissions | 20.4 | 34 |
| Manumissions that involved undue influence by slaves | N/A | 57 |

materially reproduced.[7] White testators who transmitted property and slaves to bloodline relatives ensured that the status, wealth, and material foundations of white families would be recreated in the next generation. These testators reinforced the naturalness of African American slavery and white mastery by promising future white generations that slaves and their offspring would pass seamlessly as property. Testators who challenged that model risked legal assaults on their wills and a public airing of their personal and sexual lives during a trial.

Specific patterns in the grammar of capacity emerged in trials challenging wills devising to or manumitting beneficiaries of color. Legal briefs and trial witnesses often emphasized African American beneficiaries' degeneration from the ideal of the well-behaved, obedient slave. As in most disputes, gendered behavioral ideals shaped how the community judged the worthiness of the chosen beneficiaries, particularly when disinherited bloodline family seemed worthy. Challenges involving interracial beneficiaries amplified the contradictions inherent in a slave system based on race and inheritable status as the markers of slavery. These challenges also serve as a marker of white anxieties about miscegenation and a free black class that would challenge the core justifications of slavery. For example, in *Minor's Heirs v. Thomas* (1851), Kentucky testator Jeremiah Minor almost completely disinherited his legitimate white

[7] On interracial relationships, family, and communal regulation, see Joshua Rothman, *Notorious in the Neighborhood: Sex and Families across the Color Line in Virginia, 1787–1861* (Chapel Hill: University of North Carolina Press, 2003). For broad discussion of the many forms (consensual and coerced) interracial relationships took, see Martha Hodes, ed., *Sex, Love, Race: Crossing Boundaries in North American History* (New York: New York University Press, 1999).

children, leaving his estate to his "black family." One witness testified that "his [Minor's] negro woman Fan had complete control over him and could make him do any thing she pleased."[8] This testimony highlighted Fan's subversion of the master/slave relationship. The description portrayed a usurpation of Minor's white male authority. Fan's relationship with Minor challenged the complex myths that rhetorically constituted Southern families. Focusing on gender-appropriate behavior conditioned by racial identity allowed juries and testifying witnesses to condemn testators or beneficiaries' behavior by mobilizing these myths embedded in law and that structured dominant social values.

## DEAD MASTERS AND SLAVES' LIVES

While slaves' lives were fraught with the uncertainty of sale at any time, the masters' deaths guaranteed a change in ownership and often a change in residence. Enslaved people and deceased testators' white families followed the probate process very closely.[9] Ex-slave James C. Pennington vividly described the apprehension occasioned when slaves passed between generations. "It is very rarely the case that a slave's condition is benefited by passing from the old master into the hands of one of his children," Pennington remarked. "The decline is so rapid and marked ... that the children of slaveholders are universally inferior ... mentally, morally, physically, as well as pecuniarily ... and this is a matter of most vital concern to the slaves." Many slave narratives document how masters' deaths brought profound changes, including the separation of families. Frederick Douglass described the division of his master's estate, recalling how it "sunder[ed] forever the dearest friends, dearest kindred, and strongest ties known to human beings." Other slaves remembered either direct or indirect promises from their masters that their wills would free them. At her mistress's death, Harriet Jacobs "could not help having some hopes she had left me free." When the will was read, "we learned that she

[8] "Will of Jeremiah Minor," *Thomas & c. of color v. Jeremiah Minor's Heirs & c.* (1849), Scott County Court Order Book 20, 164; Scott County Court Records, KDLA. Hereafter *Thomas v. Minor* (1849), SCCOB 20. "Testimony of Thomas Catlett," *Thomas & c. of color v. Jeremiah Minor's Heirs & c.* (1849), Scott County Court Order Book 21, 104. Hereafter *Thomas v. Minor* (1849), SCCOB 21. Both in Scott County Court Records, KDLA.

[9] Ch. 43, Art. 9 § 4. *Revised Statutes of Kentucky* (1852, printed 1860). The sample (n = 25%) is taken from Harrison County Will Books B – H (1818–1864), Harrison County Court Records, KDLA.

had bequeathed me to her sister's daughter, a child of five years old. So vanished our hopes."[10]

Other slaves' owners kept these promises. Even in those circumstances, freedom through a testamentary manumission was far from certain. In his slave narrative, former Kentucky slave Lewis Garrard Clark recalled the difficulties his mother faced in realizing her master's promise of emancipation by his will.

> Mr. Campbell promised my father that his daughter Letitia should be made free in his will. It was with this promise that he married her. And I have no doubt that Mr. Campbell was as good as his word, and that, by his *will*, my mother and her nine children were made free. But ten persons in one family, each worth three hundred dollars, are not easily set free among those accustomed to live by continued robbery. We did not, therefore, by an instrument from the hand of the dead, escape the avaricious grab of the slaveholder. It is the common belief that the will was destroyed by the heirs of Mr. Campbell.[11]

Emancipations such as Letitia's at first appear to subvert the institution of slavery and demonstrate the benevolence of some white masters who acknowledged affectionate interracial sexual relationships. Campbell's manumission of Letitia destroyed slave property and withheld mastery over Letitia and her children from legally legitimate white family members. Campbell transformed her from chattel property to legal personhood. To conclude however, that testators who manumitted slaves intentionally struck a blow against the power of white patriarchy overlooks the timing of these devises and the coercive power relations inherent in sexual relationships between male masters and enslaved women.

The sexual relationship between Campbell and Letitia was central to her emancipation. Although her son described his mother as Campbell's "wife," she remained his property. Interracial relationships existed in a legal universe that highlighted the nearly absolute power of masters

[10] James C. Pennington, "The Fugitive Blacksmith; or Events in the History of James C. Pennington," in Yuval Taylor, ed., *I was Born a Slave: An Anthology of Classic Slave Narratives, Volume Two 1849–1866* (Chicago: Lawrence Hill Books, 1999), 148; Frederick Douglass, *Narrative of the Life of Frederick Douglass, An American Slave* (Boston: Anti-Slavery Office, 1845; reprint, New York: Dover Publications, 1995), 27; Harriet Jacobs, *Incidents in the Life of a Slave Girl*, in Yuval Taylor, ed., *I was Born a Slave: An Anthology of Classic Slave Narratives, Volume Two 1849–1866* (Chicago: Lawrence Hill Books, 1999), 546.

[11] "Narratives of the Sufferings of Lewis and Milton Clarke, Sons of a Soldier of the Revolution, During a Captivity of More Than Twenty Years Among the Slaveholders of Kentucky, One of the So Called Christian States of North America" (1846), http://docsouth.unc.edu/neh/clarkes/clarkes.html.

deemed sane. Men who waited until their deaths to emancipate enslaved concubines reinforced the politics of coercion and submission between master and slave by denying enslaved women ownership of their bodies. The reference to Letitia as a "wife" and to her nine children suggests that she did not overtly or consistently resist Campbell's exercise of conjugal rights. Yet her status as slave meant she had no legal right to deny him sexual access to her body either. Although husbands had a property right in their wives' bodies, white wives had some legal recourse to divorce, separation, or appeal to family and friends for support and protection. Campbell had the legal freedom to emancipate Letitia at any time during his life, thus possibly avoiding the family dispute that negated his will. He chose to keep her in a coercive relationship in which he had almost absolute legal control until his death. These kinds of manumissions simultaneously reinforced and disturbed the sexual and racial hierarchies in the South by recognizing affectionate and sexual interracial unions while maintaining coercion and enforced obedience through enslavement.

Testators' family members also recognized the contentious and uncertain nature of manumissions in wills. As testator Jane Miller's brother commented in a letter discussing her intended manumissions, "I well know the great difficulty that had attended the carrying out of all such wills trammeled by law suits ... it amounts to a failure or very annoying detentions."[12] Testators who manumitted slaves rather than passing them to the next generation rejected legitimate bloodline kin. In nullifying their value as property, these wills passed the value of each slave to him or herself rather than to the testators' family members – a gift of self-possession to each slave, in other words. Furthermore, these wills violated the white community's patterns of cementing intergenerational bonds forged by passing humans as legal property.[13] If inheriting slaves was a means of binding white families together through slavery, manumissions often led to outright hostility within white families and between the emancipated slaves and the heirs-at-law in the courtroom.

Often, the charges of undue influence and mental unsoundness appeared together in disputes in which testators emancipated slaves or left property to interracial concubines. A typical challenge alleged that the testator's weakened mental state allowed the black beneficiaries to

[12] Letter inserted in "Testimony of James Miller," Transcript, *Sarah v. Miller* (1864), KCAR, KDLA.

[13] Walter Johnson, *Soul by Soul: Life inside the Antebellum Slave Market* (Cambridge and London: Harvard University Press, 1999), 101.

exert "unnatural" influence over the testator's disposition of property. In *James v. Langdon* (1846), the court judge observed that testator David Roper wrote his will "when his body and mind, naturally weak, were both much enfeebled by age and disease. Lucy and Hector, his two elder slaves, were attentive to his wants and he was much under their influence and control, and there is good reason to believe that Lucy used means to prejudice and embitter his mind against his children."[14] Crucial to the notion of undue influence was the legal status of the relationship between the alleged influencer and the testator.

Testamentary capacity and undue influence jurisprudence was predisposed to overturn gifts to interracial sexual partners because laws forbade interracial marriages, thus placing these relationships outside of the boundaries of legal legitimacy favored by inheritance law. Courts and local individuals found black beneficiaries suspect. The Court of Appeals tolerated – even expected – persuasion from legitimate or "natural" relations, as they ruled in *Sechrest v. Edwards* (1862). "Lawful influence," Judge Peters held, "such as arises from legitimate or social relations, must be allowed to produce their natural results even upon last wills and testaments."[15] In *The Law of Wills* (1866), oft-cited jurist Isaac Redfield saw the law as maintaining morality by excluding influence emanating from relationships not sanctioned by the law. Influence arising from legally unsanctioned relationships, Redfield believed, "do[es] violence to the morality of the law ... if we should apply this rule to unlawful as well as to lawful relations."[16] The hidden legal default privileged these beneficiaries – related through legally recognized relationships and acknowledged shared blood – in reaping material benefits. If the capacity standard required testators to recognize the "natural objects of their bounty," undue influence jurisprudence anticipated that testators would favor their heirs-at-law rather than deny them their material legacy. Lawful relations were expected to exert influence and receive the testator's bounty. The statutory and case law treated with skepticism those outside legally recognized or blood relationships. To devise otherwise, if

[14] *James v. Langdon*, 46 Ky. 193 (1846).

[15] *Sechrest v. Edwards*, 61 Ky. 163 (1862).

[16] Isaac Redfield, *The Law of Wills, Embracing the Making and Construction of Wills; The Jurisprudence of Insanity; The Effect of Extrinsic Evidence; The Creation and Construction of Trusts, So Far As Applicable to Wills, with Forms and Instructions for Preparing Wills Part I*, second edition (Boston: Little Brown and Co., 1866), 466.

not symptomatic of insanity, suggested a testator susceptible to the illicit seductions of an unworthy and often unrelated beneficiary.

## THE COURT'S CONUNDRUM: ARRESTING THE WILL OF A MAN

In spite of the law's predisposition toward a biologically defined and racially homogenous family, the Court of Appeals's early decisions indicated it would not tolerate lower courts arbitrarily usurping property owners' right to dispose of property. In overturning the Bracken County Court's 1814 rejection of Reuben Cochran's will, the Court of Appeals chastised the lower court for impinging on the testator's freedom, remarking, "we cannot think a Court justifiable in arresting the will of a man, and thereby perhaps causing his estate to pass contrary to his own wish and will."[17] Cochran devised land to his two illegitimate daughters and gave his slaves to his nephew. The court appeared particularly concerned about protecting masculine prerogative and respecting the integrity of a testator's right to exercise free will when transmitting his property. This preference, however, had its limits.

By 1822, the Court of Appeals had established its inclination to favor beneficiaries who shared kin and race with the testator and its suspicion of testamentary gifts resulting from interracial relationships. George Moore died in 1822, emancipating his black concubine (never named in the record) and devising property to her and several other unrelated beneficiaries. Moore, who never married, disinherited his brothers. They challenged the will, claiming Moore was "deranged on the subject of his relatives" and that his concubine and other beneficiaries unduly influenced Moore. The court agreed, ruling that Moore's brothers had become the objects of his "hatred and disgust," and Moore's reasons for his feelings appeared "futile and groundless." To the court, the will itself served as evidence of mental incapacity. They concluded that if Moore had held an unnatural aversion toward unrelated persons rather than those "supposed by the ties of natural affection to be the objects of his bounty, we should have no difficulty in sustaining this will." The court made clear that had Moore left his property to his relatives rather than to his concubine, who "possessed considerable influence" over him, his will would have been upheld as reflecting a sound and rational mind. Moore's will triggered an undue influence challenge because of the lack of legal

[17] *In re Cochran's Will*, 6 Ky. 491 (1814).

recognition of his relationship to his beneficiaries. The court, for its part, then equated mental incapacity with a testator who chose beneficiaries outside of bloodline kin.[18]

Joseph Cabell Breckinridge, the lawyer for the beneficiaries, presented an alternative interpretation of Moore's relationship with his concubine.[19] Breckinridge defended Moore's right as an independent citizen to pass property to whomever he chose. Breckinridge conceded that an affectionate relationship may have existed, at least from the standpoint of Moore's concubine, noting that she may have been the only "mourner that shed a tear upon his grave." This did not excuse Moore's sexual conduct, which Breckinridge agreed was despicable. Breckinridge contended, however, that Moore's interracial relationship was an act "not of madness, but of lust." Some men, he argued, "seek after the depraved indulgence of their foul and unnatural lusts, in an intercourse with the forbidden sex; or, descending one grade lower in the scale of turpitude, sport their manhood in brutal rivalship with the courser and the boar."[20] As distasteful as Moore's conduct was, Breckinridge defended it as within the boundaries of sane albeit deeply degenerate behavior. Breckinridge conceded that Moore's interracial relationship carried the same moral opprobrium as homosexuality and bestiality, but distinguished it from insanity. His castigation of Moore reinforced dominant ideas about the immorality of interracial relationships, yet held testamentary freedom as a precious right that required judicial protection to ensure the independence of all testators.

The brief presented Moore's case as a broader need to protect testamentary freedom from encroachment by designing relatives, noting the issue was one of "legal privilege." Breckinridge insisted that a testator must be allowed to disinherit relatives. He argued that if an "execrable" offense could strip a testator of "the rights of free agency," then all testators' independence was at risk. In a statement calculated to resonate with the founding values of the republic, Breckinridge appealed to the court as "votaries of civil liberty."[21] Although the court overturned the

[18] "Reply to Petition for Rehearing, Submitted by Counsel for Appellant," *Johnson v. Moore's Heirs*, 11 Ky. 371 (1822).

[19] Joseph Cabell Breckinridge (1788–1823) was a member of the Breckinridge family whose members were among Kentucky's elite politicians, military officers, and lawyers. See James C. Klotter, *The Breckinridges of Kentucky* (Lexington: University of Kentucky Press, 1986).

[20] "Reply to Petition," *Johnson v. Moore's Heirs*, 11 Ky. 371 (1822).

[21] Ibid.

will, depriving Moore's concubine of legal personhood, this early dispute illuminates how race and sex infused the definition of legal sanity and the exercise of inheritance rights. The battle being fought was not over the freedom claims of enslaved people. Rather, it was over the limits of freedom and independence for testators, who were overwhelmingly white and male, when they crossed racial barriers.

Local communities connected interracial relationships and insanity. Witness testimony in several cases heard over twenty-five years after *Johnson v. Moore's Heirs* (1822) reveal how people in Kentucky communities articulated their ideas about the proper relationship between masters and their slaves. In two of these cases, *Denton v. Franklin* (1848) and *Minor's Heirs v. Thomas* (1851), when testators publicly recognized interracial relationships as sexual or when they resulted in testamentary gifts, local witnesses expressed disgust and consternation.[22] Their testimonies – usually the bulk of the evidence upon which the jury would rule – indicated that some men attributed interracial gifts or testamentary manumissions to an unsound mind. By defining sanity in terms of testators' choices, local men from the testator's community patrolled and reinforced the boundaries of whiteness and family and defined the limits of property rights.

In *Denton v. Franklin* (1848), Edmund Talbot and Hannah, a former slave emancipated by Talbot, had conducted a connubial relationship for many years. Talbot's will emancipated his slaves, devised much of his property to them and Hannah, and left his son and two daughters small devises of land. Similarly, in *Minor's Heirs v. Thomas* (1851), Jeremiah Minor, a Scott County testator, also emancipated his slaves and left them property, referring to them as his "black family." His children contested the will. In both cases the emancipated slaves participated as legal parties and challenged an inheritance system that usually cast them as chattel property rather than legal persons. These wills and the trials that disclosed the relationships behind them suggest that the testators and their African American beneficiaries understood family outside of parameters defined by race and shared blood.[23]

Lawyers for the heirs-at-law (the testators' disinherited children) in both cases contested the wills on mental incapacity and undue influence

[22] *Denton v. Franklin*, 48 Ky. 28 (1848); *Minor's Heirs v. Thomas*, 51 Ky. 106 (1851).

[23] *Denton v. Franklin*, 48 Ky. 28 (1848); "Will of Edmund Talbot," *Talbott, Thos. D. and others v. Hardwick, B.F. and others* (April 1847), Henderson County Circuit Court Case Files, Case 7749, KDLA. Hereafter abbreviated as *Talbott v. Hardwick* (1847), HCCC Case 7749; "Will of Jeremiah Minor," *Thomas v. Minor* (1849), SCCOB 21, 106.

grounds. Strategically, they had to develop an argument that would allow a finding of insanity and overturn an individual's testamentary freedom while reaffirming generally the property rights that attended white manhood. In both cases the challengers' lawyers used a narrative of mental decline that appears in many testamentary cases. In *Denton v. Franklin* (1848), witnesses testified that in the years before the will had been written, Edmund Talbot had been "sensible," and of "sound mind." As he aged he lost mental capacity. Hector Green, the county surveyor, compared records that Talbot, a former surveyor, made years earlier with those he made later; he concluded that "his business capacity must have been much deranged & impaired in the latter years of his life." In Jeremiah Minor's case, his mental decline also was attributed to his advanced age. Martin Bramlett, Minor's neighbor, testified that until six years prior to his death, Minor was a "moral high minded honorable man," but during the last few years of his life, Minor lacked the "sense as a common boy of ten years."[24] This mental deterioration allowed the challengers to explain why the master/slave hierarchy had been inverted. The testators' progressive retreat from rationality created a debilitated mental state that allowed the slaves to influence their decisions, eventually leading them to disinherit their families. Although this strategy failed when local juries refused to overturn these wills, the Court of Appeals found the testimonies credible enough to set aside the wills and rule in favor of the heirs-at law in both cases.

Both cases focused on the sexual behavior of the African American beneficiaries. In Edmund Talbot's case, his interracial sexual relationship became the focal point of the trial. Talbot had been a local doctor and a county surveyor. He had bought and sold slaves in Henderson County, where he had resided for more than fifteen years before his death. Located in the northwestern part of Kentucky, Henderson County was primarily agricultural and had one of the largest slave populations in the region. The contestants' lawyers had to prove that this respected local officeholder, doctor, and businessman was mentally incapable of writing a will. Talbot, though, had raised the ire of the community by violating an unwritten code that tolerated white men who pursued interracial relationships with African American women as long as these relationships remained legally and socially unrecognized. The lawyers hoped to convince the jury that it would be doing its duty by sending a message to the community that

24 "Testimony of Hector Green," *Talbott v. Hardwick* (1847), HCCC Case 7749; "Testimony of Martin Bramlett", *Thomas v. Minor* (1849), SCCOB 21, 102.

while such relationships might be informally tolerated, formal recognition was unacceptable.[25]

During the county circuit court trial, witnesses testified that Hannah and Talbot shared a room and lived as husband and wife. Although Talbot had emancipated Hannah years before his death, two of Talbot's acquaintances testified that Hannah acted "unbecoming a servant," and worse, Talbot had not chastised her. Witnesses portrayed Hannah as a duplicitous slave, although she was legally free. They refused to admit that perhaps Talbot and Hannah willingly had engaged in an affectionate, companionate relationship that deviated from the subjection of the master/slave relationship, or for that matter, the subordination in the husband/wife relationship. They claimed Talbot could not exercise his authority over his dependents, permitting all sorts of social and gender transgressions. John Denton recalled that he heard Hannah "abuse his the doctors sons in law in the Dr's presence & the Dr. said nothing but permitted it." Clearly, Talbot's friends, neighbors, and business associates believed that these instances indicated not only Hannah's powers of persuasion, but also Talbot's weak and disordered mind.[26]

For those who supported slavery and saw the institution as reflecting natural relations ordained by God and law, Talbot could commit few greater sins against his community or posterity than conduct an overt interracial relationship approximating marriage. As proslavery theorist and one-time South Carolina senator William Harper noted in a frequently circulated essay:

> The licentious passions of men overcome the natural repugnance, and find transient gratification in intercourse with females of the other race. But it is a very different thing from making her ... the companion of the bosom and hearth. Him ... we should esteem as a degraded wretch. It is not only in defence of ourselves, of our country and of our own generation, that we refuse to emancipate our slaves, but to defend our posterity and race from degeneracy and degradation.[27]

[25] Transcript, *Talbott v. Hardwick* (1847), HCCC Case 7749; "Reports Communicated to Both Branches of the Legislature of Kentucky at the December Session, 1845 (Auditor's Report), Legislative Document No. 10," (Frankfort: A.G. Hodges, 1845). For a broader discussion of the ramifications of interracial relationships, see Bardaglio, *Reconstructing the Household*, 48–64.

[26] "Testimony of Joseph B. Norman," "Testimony of James Gillis," *Talbott v. Hardwick* (1847), HCCC Case 7749; "Testimony of John Denton," "Testimony of John Dorris," *Talbott v. Hardwick* (1847), HCCC Case 7749. For similar portrayals of interracial relationships by white witnesses, see Davis, "The Private Law of Race and Sex," 262–5.

[27] William Harper, "Slavery in the Light of Social Ethics," in *Cotton is King and Proslavery Arguments* (Augusta: Pritchard, Abbott & Loomis, 1860), 547–626.

As Harper suggested, Talbot and Hannah had violated a complex array of racial and gendered codes of behavior that structured social and legal relations in slave states. Hannah had assumed the role of plantation wife by sharing Talbot's bedroom and expressing judgments on the conduct of Talbot's children and their spouses. She occupied a racially determined position physically and symbolically reserved for white women. John Dorris, who had lived with Talbot for several years, claimed that Hannah "had influence over him about plantation affairs & other matters."[28] Hannah imposed on Talbot's authority as the male head of household by openly advising him on the masculine world of business affairs. Indeed, to the white residents of Henderson County, the Talbot household appeared chaotic and degenerate.

The plaintiffs pointed to Hannah as the true culprit who exploited a mentally diminished and isolated man. Implicit in this reasoning was the premise that mastery required a strong, vigilant mind or else dependents would exploit their masters' weaknesses for their own benefit. It also upheld the mental and moral superiority of white men, as long as they remained "sane," while highlighting the inherently mendacious nature of black women. Masters perceived as losing mental acuity no longer could claim the privileges and responsibilities of whiteness or mastery, including the right to make decisions involving their property distribution.

Similar tropes emphasizing the cunning nature of African Americans and the consequences of a weak and disordered patriarch emerged in *Thomas v. Minor*, the dispute over Jeremiah Minor's will. Although Minor was not accused of conducting a sexual relationship with his slaves, witnesses emphasized the slaves' immoral sexual conduct and Minor's inability to compel obedience from them. Neighbors marched out a parade of horribles to describe the conditions of the Minor farm, demonstrating the dangers posed by a mentally incapacitated master. John House, a close neighbor, testified that Minor's negro quarter was a "sink of vice and debauchery." Worse, he raised the specter of profligate white women prostituting themselves in mixed-race liaisons, stating that "they [Minor's slaves] sold liquor and entertained white women of the basest and most abandoned character notoriously of bad virtue and fame." Sexual liaisons between white women and black men presented threats to racial slavery that sex between a male master and female slave did not. Because enslaved status was passed through the mother, racial mixing could create a free mulatto underclass and raised the specter of

[28] "Testimony of John Dorris," *Talbott v. Hardwick* (1847), HCCC Case 7749.

racial degeneration. Racial purity depended on protecting white women's sexual virtue in order to create the next racially pure generation of masters, citizens, and mothers.[29]

In many cases involving interracial beneficiaries, community members linked the reasons for testators' mental decline to a variety of reasons other than old age, including illness or death of a spouse. Often, they attributed the onset of the decline to a time when the testator became isolated from white society and lived almost exclusively with African Americans. In the *Minor* case, John House testified that after Minor's wife died, "no white person lived with the old man." In *Sarah v. Miller* (1864), female neighbors testified that Jane Miller rarely visited them or participated in Trigg County social rituals. Miller's physician called her a "recluse" who lived "only with her negroes for many years before her death." Deprived of the civilizing influences of white society, these testators slowly became insane and relinquished their authority, and ultimately their property, to their slaves.[30]

Some of these cases resulted in appellate courts or juries sustaining wills naming interracial beneficiaries in spite of all social and legal obstacles. Historians have pointed to the culture of "personalism" as influencing legal outcomes in local jury trials. Within local communities, one's reputation, developed through years of close contact with neighbors and the community, could influence how juries made decisions in individual cases. David Dickson, a respected Georgia planter and businessman, left his estate to his illegitimate mixed-race daughter, Amanda Dickson. Dickson's legendary hospitality and reputation within the community may have fostered goodwill toward him and his daughter among the jurors who ultimately upheld the will.[31] In the two Kentucky cases, *Minor's Heirs v. Talbot* and *Denton v. Franklin*, local judges and juries upheld the wills in spite of condemnatory testimony. Although numerous witnesses testified that Jeremiah Minor's and Edmund Talbot's mental capacity had declined in recent years, previously both testators had enjoyed reputations as respected men who adhered to their roles as businessmen,

[29] "Testimony of John House," *Thomas v. Minor* (1849), SCCOB 21, 101. Martha Hodes, *White Women, Black Men: Illicit Sex in the Nineteenth Century South* (New Haven: Yale University Press, 1997), 4. See Bardaglio, *Reconstructing the Household*, 58–78; Victoria Bynum, *Unruly Women: The Politics of Social and Sexual Control in the Old South* (Chapel Hill and London: University of North Carolina Press, 1992), 35–42.

[30] "Testimony of John House," 101, *Thomas v. Minor* (1849), SCCOB 21; "Testimony of Dr. Burnett," Transcript, *Sarah v. Miller* (1864), KCAR, KDLA.

[31] Kent Anderson Leslie, *Woman of Color, Daughter of Privilege: Amanda America Dickson, 1849–1893* (Athens: University of Georgia Press, 1995), 30–1.

community leaders, slaveholders, and moral examples in the community. In many respects they had upheld the local gender conventions for men of their class and color.

Personal and business relationships over many years may explain the jury's willingness to overlook Edmund Talbot's and Jeremiah Minor's transgressions. As Thomas B. Catlett noted in the *Minor* will dispute, Jeremiah Minor had been a "man of good conduct" and "industry" who "managed his concerns well." In 1845, Henderson County claimed only fifteen hundred and nine white men over twenty-one years old.[32] It is probable that some jurors knew Talbot. Members of the jury also may have feared their behavior might receive the same legal scrutiny. Interfering with male testators' freedom potentially eroded the freedoms and privileges associated with masculinity, perhaps making an all-male jury more hesitant to interfere with the property rights of other local men. When the testator in a will dispute was female, male juries appeared more willing to overturn wills on insanity and undue influence grounds.

In *Sarah v. Miller* (1864), two local juries rejected Jane Miller's will, although numerous witnesses testified to her sanity and intelligence. Even so, Miller deviated from behavior appropriate to her sex and class. Unlike Jeremiah Minor and Edmund Talbot, Jane Miller had never been a typical master or adhered to gender conventions. She never married and retained legal rights to her property. Trial transcripts reveal that community members determined the standard of sanity to which Miller would be held by comparing her conduct to that of other women. Miller's neighbor, William Martin, testified to her mental unsoundness, noting that "her conduct all the time was very strange and different from any other woman I ever knew." Similarly, in testifying in favor of Miller's sanity, Reverend James Hawthorn observed that Miller was a "judicious lady with rather more ordinary shrewdness ... than is often found in ladies in the same circumstances." Comparing Miller to other women the witnesses believed were similarly situated made her deviations from ordinary female behavior more apparent. Even Hawthorn's testimony noted that she had "more ordinary shrewdness" than other women, highlighting how Miller differed from her female counterparts.[33]

[32] "Testimony of Thomas B. Catlett," 103, *Thomas v. Minor* (1849), SCCOB 21; "Reports Communicated to Both Branches of the Legislature of Kentucky, Auditor's Report (1845)," 105.

[33] "Testimony of William Martin," "Testimony of Rev. James Hawthorn," Transcript, *Sarah v. Miller* (1864), KCAR, KDLA.

Miller's behavior toward men also came under scrutiny. When asked by the contestants' lawyers if she shunned the company of men, Sheriff Daniel Landes replied that she "always tried to shun me" and referred to her as "very unsocial."[34] The language used to describe Miller's relationships with men emphasized her rejection of them and highlighted Miller's unmarried status. She thwarted traditional arrangements in which men gained control of women's property through marriage, exercised her right to write a will, and denied her brothers control of her wealth and slaves through her testamentary emancipations. Although many witnesses testified to her sanity, the trial emphasized Miller's behavior as diverging from that of other women, most of whom were married and legally dependent on men. As a woman who lived in seclusion, rejected social rituals, and avoided contact with men, Jane Miller's behavior pointed to mental incapacity. By nullifying Jane Miller's will, jurors restored her property and mastery over her slaves to its proper place: under the male control of her brother Isaac, the heir-at-law.

Once *Minor's Heirs v. Thomas* and *Denton v. Franklin* reached the appellate level, the Court of Appeals refused to overlook Edmund Talbot or Jeremiah Minor's transgressions. In both cases, the court shored up white patriarchy by reestablishing racial and sexual order. The court attributed the testators' failures to conform to the cultural and social behaviors of a white patriarch to insanity. It defined the limits of male testamentary freedom and independence, turning the focus toward not only the beneficiaries of the will, but also the white heirs-at-law who had been disinherited in the process. In *Denton v. Franklin* the court directed its displeasure at Edmund Talbot's concern for Hannah instead of his children. The court commented that "the gratification of the wishes of this colored woman, seems to be its [the will's] leading object. The natural duty of providing for his own children, whose condition and circumstances in life, required the exercise of his bounty in their favor, was entirely forgotten or disregarded." The court made distinctions based on race about the legitimacy and morality of relationships within the Talbot household and these judgments determined property rights.[35]

In the dispute over Jeremiah Minor's will, the court's decision reaffirmed that testators would not will property outside of their racial or

[34] "Testimony of Daniel Landes," Transcript, *Sarah v. Miller* (1864), 136, KCAR, KDLA.

[35] *Denton v. Franklin*, 48 Ky. 28 (1848); See Hodes, *White Women, Black Men*, 77–86 for a discussion of other instances in which courts sanctioned white men perceived as unable to fulfill the responsibilities of patriarchal authority.

kin group without provocation. The court ruled that his "children were obedient and affectionate ... which excludes the inference that his slaves were preferred to them as subjects of his bounty on account of ungrateful or improper conduct."[36] Minor had referred to his slaves in his will as his "black family," suggesting that his relationship with his slaves was affectionate. Minor's will indicated that he saw himself as a paternal figure to his slaves. The court's rejection of the interracial gifts indicated that paternalism, when expressed through inheritance, would be confined to white heirs-at-law. The lines determined by race and blood prevented Minor's slaves from reaping the benefits of his interracial vision of family. Of course, Minor's cryptic reference does not preclude that he demanded subordination from his slaves. For the antebellum court however, legitimately established bloodlines and race were the determining factors in deciding how property and freedom would be distributed.

Once *Sarah v. Miller* (1864) reached the Court of Appeals, the judges strongly supported the will. They opined that "on the subject of capacity the testimony is, both numerically and morally, overwhelming in favor or a disposing mind."[37] The court indicated that, based on the evidence, the lower courts' decisions would not pass statutory requirements for an insanity finding. Although Miller deviated from Trigg County gender roles, she did not pose the threat of sexual disorder and racial chaos brought about by the interracial liaisons described in the *Minor* and *Denton* cases. Miller also banished her freed slaves to Liberia, whereas Talbot's and Minor's emancipations left free African American property owners in local communities. Although Miller never married, her emancipations did not reward slave behavior that impinged on white mastery and masculine authority. Two local juries refused to forgive Jane Miller's eccentric behavior; unlike the *Minor* and *Denton* decisions, the Court of Appeals found little legal evidence upon which it could endorse local disapproval.

The central issue in these cases is not whether Edmund Talbot, Jeremiah Minor, or Jane Miller were insane by historical legal standards or by contemporary standards. These cases are about how Kentucky courts and communities understood the relationships between family, property distribution, and insanity when wills crossed racial lines. These cases reveal how people experienced family in configurations different from those defined by law and dominant social ideals. They suggest that some people

[36] *Minor's Heirs v. Thomas*, 51 Ky. 106 (1851).
[37] *Sarah v. Miller*, 62 Ky. 259 (1864).

understood the familial obligations that inhere in private relationships in ways that sometimes threatened the organic hierarchies that structured Southern society.

This area of testamentary capacity jurisprudence may have appeared neutral in its legal rules; in its application, local and state legal actors were deeply invested in maintaining material and affectionate bonds between generations of white families. *Denton v. Franklin*, *Minor's Heirs v. Thomas*, and *Sarah v. Miller* reveal the flexibility of the capacity standard and established the limits to which the Court of Appeals would entertain the gender politics of local communities. Local communities were willing to uphold Jeremiah Minor and Edmund Talbot's wills in spite of sexual and social transgressions because they knew Minor and Talbot. In doing so, they reaffirmed white male authority and sexual license. Local juries punished Jane Miller's independence and eccentricity, suggesting that sanity for women depended far more on female adherence to marriage and gender conventions.

These cases reveal the ongoing manufacture of law in the space between local legal proceedings and state-level, formalist appellate decision making. In *Denton v. Franklin* and *Minor's Heirs v. Thomas*, the Court of Appeals refused to let community judgments prevail against images of white patriarchs emasculated by the deprivation of reason and authority. The needs of state law prevailed over legal localism because much more was at stake than articulating the capacity standard. These cases implicated the institutional supports, the reinforcing steel that ran through the architecture of slavery. A master who allowed racial disorder and sexual chaos jeopardized the orderly transmission of wealth and the maintenance of the slave economy. The court indicated that legally unsanctioned interracial sexual relationships would not be rewarded with material benefits conferred by legitimacy, whiteness, and social acceptance. The racially determined laws of marriage, miscegenation, and legitimacy merged seamlessly with the ostensibly neutral laws of inheritance.

The reasons behind the resolution of Jane Miller's will dispute are more complex. The local trials suggest that juries were much more likely to closely regulate women's property decisions. (For a fuller discussion of this point, see Chapter 5.) Writing a will represented the recognition of a distinctly masculine obligation of maintaining the family through wealth distribution. Female testators challenged that model by asserting independence over property and creating an alternative model in which women controlled wealth distribution. In spite of numerous witness testimonies affirming Miller's sanity and even her exceptional intelligence, local juries overturned her will. As witness testimony revealed, several community members resented Jane Miller, her independence, and her preference for solitude away from male company. The Court of Appeals however, strongly endorsed her will as reflecting a "self-poised mind, unbiased by any extraneous influence."[38] The court would not allow a precedent-setting ruling based on scant legal evidence to determine the contours of mental capacity. Once her legal capacity was established, the court validated her will. Ruling in 1864, perhaps the court also recognized slavery's imminent demise. Either way, it maintained the appearance of juridical neutrality required for scrutiny by a broader audience.

These cases created a window of opportunity for a few African Americans emancipated by wills. Although in the Minor and Talbot will disputes they ultimately lost, Franklin, Thomas, and the other African American litigants claimed a legal voice through which they rejected their status as property. Sarah and Jane Miller's other slaves ultimately gained their legal freedom. Slaves who brought these emancipation suits actively participated in a legal system that fused skin color to status as property. Ironically, they validated white privilege by struggling to uphold their masters' wills, but in the process, their trials revealed alternative visions of sexual desire, family, and perhaps affection. In the cases that resulted from these relationships, some local community members asserted that only an unsound mind would choose such beneficiaries. Heirs-at-law bringing suit, witness testimony, and courts overturning wills preserved the illusion of testamentary freedom as a right that inhered in sane and rational men and women. Sanity and rationality however, were defined by racial and sexual ideologies that orchestrated the operation of probate law.

[38] Ibid.

# 3

# Arbiters of Sanity

## *Medical Experts and Jurists*

In May 1891, Owen County Circuit Court spectators watched a heated disagreement between two of Kentucky's most distinguished medical experts. At issue was Joseph F. Williams's sanity at the moment he wrote his will, leaving most of his property to the Baptist Church.[1] Five physicians testified, including Dr. F. H. Clark, superintendent of Lexington's nationally known Eastern State Lunatic Asylum (ESLA), and Dr. David W. Yandell, a University of Louisville Medical Department professor, author, and past president of the American Medical Association. Both physicians claimed to possess diagnostic expertise, yet they reached opposite conclusions. Clark asserted, "I think he was sane, capable of knowing his property and knowing his relatives." Yandell declared, "He was of unsound mind & could not make a will."[2] Although willing to decisively judge Williams's mental state, neither Yandell nor Clark had ever met him.[3] Williams's local doctor, Joe Dupuy, who had treated him

[1] "Will of Joseph F. Williams," Transcript, *Williams v. Williams* (1893), Case 22461, Box 982, Kentucky Court of Appeals Records (hereafter KCAR), Kentucky Department for Libraries and Archives, Frankfort, Kentucky (hereafter KDLA).

[2] "Testimony of FH Clark" and "Testimony of David W. Yandall," Transcript, *Williams v. Williams* (1893), Case 22461, Box 983, KCAR, KDLA. The spelling of Yandell's last name varies. Several transcripts record it as Yandall, while book publishers and contemporary archivists spell it as Yandell.

[3] The words "medical expert" as used in the nineteenth century referred to physicians who brought specialized knowledge to trial gleaned from occupational practice and education at the nation's elite medical schools. Experts participated in regional and national dialogues through medical societies, publications, and affiliations. "Irregulars," midwives, and derogatorily labeled "quacks" or "root doctors" referred to practitioners with no formal training. Local doctors had some training but did not participate in research or the national societies and did not publish in specialized journals. Classifying individuals is an

for years, testified that Williams was "insane on the subject of religion." On cross-examination, the challengers' lawyer asked Dupuy about his qualifications to diagnose insanity. Dupuy admitted, "I am only a general practitioner and have never made the subject of insanity a subject of special study." The question implied that in spite of personal experience with his patient, Dupuy was unqualified to pass judgment on Williams's mental state.[4]

Beginning in the late eighteenth century, formally trained, elite physicians identified new forms of insanity, such as neurasthenia, moral insanity, religious insanity, nymphomania, kleptomania, and a host of other "manias."[5] According to these medical experts, different forms of insanity explained everything from religious fervor to moral turpitude and deviant wills.[6] Early American doctors shared their British counterparts' zeal for medical jurisprudence, an academic and professional field that used medical knowledge to exercise legal power.[7] By the mid-nineteenth century, experts testified regularly in testamentary capacity trials, explaining to juries that deviant behavior often resulted from disease. Their influence touched off a protracted debate in elite legal and medical circles over who could best determine testamentary capacity.

To jurists, the disease model of deviance propounded by medical experts offered both promise and peril. New theories of insanity furnished modern, scientific, and seemingly objective explanations for iniquitous wills. Most eccentric behavior could be symptomatic of insanity, providing ready justification for overturning wills that deviated from traditional patterns of choosing legitimate bloodline beneficiaries. The new theories could be appropriated to reinforce the centuries-old legal structures that consolidated wealth in white familial bloodlines. Simultaneously, the new theories threatened to undermine the post–American Revolution

inexact science, but, generally, medical experts were distinguished by their appointments to faculties or other medical institutions and their participation in regional or national dialogues.

4 "Testimony of Dr. Joe Dupuy," Transcript, *Williams v. Williams* (1893), Case 22461, Box 982, KCAR, KDLA.

5 Barbara Sicherman, "The Uses of a Diagnosis: Doctors, Patients, and Neurasthenia," *Journal of the History of Medicine and Allied Sciences* 32 (1977): 33–54; Carol Groneman, *Nymphomania: A History* (New York: W. W. Norton, 2000).

6 Edward Shorter, *A History of Psychiatry: From the Era of the Asylum to the Age of Prozac* (New York: Wiley, 1997); Anne Digby, *Madness, Morality and Medicine: A Study of the York Retreat, 1796–1914* (Cambridge: Cambridge University Press, 1985).

7 James Mohr, *Doctors and the Law: Medical Jurisprudence in Nineteenth Century America* (New York: Oxford University Press, 1993), chapter one, 3–15; Cyril H. Wecht, "The History of Legal Medicine," *Journal of the American Academy of Psychiatry and the Law* 33 no. 2 (June 2005): 245–51.

foundational assumption that individuals freely decided to make moral or immoral decisions. They challenged the concept of free will by questioning any property transmission outside of bloodlines as an outcome of disease rather than an expression of free will. Jurists and experts on both sides of the debate direly warned that these new theories risked destabilizing decades, if not centuries, of inheritance law. This nationwide debate reached its zenith in Kentucky in the late nineteenth century, when a series of judicial holdings in testamentary cases cabined medical experts' courtroom authority.

This debate demonstrates that mental insanity was a fluid concept and the production of law was unstable, influenced by scientific discovery and evolving medical culture. It also culminated in a partial judicial retreat to common law and ordinary people's understandings of capacity. Local, situational evidence of capacity once again became principal, after being tested by judicial and medical attempts to impose scientific principles defined by leading authorities. Medical jurisprudence, a movement initially characterized by doctors and jurists' confident enthusiasm, fractured under its own internal contradictions. Appellate jurists came to realize that what might appear to juries as prevarication by medical experts was inherent in the medical research on insanity. Expert testimony would not yield the certainty doctors and jurists had hoped it would. Instead, it created ambiguity and dissention in both professions. While medical experts never completely disappeared from testamentary capacity trials, their influence waned significantly and was replaced by evidence from local witnesses. Eventually, medical experts reasserted their influence, but not until later in the twentieth century after the rise of clinical psychiatry.[8]

In the nineteenth century, many physicians, trained at the nation's best medical schools, believed they had a professional obligation to educate juries in scientific truth in order to ensure just legal outcomes. As one prominent New York physician commented in 1871, Benjamin Rush, the founding father of American medical jurisprudence, believed that medical testimony was an "aid in the vindication of oppressed innocence and the punishment of crime."[9] Others in the medical community were

[8] On the rise of psychiatry in the twentieth century, see Elizabeth Lunbeck, *The Psychiatric Persuasion: Knowledge, Gender and Power in Modern America* (Princeton: Princeton University Press, 1995).

[9] James J. O'Dea, M.D., "The Sphere, Rights and Obligations of Medical Experts: Read before the Society April 18, 1871," 402–43 in *Papers Read before the Medico-Legal Society of New York*, first series, third edition (New York: The Medico-Legal Journal Association, 1889), 406.

circumspect, mixing optimism with concerns about how the partisan practices of litigation would destroy their professional reputations when opposing lawyers attacked their theories, testimony, and occasionally their characters.[10] As one expert lamented in a *Popular Science* article in 1885, medical experts had been accused of "ignorance, incompetency, and in some cases, venality. It has been said that their opinions are purchasable."[11] For their part, elite jurists oscillated between a distrust of medical experts and a greater distrust of local juries, perceived as unschooled and vulnerable to infusing verdicts with their own opinions of testators' choices. Certainly, medical experts gave reason for the suspicion evinced by jurists; they disagreed vehemently, leading to confusing testimony like that heard in the Williams case.

To the most enthusiastic proponents of medical authority in courtrooms, diagnoses of insanity controlled the ingress and egress to the rights of citizenship. John Ordroneaux, the New York state commissioner on lunacy, argued in 1875 that the interests of justice permitted depriving the insane of a jury trial. Juries were reserved for citizens, he contended, and a prerequisite of citizenship was that "all men are rational beings." While the insane were, as he put it, "civilly *in* the State, they are not civilly *of* the State."[12] This position made civil participation (including any property right) dependent on a disputed standard of rationality. To Ordroneaux, experts were the appropriate arbiters of sanity and citizenship. This sort of logic created an integral role for experts in the adjudication of property transfers.

For a moment in the mid- to late nineteenth century, the Kentucky Court of Appeals appeared ready to accept new medical theories about the nature of the human mind and its relationship to independent volition. Ultimately, however, the court came to distrust medical experts' opinions as unreliable and undermining the law's respect for self-sovereignty. Kentucky judges diminished the influence of new controversial theories of insanity, in part by hardening the juridical distinction between the legal definition of "mental capacity" and medical diagnoses of "insanity." The court's judges instead concentrated on the

[10] Many thanks to James Mohr, who emphasized the "mixed motives" of medical experts and cautioned against ascribing any single agenda to them.

[11] Frank Hastings Hamilton, "Medical Expert Testimony," *Popular Science Monthly* 26 no. 37 (1885): 603.

[12] John Ordroneaux, "The Proper Status of the Insane and Feebleminded," in *Papers Read before the Medico-Legal Society of New York*, third series, 1875–8, revised edition (New York: The Medico-Legal Journal Association, 1886), 51.

immediate circumstances surrounding testators' testamentary decisions, also considering, as local juries had done, the socioeconomic outcomes of property distribution for the beneficiaries and heirs-at-law. The story of medical testimony gaining and then losing influence at the state level is also the story of waning and reviving influence of local opinions as they were assessed at the appellate level.

Testamentary capacity trials uncover how the label of insanity structured familial relations and property transmission.[13] Historians rarely approach the label of insanity as an exchange between the subject, the community, and the medical expert within a nonmedical environment. For example, 1860 federal census statistics from seventeen asylums indicated that 6.1 percent of their populations was institutionalized due to religious insanity, as was Joseph Williams, who spent seven months at Lexington's ESLA in 1859.[14] After Williams's release from the ESLA, he returned to Owen County and managed a successful farm. His continuing talk of divinely inspired visions and ongoing religious fervor led local physicians and neighbors to consider him mentally unsound. Williams's post-asylum life would have been invisible to the historical record had his heirs-at-law not challenged his will. He may have appeared in ESLA records, but without the will dispute, historians would have no knowledge of how the label of "insane" shaped his subsequent life. The years after institutionalization and before his 1887 death reveal a more complete picture of how medical experts and local people understood sanity as a range, breaking down bright line distinctions between sane and insane. Table 3.1, taken from the 1880 federal census, indicates where Kentucky's insane lived. Although the method of data collection probably missed people considered insane by their families or local doctors and probably skews toward

[13] On testamentary capacity and medical experts, see Susanna Blumenthal, "The Deviance of the Will: Policing the Bounds of Testamentary Freedom in Nineteenth-Century America, *Harvard Law Review* 119 (2006): 959–1034; Christopher J. Buccafusco, "Spiritualism and Will(s) in the Age of Contract," (February 21, 2008), available at SSRN: http://ssrn.com/abstract=1096367; James Mohr, "The Paradoxical Advance and Embattled Retreat of the 'Unsound Mind': Evidence of Insanity and the Adjudication of Wills in Nineteenth Century America," *Historical Reflections* 24 no. 3 (1998): 415–35. On insanity within families more generally, see Mary Ann Jimenez, *The Changing Faces of Madness: Early American Attitudes and Treatment of the Insane* (University Press of New England, 1987); Peter McCandless, *Moonlight, Magnolias and Madness: Insanity in South Carolina from the Colonial Period to the Progressive Era* (Chapel Hill: University of North Carolina Press, 1996).

[14] William Sims Bainbridge, "Religious Insanity in America: The Official Nineteenth Century Theory," *Sociological Analysis* 45 no. 3 (Autumn 1984): 226; Transcript, *Williams v. Williams* (1893), Case 22461, Box 982, KCAR, KDLA.

TABLE 3.1. *Living Arrangements of Insane Individuals (1880)*

| | Total | Hospitals/ Asylums for the Insane | Other Institutions | Almshouses Having No Insane Department | Jails | At Home |
|---|---|---|---|---|---|---|
| Kentucky | 2,784 | 1,404 | 2 | 56 | 14 | 1,308 (47%) |
| United States | 91,959 | 40,942 | 235 | 9,302 | 207 | 41,063 (44.7%) |

*Source*: U.S. Department of the Interior, Census Office, Tenth Census, 1880, "Report on the Defective, Dependent, and Delinquent Classes of the Population of the United States," Government Printing Office, 1888.

institutions, it shows that close to half of all insane individuals lived at home both in Kentucky and in the United States.

The most optimistic medical experts, especially those involved in introducing medical jurisprudence into medical schools in the early nineteenth century, approached the legal system as an instrument through which they could pursue enlightened social agendas. Many experts believed they could create a healthy civic body through patient treatment and shape social and legal policies that fostered public health.[15] They pressed legislatures to build and fund asylums and called upon courts to use medical knowledge to determine mental capacity standards in litigation and lunatic inquest procedures.[16] Isaac Ray, one of the foremost experts on medical jurisprudence, believed experts had a unique public obligation to bring scientific truth to law.[17] He observed that the "public seems to have a claim upon their [experts] services over and above that which arises from the ordinary relations of citizens."[18] Moreover, experts saw a particularly important connection between an orderly society and a stable property regime. As Ray commented, "humanity" demands that property be removed from the control of those deemed insane; indeed, "the peace

[15] Gerald Grob, *The Mad Among Us: A History of Care of America's Mentally Ill* (New York: Free Press, 1994); Mohr, *Doctors and the Law*.

[16] Throughout the last half of the nineteenth century, experts called for state commissions of experts who would investigate criminal and civil trials involving insanity issues. For example, see William H. Stokes, "On a Court of Medical Experts in Cases of Insanity," *The American Journal of Insanity* 10 no. 2 (October 1853): 112–22.

[17] On Ray's influence, see Mohr, *Doctors and the Law*, 144–9; John S. Hughes, *In the Law's Darkness: Isaac Ray and the Medical Jurisprudence of Insanity in Nineteenth Century America* (New York: Oceana Publications, 1986).

[18] Isaac Ray, "Hints to the Medical Witness in Questions of Insanity," *The American Journal of Insanity* 8 no. 1 (July 1851): 53.

and safety of society demand it and the ultimate good of all parties are promoted by it."[19]

Benjamin Rush, another early proponent of medical jurisprudence, thought doctors had a role in promoting a fair, orderly inheritance system in the new republic. In an 1810 public lecture, Rush reminded newly trained doctors that their profession went beyond the treatment of disease and was "intended to render other services to society. It was designed to extend its benefits to the protection of property and life.... This honour has been conferred upon it by the bench and the bar."[20] Rush, a product of a Scottish Enlightenment education, saw a clear connection between his duties as a physician and as a patriot in the new republic.[21] Kentucky's medical school faculties embraced medical jurisprudence from their inceptions. Rush's student Charles Caldwell carried west his mentor's enthusiasm for melding science to law at Lexington's Transylvania University, where he served as professor of the Institutes of Medicine, Clinical Practice, and Medical Jurisprudence.[22] By 1837, Caldwell left Transylvania University and signed on as a charter member of the Louisville Medical Institute, along with David Yandell's father, Lunsford Yandell.[23] Indeed, Kentucky was far from a medical backwater; during the nineteenth century, it claimed nationally respected experts such as Caldwell, Edward Jarvis, Daniel Drake, William Chipley, and the Yandells, all who published prodigiously in the field of medical jurisprudence, shaped national dialogues on insanity, and influenced Kentucky's social and judicial institutions.

[19] Isaac Ray, "American Legislation on Lunacy," *The American Journal of Insanity* 21 no. 1 (1864): 21.

[20] Benjamin Rush, "Lecture XVI: On the Study of Medical Jurisprudence," in *Sixteen Introductory Lectures, to Courses of Lectures upon the Institutes and Practice of Medicine* (Philadelphia, 1811), transcribed at U.S. National Library of Medicine Online, http://collections.nlm.nih.gov/muradora/objectView!getDataStreamContent.action?pid=nlm:nlmuid-2569048R-bk&dsid=OCR&mimeType=text/plain, accessed June 28, 2012. On this lecture and Rush's influence more generally, see Mohr, *Doctors and the Law*, 61.

[21] Lisabeth Hakkonssen, *Medicine and Morals in the Enlightenment: John Gregory, Thomas Percival and Benjamin Rush. The Wellcome Series in the History of Medicine, Clio Medica* 44 (Atlanta: Rodopi, 1997), 200.

[22] Ronald F. White, "A Dialogue on Madness: Eastern State Lunatic Asylum and Mental Health Policies in Kentucky, 1824–1883," Dissertation, University of Kentucky, Lexington, 1984, 33–7.

[23] Nancy Disher Baird, *David Wendel Yandell: Physician of Old Louisville* (Lexington: University Press of Kentucky, 1978), 4–5.

## THE MECHANISMS OF THE MIND

These experts worked from specific premises about how the brain functioned. Following eighteenth-century French physicians Phillipe Pinel and Jean Etienne Esquirol, most physicians divided insanity into basic categories, including melancholia, epilepsy, mania, dementia, and idiocy.[24] In the first third of the nineteenth century, experts expanded those categories to include partial insanity, monomanias (insanity on one subject), temporary insanity, and moral insanity or moral mania.[25] Until the late nineteenth century, most physicians located insanity in a theory of biological materialism or faculty psychology, distinguishing the physical brain from the mind. They explained that the reasoning, moral mind (not the brain organ) was a divine creation and incapable of defects.[26] Insanity resulted from a brain "lesion" that affected the mind, causing delusions and deviant behavior. As one contributor to *The American Journal of Insanity* explained, "the immaterial and immortal mind is, of itself, incapable of disease and decay ... The brain is the instrument which the mind uses in this life ... and like all other parts of our bodies, is liable to disease."[27] As long as the mind was housed in a healthy brain, it dictated reasonable moral behavior. Adherence to a specific moral order was an outcome of a disease-free brain. By equating the mind with the mandates of a divinely inspired order, experts medicalized a natural social and familial order.

Experts explained insane behavior as deviation from a constructed social order they identified as "natural." Rush referred to this form of insanity as "moral derangement, which is seated in the domestic affections."[28] Sixty years later, in a paper read before the New York

[24] Eighteenth-century French physicians Phillipe Pinel and Jean Etienne Esquirol originally delineated these categories. For examples of American experts applying these categories, see William A. Hammond, M.D., "Opinion Relative to the Testamentary Capacity of the Late James C. Johnston, of Chowan County, North Carolina," in *Insanity in its Medico-Legal Relations* (New York: Voorhis and Co., second edition, 1875. Original date, 1867), 8 and Edward Patterson, "Monomania as Affecting Testamentary Capacity," in *Papers Read before the Medico-Legal Society of New York*, third series, 1875–1878, revised edition (New York: The Medico-Legal Journal Association, 1886), 20.

[25] See Roy Porter, *Madness: A Brief History* (Oxford: Oxford University Press, 2002), especially chapter six, "The Rise of Psychiatry."

[26] Gerald Grob, "Presidential Address: Psychiatry's Holy Grail: The Search for the Mechanisms of Mental Diseases," *Bulletin of the History of Medicine* 72 no. 2 (1998): 192.

[27] No Author, "Definition of Insanity – Nature of Disease," *The American Journal of Insanity* 1 no. 2 (1844): 99.

[28] Rush, "Lecture XVI: On the Study of Medical Jurisprudence."

Medico-Legal Society, Dr. Charles Lee referred to insanity of the "natural feelings, affections and habits." Lee argued that sane testators transferred property along bloodlines when he called suspicious "a *civil act, as a will*, depriving a parent, brother, sister, or other relative, of an inheritance which would naturally, rightfully, and legally fall to them."[29] Lee saw inheritance as an act reaffirming the naturalness of interfamilial property transmission. In one Kentucky trial, Yandell described testator Bannister Taylor's "unnatural actions," emphasizing that Taylor lacked the feelings of "natural love," instead harboring an "unnatural hate" toward his daughter. Indeed, experts used this aspect of the grammar of capacity – the rhetoric of naturalness – to distinguish behavior that deviated from a divinely ordered cosmology.[30] These premises fused moral values to scientific authority. Medical science supported religion by making "natural" specific models of social and familial organization.

Insanity threatened society in several ways: it could lead to violent criminal acts, social instability, and even a return to atavistic states of barbarism. By 1840, experts expressed fears that insanity was becoming more prevalent. Immoral environments created by the vicissitudes of evolving civilization, they argued, propelled the increase. As Louisville expert Dr. Edward Jarvis noted (quoting French physician Esquirol), "insanity is a disease of civilization and the number of the insane is in direct proportion to its progress." In his article titled "On the Supposed Increase of Insanity," Jarvis outlined his fear that the "neglect of the natural laws of self-government" would lead to "more dissipation."[31] Removed from tradition-bound, static social orders, individuals engaged in behavior inconsonant with natural laws.

White people were especially vulnerable to the deleterious effects of rapidly developing civilization, underscoring the degree to which conceptions of sanity turned on racial ideology. Jarvis observed that among people of color, insanity rarely existed because they lacked the capacity

[29] Charles A. Lee, M.D., "A Medico-Legal Opinion Relative to the Sanity of Carlton Gates, in *Papers Read before the Medico-Legal Society of New York*, first series, third edition (New York: The Medico-Legal Journal Association, 1889), 208. Read before the society September 8, 1870.

[30] See Gary S. Belkin, "Moral Insanity, Science and Religion in Nineteenth Century America: The Gray-Ray Debate," *History of Psychiatry* 7 (1996): 591–613, for a discussion of how theological views permeated scientific discourse, even between medical experts who disagreed on insanity etiologies.

[31] Edward Jarvis, "On the Supposed Increase of Insanity," *The American Journal of Insanity* 8 no. 4 (April 1852): 362.

for progress. Citing Native American and African civilizations as evidence, he concluded that insanity "is seldom found in the savage state, while it is well known to be frequent in the civilized state."[32] To Southern doctors in particular, racial ideology influenced how they understood the links between mental health, households, and social stability.[33] Many Southern doctors argued that African Americans were prone to drapetomania, a form of insanity caused by an obsession with freedom.[34] They also contended that freedom made African Americans more susceptible to madness, because their simplistic thought processes precluded adjusting to the stresses of self-sovereignty.[35] In an 1837 speech, physician Charles Caldwell promised that students at the newly opened Louisville Medical Institute would receive "*no sinister and perverting impressions respecting any of the domestic institutions of the south* [italics his]."[36] The Louisville Medical Institute would educate good doctors who, steeped in Southern cultural sensibilities, affirmed the naturalness of slavery.

Kentucky medical experts interpreted their observations to justify a social hierarchy stratified by race and class. In 1852, Jarvis called attention to how education and unchecked social change threatened mental health.[37] He noted that in caste-based societies, where children pursue

[32] Ibid., 350.

[33] The notoriously flawed 1840 census suggested that few insane blacks lived in the South. In Maine, however, every fourteenth African American was insane, leading Southern proslavery politicians and some experts to suggest that freedom caused insanity in African Americans. Gerald Grob, *Edward Jarvis and the Medical World of Nineteenth-Century America* (Knoxville: University of Tennessee Press, 1978), 70–4. For analysis of the census, see No Author, "Startling Facts from the Census," *The American Journal of Insanity* 8 no. 2 (October 1852): 153–5. Jarvis, while concerned about the links between insanity and advanced civilization, refuted the statistical methodology, finding it "groundless" and a "stumbling block" to pursuing truth through science. Edward Jarvis, "Insanity among the Colored Population of the Free States," *The American Journal of Insanity* 8 no. 3 (January 1852): 268–82.

[34] Samuel A. Cartwright, "Report on the Diseases and Physical Particularities of the Negro," *The New Orleans Medical and Surgical Journal* 7 (1851): 707–8. Cartwright's article was reprinted in *DeBow's Review* and in other regional papers. See *Pensacola Gazette* (Pensacola, Florida), September 27, 1851.

[35] John S. Hughes, "Labeling and Treating Black Mental Illness in Alabama, 1861–1910," *The Journal of Southern History* 58 (August 1993): 435–60.

[36] Charles M. Caldwell, "A Succinct View of the Influence of Mental Cultivation on the Destinies of Louisville, An Introductory Lecture Delivered at the Opening of the Louisville Medical Institute," 1837.

[37] Grob, *Edward Jarvis and the Medical World of Nineteenth-Century America*, 45. Jarvis opposed the institution of slavery, but believed in the inherent inferiority of African Americans.

their fathers' occupations, "undue mental excitements and struggles do not happen, and men's brains are not confused with new plans ... as education prevails, and emancipates the new generations ... and the manifold ways of life are open to all ... men may ... become insane."[38] ESLA superintendent William Chipley echoed Jarvis's fears when he worried that the social upheaval caused by the Civil War would have profound negative effects on Kentuckians. Chipley contrasted the "virtuous, quiet, humble life of the past" against concerns about the effects of rapid social reorganization brought by political and social changes. Chipley believed that an "increase of mental diseases is one of the unhappy results of the unhallowed efforts of wicked men to revolutionize established government by violence."[39] By the late nineteenth century, this sort of reasoning developed into a full-fledged critique that the environmental influences of a rapidly changing civilization posed dire public mental health threats. The connection between progress and insanity required that experts use their knowledge to preserve social order against the intransigent forces of chaos that accompanied change.

Like politicians and jurists, many experts saw disrupted familial relations and insanity as mutually causative. Jarvis contended that "a large portion of the cases of lunacy arise directly from the trials, difficulties and misunderstandings of home."[40] Insane people living at home presented a "burden upon their families, a terror on society."[41] Other experts concurred. In his 1879 "Report to the Legislature," ESLA superintendent R. C. Chenault listed religious excitement, domestic trouble, separation from husband, wife, or parents, and loss of property as "alleged causes" of insanity among the patients confined there. Experts noted with trepidation that while physical causes of insanity remained constant or even decreased, the moral causes of insanity increased alarmingly.[42] This concern about moral insanity epitomized broader fears of social and moral degeneration caused by seemingly irrational forces.

[38] Jarvis, "On the Supposed Increase of Insanity," 361.

[39] "Reports of American Insanity," *The American Journal of Insanity* 21 no. 4 (April 1865): 567–8.

[40] Edward Jarvis, "What Shall We Do With Our Insane?" *The Western Journal of Medicine and Science* 5 no. 2 (February 1842): 81. Jarvis spent a few years in Louisville before moving to Massachusetts, where he wrote the 1855 *Massachusetts Report on Insanity and Idiocy*, which his peers considered the most comprehensive examination of insanity in the nineteenth century.

[41] Jarvis, "What Shall We Do With Our Insane?" 82.

[42] Jarvis, "On the Supposed Increase of Insanity," 333–64.

## EXPERTS IN THE COURTROOM

Experts' insistence on the connections between cerebral lesions and insane behavior obscured how diagnostic paradigms were infused with judgments about the legitimacy of social and legal relations. Some experts testified about dead testators they had never met. They relied on behavioral indicators, creating tautological declarations in their testimonies. A diseased brain indicated insanity, which was made obvious by aberrant behavior caused by a diseased brain. For example, many experts reasoned that brain deterioration produced delusions that rendered a testator particularly susceptible to undue influence. While delivering a paper to the New York Medico-Legal association, Isaac Ray cautioned other experts:

> When we consider the enfeebling effect on body and mind of a long last illness ... and of the utter prostration of the will produced by pain and a sense of complete dependence, we can scarcely conceive of conditions better fitted for the exercise of undue influence. An old man marries a young woman, and within a year or two dies, leaving a will greatly in her favor, much to the disappointment of relatives who would otherwise have received the whole of the estate.[43]

Ray deemed suspect the marital relationship between the testator and beneficiary, largely due to their age difference and the testator's weakened mind. Ray pathologized testators' late life marriages. Like litigants who argued to exclude second wives from economic membership in families (see Chapter 1), Ray endorsed a system of property transmission based on bloodline heirs.

In his testimony in *Taylor v. Minor* (1885), Yandell illustrated how testators' deviation from prescriptive social roles might indicate insanity. Testator Bannister Taylor disinherited his daughter who had married against his wishes. Yandell testified that "[I]nsanity of any kind is made manifest in a departure from the ordinary methods of acting speaking or thinking. If we were to see a Bishop in his shirtsleaves [*sic*] moving around the haunts of the Irishman ... if persisted in towards we would know that it was so far a departure ... that we would be forced to the conclusion that the person was insane."[44] By comparing a temperate, restrained bishop to a degenerate Irishman who frequented "haunts,"

[43] Isaac Ray, "Testamentary Capacity," in *Papers Read before the Medico-Legal Society of New York*, third series, 1875–8, revised edition (New York: The Medico-Legal Journal Association, 1886), 434.

[44] "Testimony of DW Yandell," Transcript, *Taylor v. Minor* (1885), Case 16241, Box 671, KCAR, KDLA.

Yandell reinforced class and ethnic expectations. Consistent deviation from acceptable behavior indicated insanity. Yet Yandell's testimony did allow for some deviation from ascribed social roles. Yandell believed that this behavior indicated insanity only if it "persisted." Occasional lapses had little consequence, muddying a clear line at which deviance became insanity.

Lawyers called upon medical experts to explain the subtle gradations of the newly recognized forms of insanity. Nationally prominent expert Dr. William Hammond distinguished insanity as a disregard of heirs-at-law due to "general or partial derangement of one or more faculties of the mind, which, whilst not abolishing consciousness, prevents freedom of mind or action."[45] This theory of partial insanity allowed experts to exercise scientific and moral authority by distinguishing between immorality and insanity. In perhaps the most influential medical jurisprudence treatise of the nineteenth century, Ray popularized the theory that only the brain's affective faculties could be diseased, appearing to leave undisturbed the intellectual faculties.[46] Ray characterized this form as a "mental disease that is chiefly confined to the moral sentiments and affections, the intellectual *powers* evincing no appreciable derangement."[47] Ray contended that this moral insanity "furnishes good ground for invalidating civil acts, for notwithstanding the apparent integrity of the intellectual powers."[48]

These claims allowed experts to focus solely on the testators' conduct within affective relationships, allowing them to separate sane conduct in business or intellectual pursuits from interpersonal relationships. In *Pecantet v. Grayson* (1872), Eliza Atkinson left her estate inherited from her husband to Colonel Grayson, whose family took care of her during her final illness. (*Pecantet v. Grayson* is also discussed in Chapters 1 and 5.) Atkinson disinherited her husband's son by his first marriage. Atkinson had deviated from prevailing gender expectations of a sober,

[45] Hammond, "Opinion Relative to the Testamentary Capacity of the Late James C. Johnson, of Chowan County, North Carolina," 9.

[46] Ray was not the first to develop a theory of faculty psychology, which he attributed to Pinel.

[47] Isaac Ray, "Hints to the Medical Witness in Questions of Insanity," *The American Journal of Insanity* 8 no. 1 (July 1851): 53.; Isaac Ray, *A Treatise on the Medical Jurisprudence of Insanity* (Boston: Charles C. Little and James Brown, 1838). Ray's treatise went through several editions throughout the nineteenth century. Although moral insanity was discredited by 1900, Ray remained committed to it through the 1880s.

[48] Ray, *A Treatise on the Medical Jurisprudence of Insanity*, 258.

sedate widow by enjoying a flamboyant widowhood characterized by, as the Court of Appeals noted, "passions for men and ardent spirits."[49] Atkinson's personal physician, Dr. J. L. Dismukes, testified that Atkinson's "emotions and affections were perverted evidently while there was considerable vigor and activity of intellectual powers."[50] Dismukes supported his diagnosis of "partial insanity" by referring to her behavior as "strikingly unfeminine in several particulars," noting that the "exciting causes" of her insanity were "*Nymphomania* ... with the *vanity of fashion*." Insanity theories that separated intellectual from moral and affective behaviors supported diagnoses that focused narrowly on one aspect of a testator's deviant behavior.

Experts inscribed economic imperatives on the moral ideology of sanity. Through the grammar of capacity they declared as medical truth the idea that familial affection would be expressed through testamentary gifts, especially when deserving heirs-at-law appeared economically deprived. Dismukes testified that Atkinson had "an insane aversion and hatred for those of natural ties, that ought to be nearest and dearest. I would suspect the sanity of any-one, who without known and sufficient cause, had an aversion toward one or those who should be the object of ones bounty and affection."[51] In *Williams v. Williams* (1893), when the challengers' attorney asked Yandell if Williams could make a will considering his religious convictions, he replied, "There is nothing thicker than blood. If a man gives his property to the church and leaves out his kin I don't think he is sane. It would be different if they were rich: but if they were poor, don't think he could do it under those circumstances."[52] Yandell linked insanity to deviation from patterns of family wealth preservation in which fathers valued upward economic mobility for their children. By asserting that "there is nothing thicker than blood," Yandell equated sanity with wealth transmission within the family. Williams's religious fervor was the ostensible indication of insanity; yet his will would have gone unchallenged had he left his wealth to his heirs-at-law (Figure 3.1).

[49] *Pecantet v. Grayson*, 6 Ky. Op. 80 (1872).

[50] "Testimony of Dr. JL Dismukes," Transcript, *Pecantet v. Grayson* (1872), Case 5727, Box 225, KCAR, KDLA. Dismukes was a graduate of the University of Pennsylvania medical school, where Benjamin Rush taught. He testified as an expert and was also Atkinson's personal physician, giving him the opportunity to comment directly on her conduct.

[51] Ibid.

[52] "Testimony of David W. Yandall," Transcript, *Williams v. Williams* (1893), Case 22461, Box 983, KCAR, KDLA.

FIGURE 3.1. Dr. David W. Yandell, Physician, Expert Witness, and President of the American Medical Association in 1872. Yandell testified at several testamentary capacity trials in mid- to late nineteenth-century Kentucky.
*Source*: Filson Historical Society, Manuscripts and Photographs Division, Louisville, Kentucky.

## "THE PROCRUSTEAN BED": DOCTORS AND REPUTATION IN COURTROOMS

Some experts believed bringing medical knowledge into courtrooms was essential. Family members, beneficiaries, or the testator could conceal the testator's insanity. As Dr. Caldwell (not Charles Caldwell), a local doctor testifying in *Taylor v. Minor* (1885), noted, "A person may be a monomaniac upon a given subject and it may not even be detected by his friends and near neighbors for many years."[53] Family members also concealed insanity, requiring experts to uncover these deceptions. Families would protect members to avoid the stigma associated with insanity by

[53] "Testimony of Dr. Caldwell," Transcript, *Taylor v. Minor* (1885), Case 16241, Box 671, KCAR, KDLA.

tolerating, as one expert characterized it, "the outrageous conduct of one of their number uncomplainingly, while the outside world does not suspect a thing is wrong."[54] In *Williams v. Williams* (1893), ex-slave Cynthia Williams recalled, "I knew they kept his crazyness [*sic*] a secret from blacks."[55] That Cynthia Williams identified Joe Williams's behavior as "crazyness" indicates that, at least on the Williams farm, slaves and whites shared recognition of mental incapacity and its effects on authority. The white Williamses may have concealed Joe Williams's deviant behavior in order to maintain his (and their) authority. At the trial, Yandell confirmed that insanity could be missed by laypeople, testifying that a man "may be all right on every thing else ... but will show his insanity when he comes to that [religion]."[56] The potential for deceit by those afflicted or their families required a trained expert to identify mental afflictions.

If testators or beneficiaries could conceal insanity, challengers could press cases with scant or conflicting evidence. In *Spears v. Sales* (1867), for example, the contestants' attorneys made a case for the frequency of unrecognized insanity, citing the "able treties" [*sic*] of medical jurisprudence to claim that insanity "is seen in the domestic circle of the afflicted person and *those composing that circle know its existance* [*sic*] and feel its terrible power, when others cannot observe it. This affection is *far more common* in the ordinary walks of society than is generaly [*sic*] imagined."[57] Such expansive definitions of insanity meant that diagnosing insanity required vigilance and expertise. The challengers advanced this argument as a strategy to counter conflicting testimony by, as the court phrased it, "all the witnesses who testified in the case, except his wife, say he was competent to ... manage his own affairs with as much skill and judgment as men of common sense."[58] By arguing for the frequent yet undetected occurrence of insanity in "ordinary walks of society," the attorneys characterized local witnesses as easily deceived, making experts necessary. All testators were potentially insane.

Many medical experts and jurists agreed that local juries lacked the sophistication and knowledge required to pass judgment on the

[54] Henry Smith Williams, "Social Relations of the Insane," *North American Review* 157 (November 1893): 613.

[55] "Testimony of Cynthia Williams," Transcript, *Williams v. Williams* (1893), Case 22461, Box 982, KCAR, KDLA.

[56] "Testimony of David W. Yandall," Transcript, *Williams v. Williams* (1893), Case 22461, Box 982, KCAR, KDLA.

[57] "Appellee's Brief," in *Spears v. Sale* (1867), Case 1251, Box 45, KCAR, KDLA.

[58] *Spears v. Sales*, 2 Ky. Op. 150 (1867).

deceased's mental condition. In these assertions, the tensions and contradictions between legal localism and rationalized law created and administered by professionals become clear. Decisions reached by juries, many experts contended, were likely to reflect local prejudices, lack of medical knowledge, or a replacement of the testator's judgment with their own. "The most erroneous verdicts," Ordroneaux argued in 1875, "against facts, commonsense and evidence have been rendered by juries in civil and criminal issues of insanity."[59] Instead, Ordroneaux believed, "a panel of three upright judges" should pass judgment rather than "twelve unlearned laymen." Other experts called for independent panels of physicians to pass judgment on insanity issues. One author argued that "unscientific" and "probably illiterate men" composed juries unable to "properly apply medical principles without medical education and experience."[60] As purveyors of specialized knowledge, experts were essential to determining sanity. These sorts of arguments reflected the impetus among formally trained doctors to define and protect their areas of specialized knowledge.[61] In this area, developments in the medical profession encouraged the rationalization and standardization of law at the state and national levels. Other experts challenged esoteric definitions of insanity and rejected the assertions that laypeople were unable to recognize insanity. In *Taylor v. Minor* (1885), Dr. Cleaver, the expert testifying for the proponents of the will and summoned to counter Yandell, asserted that, in its early stages, insanity "may be difficult to detect but it soon so

[59] John Ordroneaux, "The Proper Status of the Insane and Feebleminded," in *Papers Read before the Medico-Legal Society of New York*, third series, 1875–1878, revised edition (New York: The Medico-Legal Journal Association, 1886), 64.

[60] No Author, "Review of *The Law of Wills* by Isaac Redfield," *The American Journal of Insanity* 21 no. 3 (January 1865): 406–7.

[61] Medical historians have developed a substantial literature on the self-conscious movement to professionalize medicine and distinguish formally trained physicians from other practitioners. See John Harley Warner, "The Fall and Rise of Professional Mystery: Epistemology, Authority, and the Emergence of Laboratory Medicine in Nineteenth-Century America," in Andrew Cunningham and Perry Williams, eds., *The Laboratory Revolution in Medicine* (Cambridge: Cambridge University Press, 1992), 310–41; Ivan Waddington, "The Movement toward the Professionalisation of Medicine," *British Medical Journal* 301 (October 1990): 688–90; Susan Lawrence, "Iowa Physicians: Legitimacy, Institutions, and the Practice of Medicine, Part One: Establishing a Professional Identity, 1833–1886," *The Annals of Iowa* 62 (Spring 2003): 151–200; Paul J. Starr, *The Social Transformation of American Medicine* (New York: Basic Books, 1982); William F. Bynum, *Science and the Practice of Medicine in the Nineteenth Century* (New York: Cambridge University Press, 1994); Ian Dowbiggin, *Inheriting Madness: Professionalization and Psychiatric Knowledge in Nineteenth-Century France* (Berkeley: University of California Press, 1991).

far overpowers the mind as to disclose itself to common observation."[62] These experts disputed the existence of partial insanity, arguing the brain was a holistic organ; insanity affected all aspects of brain function, which led to observable behavioral changes. This disagreement over diagnosing insanity created a need for both litigants to present experts if funds permitted, or to risk having the opposing litigants' expert pronouncements go unanswered. Among experts, however, the debate was genuine, stemming from disagreements over the brain's physical structure.

As experts gained public visibility, controversy followed. Newspaper reports and word of mouth suggested that liberal use of the new theories propounded by experts unjustly deprived citizens of property and encouraged disgruntled heirs-at-law to assail carefully planned wills.[63] As one *New York Times* journalist lamented, "Many a poor fellow has lost his reputation, property, and even liberty by the unskilled and purchased opinion of an expert."[64] In 1864, Elizabeth Packard led a highly publicized campaign for legal protections against involuntary commitment to insane asylums after her husband, aided by an Illinois asylum superintendent, committed her for three years. The campaign and the call for subsequent state "Personal Liberty" laws highlighted the potential collusion between experts and designing relatives seeking to use an insanity diagnosis to remove troublesome relatives.[65] The idea that experts conveyed flawed knowledge or deliberately conspired to deprive people of property rights and freedom tarnished experts' credibility and brought into question their diagnostic authority.

Medical experts had long understood that the confrontational arrangement of trial courts created a situation that led opposing lawyers to assail their credibility during grueling cross-examinations. W. J. Conklin, a professor of physiology, complained it was "unfair" to fault experts with confusion caused by conflicting testimony, contending that it was counsel's task to "make the *evidence conflicting*."[66] Even before expert

[62] "Testimony of Dr. Cleaver," Transcript, *Taylor v. Minor* (1885), Case 16241, Box 671, KCAR, KDLA. Cleaver's credentials did not rival Yandell's as a medical expert. Cleaver had worked at Louisville University and "had taken considerable pains to acquaint myself with the subject of sanity and insanity."

[63] Mohr, "The Paradoxical Advance and Embattled Retreat of the 'Unsound Mind,'" 415–35. See also Mohr, *Doctors and the Law*, esp. chapters eleven and twelve.

[64] *New York Times*, "Medical Experts in Court," December 12, 1884.

[65] Hendrik Hartog, "Mrs. Packard on Dependency," *Yale Journal of Law & the Humanities* 1 (1988): 79–103; Mohr, *Doctors and the Law*, 165–8.

[66] W. J. Conklin, "The Medical Expert," *The Ohio Medical and Surgical Journal* (April 1878): 133.

testimony became widespread, lawyers capitalized upon the equivocation and theoretical disputes that characterized experts' theories of insanity. In *Johnson v. Moore* (1822), the beneficiaries' attorneys harshly criticized the value of expert testimony, condemning

> the varying and conflicting systems of the schools, which profess to disclose the causes, characteristics, grades and effects of mental maladies. From the days of Hippocrates to those of Rush, what has been added, on this interesting and unlawful inquiry, to the stock of human knowledge but a succession of short-lived theories, founded on conjecture, and ending in the establishment of constructive madness.[67]

Isaac Ray, an ardent advocate of expert witnesses, warned in 1851 that if unprepared, experts were in danger of "*breaking down* on the witness stand" [italics his] under cross-examination.[68] James O'Dea told the Medico-Legal Society of New York in 1871 that "hostile criticism is usually to be expected from lawyers in the interests of their clients, but it is too often carried beyond the bounds of moderation."[69] O'Dea also faulted judges, noting that the "heat engendered by a closely-contested case may palliate" lawyers' excesses, but "there is no such apology for the conduct of judges who allow scientific testimony to be indecorously handled."[70] Indeed, medical and legal professionals saw the increase of expert witnesses as a part of a greater struggle over the authority to define insanity rather than leave it to the vicissitudes of lawyerly arguments. As one expert wrote, "the profession of medicine can not prostrate itself to the procrustean bed of ancient legal prejudices."[71] Far removed from the cooperative impulses that propelled early medical jurists, by mid-century, many medical experts felt besieged as they tried to bring the truths of science to law.

Even as some medical experts sounded the alarm over a possible drubbing in courtrooms, references to moral insanity, partial insanity, different forms of monomania, and other newly discovered forms of insanity became common in courtrooms. Jurists and medical experts agreed that moral behavior reflected sanity. Many experts, however, defined insanity broadly, pronouncing mentally unsound testators whose dispositions

[67] "Petition for Rehearing," in *Johnson v. Moore*, 11 Ky. 371 (1822).
[68] Ray, "Hints to the Medical Witness in Questions of Insanity," 54.
[69] O'Dea, "The Sphere, Rights and Obligations of Medical Experts," 414.
[70] Ibid., 415.
[71] Eugene Grissom, "True and False Experts," *The American Journal of Insanity* 35 (July 1878): 36.

coincided with the juridical goal of maintaining a stable inheritance system.[72] Even in cases in which experts did not testify, litigants' lawyers cited their treatises. Lacking the specialized training of insanity experts, local physicians referenced new theories to leverage experts' medical and social authority. The frequency with which lawyers cited experts and their theories sent a message to juries and courtroom spectators; medical experts were best equipped to explain insanity.

## THE RISE AND DECLINE OF THE MEDICAL MODEL OF TESTAMENTARY CAPACITY

From Kentucky's earliest cases, Court of Appeals judges viewed with ambivalence the credibility and usefulness of medical testimony. As the nineteenth century progressed, the pervasive discussions of the value of medical testimony taking place in national dialogues, medical schools, and in courtrooms forced jurists and doctors to grapple with how the culture of medicine uneasily became entangled in the culture of law. *In re Cochran* (1814), the first testamentary capacity case in which Court of Appeals judges responded to physician testimony, Judge Logan cautioned against assigning too much value to a local doctor's diagnosis of insanity. He dismissed the testimony, holding that "The knowledge of the physician does not relate to the time the will was made ... and it is therefore by inference only that his testimony is made to apply to that day.... [I]ndulging in presumption of such dubious complexion, we cannot think a Court justifiable in arresting the will of a man."[73] Logan evinced concern about the testimony challenging a long-standing legal principle in testamentary capacity jurisprudence. Capacity determinations were confined to the moments in which testators wrote and then signed their wills. Although judges did not always adhere to this principle, it offered a justification for disregarding deviant behavior before or even after the will was written if the will comported with broader juridical goals. By upholding "the will of a man," through this specific evidentiary standard, Logan reinforced the masculine prerogative of property control. The court ruled similarly in *In re Weir's Will* (1840), disregarding the testator's physician's diagnosis of "melancholy mania." The court praised the will as a "rational act, rationally done," finding that "every just and enlightened mind would concur

[72] Mohr, "The Paradoxical Advance and Embattled Retreat of the 'Unsound Mind,'" 415–35.

[73] *In re Cochran's Will*, 6 Ky. 491 (1814).

in approving [the will] as about the best a man, standing in his relations, and being in principle an emancipator, could have made."[74] Interpreting moral judgments as rational acts, the court expressed little concern with other manifestations of deviance. As local doctors and medical experts testified that insanity was chronic and terminal, the judge carved out a narrow definition of legal capacity that ensured a moral tone in testamentary jurisprudence and protected individual testators' self-sovereignty and property rights from medical determinism.

This judicial caution ran through antebellum cases. Court of Appeals judges continually expressed misgivings with the application of science to law, choosing instead to evaluate the entirety of social and economic circumstances under which testators wrote deviant wills. In 1829, Francis M'Daniel's slaves defended their testamentary manumissions against a mental incapacity challenge from M'Daniel's children. Three doctors testified, all reaching different opinions. The court dismissed the physicians' opinions, contending that the mind was a subject "which the most experienced and erudite understand but very imperfectly."[75] The court decided that "the opinions of [these] witnesses are not entitled to much influence," holding that a disposing mind would be determined by the "facts of each case, than by any comprehensive definition."[76] After evaluating the circumstances of the case, the court upheld the will, sanctioning the slave manumissions and overturning the local jury verdict. M'Daniel's wife had made a deathbed request that he manumit the slaves in his will. The will itself evinced no sexual or familial improprieties as M'Daniel had divided the remaining property among his children. The court expressed little concern over M'Daniel's mental condition outside of the testamentary expressions of his familial obligations, holding, like it would eleven years later in *In re Weir's Will*, that a will reflecting "rationality and equality ... [was] conclusive of sanity."[77] The will itself rather than physician opinion, local witness opinion, or jury verdict constituted crucial evidence in determining sanity. The Court of Appeals linked its determination to the cultural messages transmitted by the testator's property distribution and the will's economic effect on the family. Upholding Francis M'Daniel's will positioned early the bench as the final arbiter of capacity against incursions by medical authorities.

[74] *In re Weir's Will*, 39 Ky. 434 (1840).
[75] *In re McDaniels*, 25 Ky. 331 (1829).
[76] Ibid.
[77] *In re Weir's Will*, 39 Ky. 434 (1840).

As theories of insanity grew more expansive and science gained more credibility, judges became willing to appropriate medical theory when it suited their needs. Their use of medical research made their legal findings appear rooted in science and sensitive to how evolving standards of evidence could be shaped by newly acquired knowledge. Law appeared responsive to science while maintaining its own juridical goals. Using the theory of "lucid intervals," judges applied medical theory toward justifying testators' independence in the face of medical and behavioral evidence indicating insanity. In a lucid interval, the testator, sometimes only momentarily, regained sanity long enough to write a valid will.[78] The Court of Appeals first acknowledged the ramifications of lucid intervals in 1824, holding that the testator "enjoyed, no doubt, in that period, some intervals, in which his mind might be deemed competent for the purpose of making his will; but to justify the establishment of the will, it ought to be shown by clear and satisfactory testimony, to have been made in one of those lucid intervals."[79] Again, in *In re Weir's Will* (1840), the court (overlooking its circular logic) found that the "will itself proves that, when he wrote it, he had a lucid interval."[80] And again in *Overton's Heirs v. Overton's Executors* (1857), the court accepted the "presumption of a lucid interval with a lunatic," as long as the will was "sensible, proper, and judicious." Many medical experts, however, approached cautiously the testators' temporary restoration of rationality during lucid intervals, believing that once the physical brain became diseased, insanity existed unless treatment restored a healthy brain.[81] In accepting the existence of lucid intervals, the court carved out latitude to rule in light of contradictory evidence. When wills appeared fair, doctrines like lucid intervals served as judicial explanations for otherwise deviant conduct that may have indicated insanity.

By mid-century, mirroring national trends, local doctors, lawyers, and the increasing appearance of experts as witnesses had infused the grammar of insanity with a culturally compelling medical lexicon. The most frequent explicator of medical knowledge, the local attending physicians

[78] Discussions of lucid intervals appeared in influential medical jurisprudence treatises from the early nineteenth century. See Theodric Romyn Beck, *Elements of Medical Jurisprudence*, second edition (London: W. Lewis, 1825); Ray, *Treatise on the Medical Jurisprudence of Insanity*.

[79] *In re Cochran's Will*, 17 Ky. 263 (1824). This case is not related to *In re Cochran's Will* (1814) cited at n. 73.

[80] *In re Weir's Will*, 39 Ky. 434 (1840).

[81] See Hammond, "Opinion Relative to the Testamentary Capacity of the Late James C. Johnson, of Chowan County, North Carolina," 35.

with varying degrees of education, almost always testified about any diseases for which they treated the testator and the possible effects these ailments had on mental capacity. When local doctors knew the testator and the heirs-at-law, they drew upon their community prestige, local knowledge of social relations, and medical authority in a way medical experts brought in from outside the community could not. As men who lived within local communities, local doctors were ideally poised to draw upon powerful community ideas about "natural" family relations.

By 1860, the use of expert witnesses had become more pervasive nationally and in Kentucky. These experts came from prestigious institutions and had years of experience in research and practice. New medical theories of insanity regularly appeared in experts' testimonies and lawyers' briefs. The debates over medico-jurists' theories challenged state courts to develop legal reasoning that explained the nature of free will.[82] Court of Appeals judges wrestled with how to establish the line between individuals who had mental capacity but were morally depraved, and those who lacked mental capacity and therefore were not responsible legally for their actions. The Kentucky Court of Appeals judges approached cautiously the implications of recognizing new forms of insanity. For example, in 1863, the court hesitated to accept moral insanity as a diagnosis in a criminal trial, calling it an "abstruse and perplexing subject."[83] If the court accepted moral insanity as an explanation for immoral behavior, it feared nothing less than "destroy[ing] social order as well as personal safety."[84] Although the tests for mental capacity differed for criminal and civil cases, both types of trials dealt with the same issue: free will. In criminal trials, the legal test asked whether defendants had mental capacity to distinguish right from wrong. Testamentary capacity cases asked a similar question: if the testator had the capacity to assume legal responsibility to distribute property. Both tests turned on how to measure the ability or "capacity" to exercise free will.

By 1864, the court appeared to make an abrupt about face from its previous skepticism, giving a detailed exposition of the brain's structure based on the morphology put forth by moral insanity proponents. In *Smith v. Commonwealth* (1864), a murder trial in which a jury sentenced defendant Robert Smith to hang, the court overturned the

[82] Blumenthal, "The Deviance of the Will"; Mohr, *Doctors and the Law*; Robert E. Mensel, "Right Feeling and Knowing Right: Insanity in Testators and Criminals in Nineteenth Century American Law," *Oklahoma Law Review* 58 (Fall 2005): 397–437.

[83] *Scott v. Commonwealth*, 61 Ky. 227 (1863).

[84] Ibid.

verdict on the ground that the lower court judge's instructions to the jury excluded considering moral insanity. The court's holding deserves quoting at length:

> Moral insanity is now as well understood by medico-jurists, and almost as well established by judicial recognition, as the intellectual form. Mentally, man is a dualism consisting of an intellectual and a moral nature. It is this peculiar nature that exalts him above the animal and makes him, legally and morally, a responsible being.... [I]t would be as useless and cruel to hold him accountable, either criminally or morally, for an act done without a free, rational, and concurrent will.[85]

The court appeared to reverse its previous cautious approach to medical jurisprudence. The reference to "judicial recognition" of moral insanity was more than rhetorical flourish. Other state courts had begun to allow new insanity theories as criminal defenses and as grounds for testamentary challenges. Most famously, Lincoln assassination conspirator Lewis Payne used a moral insanity defense.[86] In the notorious 1859 trial of New York congressman Daniel Sickles for the murder of Phillip Barton Key (son of Francis Scott Key), the defense successfully pleaded not guilty due to temporary emotional insanity.[87] The 1862 will dispute over New York millionaire Henry Parish's estate focused largely on expert testimony, as Parish was physically paralyzed and unable to speak when he wrote his will. Experts testified using the latest insanity theories of medical jurisprudence to speculate on Parish's mental condition.[88]

Indeed, the court appeared to amend its skepticism, accepting the verisimilitude of new theories of insanity. In *Pecantet v. Grayson* (1872), Dr. Dismukes testified to a version of brain morphology that separated the intellectual from the moral faculties. Judge Pryor concluded that Eliza Atkinson was "a monomaniac" on the subject of men and on the disposition of her property. He noted that "The testimony of her physicians indicates that this affection for men was the offspring of a passion produced for a disease peculiar to her sex."[89] The court overturned the jury verdict and Atkinson's will. In doing so, it rejected the jury as the final arbiter

[85] Ibid.

[86] Robert Waldinger, "The Sleep of Reason: John P. Gray and the Challenge of Moral Insanity," *Journal of the History of Medicine* 34 no. 2 (April 1979): 163.

[87] *The United States v. Daniel E. Sickles*, 2 Hay. & Haz. 319 (1859). See also Hartog, "Lawyering, Husbands' Rights and the 'Unwritten Law'"; Mohr, *Doctors and the Law*, 150–3.

[88] *Delafield v. Parish*, 25 N.Y. 9 (1862). See Mohr, *Doctors and the Law*, 65.

[89] *Pecantet v. Grayson*, 6 Ky. Op. 80 (1872).

of capacity, relying instead upon the physicians' reading of Atkinson's behavior as a manifestation of "monomania." The same year, in *Moore v. Moore* (1872), the court touted the value of medical experts' testimony in cases with conflicting evidence. Judge Lindsay referred to the opinions of three doctors as the work of "scientific gentlemen," contending that "the failure of these educated physicians to discover insanity … disposes of the vagaries" of four witnesses who testified to R. C. Moore's insanity.[90] The court appeared to place more confidence in the words of doctors as opposed to the recollections of local witnesses to discern mental capacity.

Not all medical experts welcomed the new turn in the expansive judicial recognition of insanity. A vitriolic debate raged between the proponents of moral insanity and single faculty insanity and those who believed, as insanity expert George Cook put it, that "the mind is a unit … we do not believe that it is made up of isolated faculties, one or more of which may be impaired of destroyed, leaving the remainder."[91] The debate continued for several decades in *The American Journal of Insanity* and at the professional conferences of physicians. In 1866, the annual meeting of the Association of Medical Superintendents of American Institutions for the Insane (AMSAII) erupted into a heated controversy over moral insanity and its legal implications, which Dr. D. T. Brown characterized as the "bug-bear" of the association.[92] Even Isaac Ray, a lifelong advocate of moral insanity, conceded that lawyers would ask testifying physicians about the existence of moral insanity "for the purpose of attaching to him an unpopular doctrine."[93]

Kentucky's William Chipley, the medical superintendent of ESLA, vehemently denied the existence of moral insanity or insanity that affected a single faculty. After testifying for the prosecution in *Smith v. Commonwealth* (1864), he wrote a lengthy rebuttal of the court's opinion in *The American Journal of Insanity* (1866). Chipley reasoned that if medico-jurists "admit perfect soundness of the intellectual faculties, and there are no criteria by which you can distinguish the act from one …

90 *Moore v. Moore*, 6 Ky. Op. 36 (1872).

91 George Cook, M.D., "Mental Hygiene," *The American Journal of Insanity* 15 no. 3 (January 1859): 274.

92 "Proceedings of the Association: Twentieth Annual Meeting of the Association of Medical Superintendents of American Institutions for the Insane," *The American Journal of Insanity* 23 no. 1 (July 1866): 75–145.

93 Isaac Ray, "Hints to the Medical Witness in Questions of Insanity," *The American Journal of Insanity* 8 no. 1 (July 1851): 63.

perpetrated by a wicked and abandoned man."[94] Chipley testified again in *Pecantet v. Grayson* (1872) against the existence of single faculty insanity, saying that in the thousands of cases of insanity he had treated, he had seen "no case where I have found persons insane upon a single subject." Still, he did not doubt that Eliza Atkinson was insane. Her cavalier approach toward marriage and her estate were too egregious to reflect sane behavior. Instead of concurring with Dismukes's diagnosis of monomania, he attributed her insanity to her consumption of opiates and intoxicating drink, which resulted in a will reflecting "vacillation and weakness of intellect."[95] To Chipley, like others opposed to moral or single faculty insanity, these doctrines allowed challengers to wills and criminal defendants to erode the responsibility that accompanied the exercise of free will. Moral insanity and single faculty insanity allowed experts to explain away immoral acts as manifestations of disease.

Within a decade, the Court of Appeals began to reconsider who conveyed legitimate knowledge and authority, and backed away from privileging medical testimony. *Wise v. Foote*, an 1883 dispute over testator James G. Arnold's will, occurred as national controversies including the Vanderbilt and Fillmore will disputes roiled legal and medical communities. Whereas in *Moore v. Moore* (1872) the court held that medical testimony "disposes of the vagaries" of the testimony of two nonexpert witnesses, in *Wise v. Foote* the court affirmed the worth of nonexpert opinions or local witnesses' opinions. Chief Justice Hargis positioned as authoritative those who knew Arnold. Unlike the decision in *Pecantet* in which the court overturned the jury verdict, it guarded the jury's decision. In *Wise v. Foote*, the challengers had questioned the validity of the opinions of "witnesses who were not experts." The challenge was based on the assumption that nonexperts could present only facts and should not infuse their testimonies with their assessments of the testator's capacity. Chief Justice Hargis ruled that nonexpert witness opinions were "relevant," if the witnesses "knew the testator, and had any opportunity of observing him; the weight and value of such opinions being for the consideration of the jury."[96] *Wise v. Foote* signaled a return of juridical power to local people and juries, subject of course, to appellate review.

[94] William S. Chipley, "In the Court of Appeals, State of Kentucky: Smith vs. Commonwealth," *The American Journal of Insanity* 23 no. 1 (July 1866): 35.

[95] "Testimony of William S. Chipley," Transcript, *Pecantet v. Grayson* (1872), Case 5727, Box 225, KCAR, KDLA.

[96] *Wise v. Foote*, 81 Ky. 10 (1883).

In *Ross v. Weaver* (1881), Anne Cooke, a purported brothel owner, disinherited her sister Jane Weaver and left most of her estate to her "paramour," James Ross. (This case is also discussed in Chapter 5.) Not only did Cooke have a reputation for prostitution, she openly and unrepentantly lived in an unmarried consensual sexual relationship. Local doctor L. C. Porter testified he thought Cooke "was intellectually sane and capable of making a will but she was morally insane." Porter's diagnosis suggested that Cooke did not willingly act immorally. She lacked free will, which justified disregarding her will. In a statement rare for its candor, Porter testified that "if the will was made correctly or good he would say she was competent but if it was a bad will he should say she was incompetent."[97] Porter sought to chasten Anne Cooke's flaunting of community values by marking her conduct as "morally insane" and impeding her ability to transmit property. By testifying that it was a "bad will," Porter condemned Cooke's choice of Ross as her beneficiary. Porter's diagnosis reflected his moral judgment of her conduct, derived from personal observation as a community member and as her attending physician.

Rather than adhere to the narrow legal test for capacity, which Porter grudgingly admitted Cooke passed, he invoked several sources of authority upon which he based his opinion. He presented his diagnosis as medical truth, connecting physical disease to her volitional ability. He contended that "Her disease was a ... utarine affection [*sic*]. From her debilitated condition she was amenable to the influence of others but her mind was clear." The Court of Appeals judges, however, protected Cooke's testamentary freedom from incursions derived from such a dubious diagnosis. Judge Pryor simultaneously confirmed Porter's censure of Cooke's conduct while abrogating Porter's medical authority. He held that Cooke's "depravity," rather than any medical reason, induced Porter to testify to her moral insanity. He concluded that "although she may have been an abandoned woman she nevertheless had the right to dispose of her estate as she saw proper, and it was simply a question of her mental capacity." Pryor rejected medicalizing Cooke's moral egress as insanity and disconnected Porter's judgment of the justice of the dispositions from his diagnosis of moral insanity.

Judges monitored closely local doctors' judgments when they presented them as medical truth. In *Bledsoe's Executrix v. Bledsoe* (1886), several local doctors testified that testator Samuel Bledsoe had Bright's disease, a

[97] "Testimony of Dr. LC Porter," Transcript, *Ross v. Weaver* (1881), Case 13247, Box 527, KCAR, KDLA.

degenerative kidney disease.[98] Doctors Connell and Brown pronounced Bledsoe insane, pointing out his "excentricities." As further proof, Dr. J. W. Connell quoted national medical expert Dr. W. A. Hammond, who "gives excentricity [*sic*] as an evidence of insanity."[99] (Although Connell may not have known, several national medical experts recently had discredited Hammond as a mercenary witness willing to diagnose anyone insane.[100]) Dr. James A. Brown testified that Bright's disease "dulls the mental faculties," leading to insanity manifested in "prejudice of parent against a child without cause is considered as one of the highest evidences of insanity."[101] Other local doctors, however, disagreed with the insanity etiologies put forth by Brown and Connell. Dr. J. T. Robinson, who knew Bledsoe for twenty years, agreed that Bledsoe suffered from Bright's disease. Robinson admitted that he believed Bledsoe had "peculiarities," but did not associate them with the kidney ailment. Robinson contended that in Bright's patients, the "mind is not affected by the disease til it produces coma."[102] Another doctor testified that Bright's disease had no direct "effect on the brain til it produces convulsions."[103] These two doctors presented the relationship between Bright's disease and insanity contrary to the local physicians called by the challengers. This sort of conflicting testimony illustrates multiple constructions of insanity that physicians articulated in local courtrooms. All twelve jurymen were unequivocal; they returned a verdict overturning the will and restoring an equal distribution of property among Bledsoe's disinherited sons.

Reviewing the evidence, the Court of Appeals overturned the verdict, questioning the persuasiveness of the evidence to justify denying Bledsoe's testamentary freedom. Judge Holt's decision conveyed his skepticism of the trial evidence and stopped the lower court from creating an informal higher standard of capacity contingent on local opinions of Bledsoe's character or will. Although Holt admitted the evidence was

98 See Chapter 1 for an extensive discussion of other aspects of *Bledsoe's Executrix v. Bledsoe*, 1 S.W. 10 (1886).

99 "Testimony of Dr. JW Connell," Transcript, *Bledsoe's Executrix v. Bledsoe* (1886), Case 716, Box 17095, KCAR, KDLA.

100 Clearly, Connell was unaware of Hammond's reputation or figured the jury would not know. Eugene Grissom, "True and False Experts," *The American Journal of Insanity* 35 (1878): 1–36, and Mohr, *Doctors and the Law*.

101 "Testimony of Dr. JW Connell," Transcript, *Bledsoe's Executrix v. Bledsoe* (1886), Case 716, Box 17095, KCAR, KDLA.

102 "Testimony of Dr. JT Robinson," Transcript, *Bledsoe's Executrix v. Bledsoe* (1886), Case 716, Box 17095, KCAR, KDLA.

103 Ibid.

"quite conflicting," he chastised the lower court for instructing the jury on a higher test of sanity than that sanctioned by the court. The lower court judge instructed that there must be "strong, *convincing* evidence" of a "rational mind" when a testator distributed property unequally among his children. Holt insisted that trial judges cannot "mislead the minds of the jury from the real issue of capacity or undue influence. These are the only questions upon which the jury should be instructed."[104] The court struck a blow for testamentary freedom, holding that if a testator has capacity, "he may make as unequal a disposition of it among his children as he pleases, or even disinherit them." The court upheld testators' rights and at the same time reinforced the informal regulatory power of male heads-of-household who had testamentary rights.

*Bledsoe* and *Ross v. Weaver* should not be read as ringing endorsements of testatorial privilege to indiscriminately disinherit heirs-at-law. Nor should these cases be read as a complete rejection of the acceptability of local physician testimony. Local doctors continued to appear regularly, often without comment from the bench. In *Bledsoe* and *Weaver*, the court made clear that it weighed carefully how local judges explained the standard of capacity to juries, particularly in instances when the jury or witnesses appeared to allow their own opinions of the testator or the justness of the will to influence testimony or verdicts. The court was emphasizing a concern with consistency and to some extent, formalism. Although many people thought Samuel Bledsoe was a cantankerous man of "bitter prejudices," Bledsoe's gifts reflected his paternal obligations to his daughter Manerva, who had spent years as his caretaker, and who most likely had few prospects for financial security as an unmarried woman. In *Ross v. Weaver* the court determined that Anne Cooke's heirs-at-law had not performed adequately their familial obligations to her. These cases show how court judges consistently reviewed and assessed the sources of knowledge that influenced the jury. By the last quarter of the century, the court reined in local doctors who would use medical authority to expand their moral and social influence over juries. It reinforced a legal definition of capacity removed from overly deterministic conclusions.

By 1889, the court had completely reversed its previous embrace of "scientific gentlemen" and their new theories of insanity. Court of Appeals Judge Lewis vilified experts' theoretical extrapolations, returning the court to its commitment to be the final arbiter of sanity based on its interpretation of the "facts" of the case. In *Bush v. Lisle*, Judge

[104] *Bledsoe's Executrix v. Bledsoe*, 1 S.W. 10 (1886).

Lewis traduced the value of expert testimony as "worse than useless, it is misleading, when given on a subject about which there is proof so convincing as to leave no reasonable ground for dispute."[105] The court believed that the "convincing" evidence presented was generated through direct observation by witnesses close to Lisle. Lewis noted that "those acquainted with him testified he possessed a clear, vigorous intellect and strong will." In this case, however, the court refused to sanction the jury's determination that Lisle, although suffering from tertiary stage syphilis, was mentally incapacitated. It explained the jury's decision as "their attention was diverted from facts proved to abstract theories of physicians."[106] Indeed, the court's holding simultaneously recognized that medical experts influenced juries while negating their assumed authority by rejecting the verdict.

By the turn of the twentieth century, Kentucky courts, like most other state courts, wholly rejected moral insanity or single faculty insanity as a viable explanation for deviant civil or criminal behavior. Medical experts had overwhelmingly repudiated moral insanity as well, some turning instead to theories of innate, hereditary degeneracy. By the early twentieth century, the psychological theories of Sigmund Freud and Jean Charcot revolutionized how doctors understood deviance. In 1899, in a dispute over Jeffery Power's will, the court opined that American jurisprudence held that "any unsoundness of mind which appears not to affect the general faculties ... is deemed not sufficient" to overturn a will. In a 1911 murder trial, the court put to rest any imputation that it would accept moral insanity as a plausible defense, holding that "the doctrine of moral insanity as a protection against punishment has been repudiated by all courts as dangerous to the safety of society."[107]

Far from their optimism in the first half of the nineteenth century, judges, jurists, and doctors came to recognize the hazards in assimilating medical theories into legal decision making. Medical jurisprudence had different ramifications for doctors and for jurists. As the contradictions, scientific uncertainties, and multiple interpretations of the human mind became clear, doctors appeared to their legal counterparts to equivocate, even prevaricate. Such was not the case. Medicine and law had different missions and different commitments to the process of creating and mobilizing knowledge and law. Even as the Kentucky bench's composition

[105] *Bush v. Lisle*, 89 Ky. 393 (1889).
[106] Ibid.
[107] *Banks v. Commonwealth*, 145 Ky. 800 (1911).

changed, judges remained committed to a conservative inheritance system that favored equality and benevolence among families defined by blood and legal relation. The court continued to encourage familial wealth transfers and protect the regulatory effect testation had on heirs'-at-law conduct. On the other hand, justices consistently reaffirmed testamentary freedom as a property right that inhered in sane men. As the court testily reiterated in 1890, "the testator has the legal right to dispose of his estate as he may wish, even to discard, *in toto*, the natural objects of his bounty, and give his estate to a stranger, without assigning or having any good reason for so doing, whatever. This is his perfect right of alienation."[108] Judges would not overturn wills in which testators appeared to meet the requirements of the legal test for capacity, especially when testators willed property to worthy heirs or explanations existed for their testamentary behavior.

[108] *Zimlich v. Zimlich*, 90 Ky. 657 (1893).

# 4

# Physical Impairments and Degenerate Minds

## *The Body as Evidence*

In 1845, Polly Bullitt's half-siblings filed a will challenge in the Louisville Chancery Court claiming that Polly was born an idiot, mentally incapable of meeting Kentucky's low standard of testamentary capacity. Tried twice in the Louisville court before being heard by the Court of Appeals, *Howard v. Coke* (1846) was no ordinary will dispute. It involved the Bullitt family, a wealthy, socially prominent family who had deep roots in Kentucky's political circles, economy, and frontier history. The *Louisville Courier* reported on the case, perhaps because Henry Clay, Kentucky's most famous lawyer and orator, came out of retirement to argue against the will. Much of the testimony focused on describing Polly Bullitt's body and appearance. Lawyers asked witnesses to "State what was the appearance of her figure, and what was the expression of her countenance?"[1] One of Polly's childhood neighbors replied, "She stooped a little; and was slovenly in her dress.... She was cross eyed and twisted or distorted in her features when in conversation."[2] Counsel asked physicians to "State the relation which physical deformity of Idiots and Imbeciles usually bears to their mental capacity?" which followed a question about the relationship between idiocy and "cross-eyes; decayed teeth, a hanging down

[1] "Interrogatories for Plaintiffs No. 1," in Box 28, FL 251, *Howard v. Churchill*, Bullitt Family Papers, Filson Historical Society, Louisville, Kentucky. Hereafter BFP, FHS. When the case reached the Court of Appeals, it was retitled *Howard v. Coke*, 46 Ky. 655 (1847). Many of the papers from the *Howard v. Coke* trial were transcribed from the original transcripts in the 1930s by Alexander Bullitt's secretary. In many instances, the original deposition or letter was preserved with the transcription. In a few cases, the original document was not in the file.

[2] "Testimony of Richard Phillips," *Howard v. Churchill*, Box 29, FL 264, BFP, FHS.

of the lower jaw."[3] A consistent theme emerged throughout the case in which Polly Bullitt's appearance became an outward representation of her inward mental incapacity.

This chapter explores how testators' bodies and physical impairments provided evidence about mental capacity. The testators' bodies served as external indicators – texts to be read – through which the state of the testators' sanity, intellect, and morality could be ascertained. Some testators were hearing or sight impaired or born with congenital physical disabilities. Others suffered from the physically disabling effects of disease. Many testators experienced physical impairment as they aged. In the grammar of capacity, loss of hearing or sight and advanced age was equated with diminished mental capacity. Challengers alleged undue influence by opportunistic caregivers who took advantage of physically dependent testators. The Court of Appeals's assessment in 1868 that testator Walter Thomas suffered from "infirmities of four score years, and the disease of the eyes, which deprived him of his sight, had brought the strong man down to comparative helplessness, and dependence upon others" typified the court's deliberations.[4] These cases reflected concern that aging potentially created dangerous dependency that precluded individuals from making independent decisions.

Nineteenth-century Kentucky cases reveal jurists and medical experts struggling to determine the extent of testators' mental awareness when they were very sick, sometimes near death, and often in excruciating pain. In *Bush v. Lisle* (1889), the challengers portrayed testator Frank Lisle as a "physical wreck," a blind syphilitic morphine addict who embodied "moral degradation" and "imbecility."[5] Current medical research confirms that during tertiary stage syphilis, most likely someone in Lisle's condition would have experienced significant neurological brain damage. Yet the Court of Appeals upheld Lisle's will after a jury rejected it, partly because Lisle named his sister's family as his beneficiaries. They had nursed the bedridden Lisle for years. In *Bush v. Lisle* (1889) and other cases, the court sought to strike a balance between protecting testators' right to

[3] "Interrogatories for Plaintiffs No. 8," *Howard v. Churchill*, Box 28, FL 251, BFP, FHS.

[4] *Thomas v. Thomas*, 2 Ky. Op. 338 (1868). Thomas had deeded property to his beneficiaries just before his death rather than write a will. Although the case was a capacity challenge to several deeds, the court treated it like a testamentary capacity challenge by considering who were the "natural objects" of Thomas's bounty.

[5] "Brief for Appellees by Breckenridge and Shelby," *Bush v. Lisle* (1889), Case 19613, Box 839, Kentucky Court of Appeals Records (hereafter KCAR), Kentucky Department for Libraries and Archives, Frankfort, Kentucky (hereafter KDLA).

choose beneficiaries and defending sick and aged testators' families from unjust disinheritance. The court sought to reaffirm a kin-based informal network of caregiving, articulated and strengthened through inheritance practices.

Cases in which beneficiaries took care of disabled testators presented Janus-faced challenges to beneficiaries and heirs-at-law alike. Described one way, caregivers made great emotional and financial sacrifices to care for ailing and disabled relatives. Described another, caretakers controlled the food, medicine, and survival of impaired testators, making them physically and psychologically dependent. Testators lost free will. Heirs-at-law challenged wills by contradicting beneficiaries' images of themselves as selfless, noble caregivers. Challengers portrayed caregiving as an oppressive relationship that fostered physical and mental dependency and that was ideally suited to exercising undue influence.

These cases occurred within a matrix of social values in which challengers used the negative connotations associated with physical and functional impairments to provide evidence of insanity. Beneficiaries argued against these narratives, affirming testators' free will and moral integrity and downplaying their physical impairments. These arguments rarely challenged directly the assumption that an aged or impaired body represented an impaired mind. Rather, they argued for the exceptionalism of a particular testator or claimed that the physical impairments or disease were misdiagnosed, thus assigning the testator an inaccurate label of mental unsoundness. In *Bush v. Lisle*, the proponents' attorney argued that, contrary to the challengers' contention, Lisle "had full use of his arms, and suffered no pain, except from his knees down. It is attempted to be shown that he was paralized [*sic*], but Dr Allen shows that this is not true."[6] Although the attorneys conceded that Lisle was blind, they mitigated the extent to which he was physically incapacitated and dependent on the Bush family.

Disability studies scholar Lennard Davis argues that "disability presents itself to 'normal people' through two main modalities – function and appearance."[7] Bodily difference and functional impairment such as blindness or deafness became part of the grammar of capacity as representations of inferiority. Physical differences perceived as deviance justified

6 "Brief for Appellants," *Bush v. Lisle* (1889), Case 19613, Box 839, KCAR, KDLA.

7 Lennard J. Davis, *Enforcing Normalcy: Disability, Deafness, and the Body* (New York: Verso Press, 1995), 11–12.

social and legal exclusions.[8] Disability has been central to establishing the boundaries of citizenship. African Americans, immigrants, and women have been denied full citizenship, justified partially through associating them with defectiveness and disability.[9] As another scholar observes, defining disability implicates "social practices that involve the unequal exercise of power and have major economic, social, and psychological consequences in some people's lives."[10] In testamentary capacity trials, evidence of disability made testators suspect, jeopardizing the execution of their wills.

Throughout testamentary capacity trials, physical and functional deviance was identified, discussed, and categorized. Medical treatises written in the last half of the nineteenth century applied evolutionary Darwinism, theories of atavism, and scientific racism to assess mental capacity.[11] In the mid-nineteenth-century South, Dr. Samuel Cartwright argued that slaves' "physical organization" made them suited for slavery. If freed, they suffered "a disease that locks up understanding."[12] Although even some of Cartwright's contemporaries considered his medical views extreme, he was in the mainstream when he emphasized that bodies differing from the white male normative body were potentially inferior and unfit to exercise the free will that accompanied civil freedom. Simultaneously, earlier and long-standing powerful popular cultural views portrayed disabled people as afflicted, pathetic, and deserving of sentimentalized sympathy.[13] Both the scientific and sentimental images of the physically impaired body depicted dependency. The ability to think independently

[8] Douglas C. Baynton, "Disability and the Justifications of Inequality in American History," in Paul K. Longmore and Lauri Umanski, eds., *The New Disability History: American Perspectives* (New York and London: New York University Press, 2001) and Rosemarie Garland Thomson, *Extraordinary Bodies: Figuring Physical Disability in American Culture and Literature* (New York: Columbia University Press, 1997).

[9] Baynton, "Disability and the Justifications of Inequality in American History," 33–57; Yvonne Pitts, "Disability, Scientific Authority, and Women's Political Participation in the Turn of the Twentieth Century United States," *Journal of Women's History* 24 no. 2 (2012): 37–61.

[10] Susan Wendell, *The Rejected Body: Feminist Philosophical Reflections on Disability* (New York: Routledge, 1996), 23.

[11] See, for example, Henry Maudsley, *Body and Will, Being an Essay Concerning Will in its Metaphysical, Physiological, and Pathological Aspects* (New York: D. Appleton and Co., 1884). For historians' discussions, see Cynthia Eagle Russett, *Sexual Science: The Victorian Construction of Womanhood* (Cambridge: Harvard University Press, 1989).

[12] Samuel Cartwright, "Report on the Diseases and Physical Particularities of the Negro Race," *New Orleans Medical and Surgical Journal* 8 (1851): 692–713.

[13] Mary Klages, *Woeful Afflictions: Disability and Sentimentality in Victorian America* (Philadelphia: University of Pennsylvania Press, 1999), 4.

was linked to the ability to act independently, expressed through a disciplined, controlled body.

In the courtroom, physical appearance and functionality served as legal evidence in determining who had the right to distribute property. Nineteenth-century treatise writer Isaac Redfield commented that it was "a settled rule of English law, until a comparatively recent period, that deaf and dumb persons were, prima facie, incapable of writing a will." Redfield noted that by 1866 testamentary rights extended to deaf and mute persons, but only after clearly showing that the testator made the will "understandingly."[14] The burden of proof for these testators rested on showing capacity, not a lack of capacity. Jurists, physicians, and witnesses rhetorically dissected physically and functionally different bodies to determine if the disability excluded the testator from the category of mentally sound, or, if, in spite of the disability, the testator possessed the requisite sanity to write a valid will.

The focus on different or disabled bodies in testamentary capacity trials appeared long before the medical turn toward scientific racism and the creation of a medical taxonomy of deviance in the mid to late nineteenth century. Although the science evolved, the basic premises equating physical impairment with mental weakness remained constant. In *In re Howard* (1827), Samuel Howard challenged his sister Alsey Howard's will, claiming she was insane. Howard, who was "deformed ... since infancy," had left her property to her mother, Sarah Howard. After the Jessamine County Court overturned the will, Sarah Howard appealed to the Court of Appeals. Samuel Howard's attorneys used Alsey Howard's physical impairments as evidence of her insanity. Chief Justice Bibb agreed that "owing to bodily deformity and decrepitude, she never was sent to school, that she avoided the company of strangers, and had fits at times."[15] In this case, however, the court separated Howard's physical differences from her mental capacity. Chief Justice Bibb held that, in spite of her physical disabilities, "her mind was not deformed, nor her affection benumbed, nor her intellect benighted."[16] Bibb's statement created parallels between physical disability and mental disabilities when he observed that her "mind was not deformed" although her body was. His

[14] Isaac Redfield, *The Law of Wills, Embracing the Making and Construction of Wills; The Jurisprudence of Insanity; The Effect of Extrinsic Evidence; The Creation and Construction of Trusts, So Far As Applicable to Wills, with Forms and Instructions for Preparing Wills Part I*, second edition (Boston: Little Brown and Co., 1866), 43–4.

[15] *In re Howard's Will*, 21 Ky. 199 (1827).

[16] Ibid.

other adjectives, which also describe paralysis and an intellect shrouded in darkness ("benumbed" and "benighted"), link physical impairments and mental incapacity.

Ironically, to the court judges, Howard's consciousness of her deformities and her desire to hide them indicated mental soundness. They held that "her consciousness of her deformity, and retreat from the approach of strangers, is a proof of sanity."[17] As Davis notes, "strong feelings of revulsion" are central to the process of constructing disability and implementing its imagery in social discourse.[18] Howard's self-imposed seclusion and her recognition of the stigma attached to her body indicated a sound mind. Judge Bibb noted approvingly that Howard "had been from infancy weak and decrepid, [*sic*] and her mother, with great care and pains, had nursed her from infancy to old age. This is surely proof, strong and undoubted, of memory, of reason and of social affections and moral sense."[19] Howard's mother was a deserving beneficiary and the court refused to disturb Howard's plan to reward properly her caretaker.

The opinions of neighbors supplied additional authoritative evidence about Howard's sanity. The neighbors noted that "those who knew her well and resided near her" agreed unequivocally upon her sanity. The reputation of an attesting witness to the will as a "man of integrity, of irreproachable character" mitigated any doubts raised by Howard's exceptional body. Independent witnesses who explained Howard's physical differences and vouched for her sanity allowed the judges to portray Howard as pitiable but not insane. Howard's brother, the challenger, had come from Tennessee to challenge the will, leading Bibb to view his motives "with great jealousy." Bibb's opinion incorporated localist sentiment by recognizing the consensus of the local community over that of outsiders with ulterior motives.

## THE DIFFERENCE BETWEEN IDIOTS AND IMBECILES

In the dispute over Polly Bullitt's 1845 will, the case ostensibly turned on whether Polly Bullitt was an "idiot." Some witnesses believed that although Bullitt was not "sprightly," she "had a knowledge of her property and was not an idiot."[20] For centuries, the term *idiot* had been part

[17] Ibid.
[18] Davis, *Enforcing Normalcy*, 11–12.
[19] Ibid., 203.
[20] "Deposition of Mrs. Sarah E. Clark," FL 256A, BFP, FHS.

of legal, medical, and colloquial language, used derogatorily to connote mental or moral failings. The Court of Appeals judges viewed the capacity of those declared idiots in the harshest terms. In an 1834 case over a wife's dower claim to her dead husband's estate, the court referred to idiots as "to all intellectual purposes, dead; and such a being, destitute of intellectual light and life, is as incapable as a dead body of being a husband or a wife, in a legal, rational or moral sense."[21] In this case, the court rejected the wife's dower claim because her marriage was never legally valid due to her husband's idiocy. The question in the Bullitt case was whether Polly belonged in the idiot category. In order to garner evidence, both sides focused on her body, her facial expressions, and her ability to perform gendered tasks such as sewing, singing, and socializing.

Bullitt came from a prominent Kentucky family with ties to the Founders. Her grandmother Annie Henry was Patrick Henry's sister. Her father, Alexander Scott Bullitt, built Oxmoor, one of Kentucky's largest slaveholding plantations, and served as the first lieutenant governor of Kentucky. Bullitt's mother and father died when she was young, leaving her with substantial property, including slaves.[22] After her parents' deaths, relatives sent Polly to the Catholic Sisters of Charity's Nazareth Female Academy, where she spent much of her life.[23] Shortly before her death, Bullitt dictated a will in which she left her estate to several charities and relatives on her mother's side, disinheriting the Bullitts, her paternal descendants. They contested the will. Polly Bullitt's nephew Joshua Fry Bullitt, later joined by Henry Clay, litigated the case against the Guthries, who were the primary beneficiaries and her mother's descendants from a marriage prior to Alexander Scott Bullitt.

Exploring local and legal conceptions of idiocy reveals another borderland on the legal landscape of testamentary capacity jurisprudence. Although few cases involved allegations of idiocy, these cases demonstrate preoccupation with how concepts of bodily control and physical integrity shaped rationality. In legal and medical terms, idiocy or imbecility differed from insanity, which was perceived as a disease of the mind or the will that usually produced delusions that replaced rationality in an otherwise ordinary adult.[24] Insanity developed from a "lesion to the

[21] *Jenkins v. Jenkins Heirs*, 32 Ky. 102 at 104.

[22] Untitled, FL 250, BFP, FHS.

[23] "Deposition of Mrs. Helen Martin" (Polly's half sister), Box 31, FL 280, BFP, FHS.

[24] During the nineteenth century, individuals with the genetic abnormality trisomy-21, which causes Down's syndrome, were identified as idiots or imbeciles. In 1867, John Langdon Down coined the term *Mongolism*, diagnosing these individuals as atavistic

faculties subsequent to their development."[25] In the early nineteenth century, medical jurists understood idiocy as an "obstacle to the development of the faculties, supervening in infancy," and resulting in a perpetual childlike state. In 1824, the Kentucky legislature differentiated the developmentally impaired from the insane, mandating that the Eastern State Lunatic Asylum distinguish between the "sick or imbecile" and those people "actually lunatic, or of unsound mind."[26] Only the latter were admitted. The statute permitted nonviolent idiots to remain with their parents in local communities. These distinctions suggest that legislators considered idiots relatively harmless but unworthy of state asylum funds, probably because many physicians considered idiocy congenital and hopeless rather than curable through the moral therapy offered at ESLA.

By the 1840s, popular and medical literature portrayed idiots as moral failures and objects of pity and disgust. In 1848, Samuel G. Howe, an early advocate of educating idiots, inveighed that without training, idiots were a "spectacle of human beings reduced to a state of brutishness, and given up to the indulgences of animal appetites and passions."[27] Howe believed that through institutionalized education, some idiots could learn language, basic manners, and rudimentary social skills. By 1860, the Kentucky legislature opened a separate institution for "feeble-minded children" in Frankfort, following similar efforts in Massachusetts, Connecticut, and New York.[28] Like most institutions for the feebleminded, Kentucky's school attempted to teach "some kind of useful labor" to prevent idiots from becoming "idle and vicious."[29]

Mongoloids. During the late nineteenth and early twentieth centuries, the diagnosis of a "moral imbecile" emerged. Not until 1966 would the World Health Organization replace the term *mongoloid idiot* with Down's syndrome. Most disability scholars now use the term *mental disability* or *intellectual disability* to describe congenital disabilities once labeled idiocy, Mongolism, or mental retardation.

[25] Isaac Ray, *A Treatise on the Medical Jurisprudence of Insanity* (Boston: Charles C. Little and James Brown, 1838), 71.

[26] 1824 Ky. Acts, Title 95 § 2.

[27] Samuel Gridley Howe, "A Selection from 'Report Made to the Legislature of Massachusetts (1848),'" in Steven Noll and James Trent, Jr., eds., *Mental Retardation in America: A Historical Reader* (New York: New York University Press, 2004), 24.

[28] *Private Institution for the Education of Feeble-Minded Youth Twenty-Fifth Biennial Report* (Barre, MA: Charles Rogers, 1898), http://www.disabilitymuseum.org/lib/docs/1707.htm?page=3, accessed May 21, 2006.

[29] J. Q. A. Stewart, "The Industrial Department of the Kentucky Institution for the Education and Training of Feebleminded Children," *Proceedings of the Association of Medical Officers of American Institutions for Idiotic and Feeble-Minded Persons* (1882): 236–9.

Medical and legal experts categorized intellectual disability according to the perceived degree of mental development. At the time of the Bullitt will dispute, the most common division was between "idiocy" and "imbecility."[30] Medico-jurists agreed that many idiots lacked any mental ability, but imbeciles might have some reasoning capabilities. Jurist Isaac Ray contended in his 1838 medical jurisprudence treatise: "In reasoning power, idiots are below the brute," but imbeciles "possess some intellectual capacity."[31] He also believed that accurately distinguishing between degrees of idiocy or imbecility was difficult to quantify in a legal test. Instead, Ray identified idiots through their bodies rather than their mental functions, describing them as "the lips are thick, and the mouth kept open, the saliva suffered to escape ... and defective teeth are displayed; the limbs are crooked." Ray interpreted their bodies as repellent, describing their visages as "dull or glaring eyes, gaping mouth, their wild and hideous laugh, their inarticulate sounds ... and utter unconsciousness of social and domestic relations."[32] The observation that idiots were unaware of "domestic relations" prima facie disqualified them from knowing the "natural objects of their bounty." Finally, Ray concluded that the idiot's nonconforming and uncontrolled body transgressed the boundaries of humanness: a "wild and hideous" laughing monster in human form.

Similar to defining insanity, legal experts struggled with the rules for determining the boundaries of idiocy, finding medical classifications inadequate for legal application. Citing Ray, jurist Isaac Redfield agreed in *The Law of Wills* (1866) that among people "denominated idiots ... there is no capacity to contract, or execute a valid testament."[33] Redfield conceded that the determination of a legal idiot was "incapable of strict definition," making it a question "triable by jury."[34] Like insanity issues, the determination of idiocy involved a range of behaviors and appearances outside behavioral norms. As historian James Trent points out, it is important to understand "mental retardation as a 'thing,' the object of scientific understanding and intervention."[35] Although taxonomies

[30] As the nineteenth century progressed, these categories gained in complexity and degree. See, for example, H. B. Wilbur, "The Classifications of Idiocy," *Proceedings of the Association of Medical Officers of American Institutions for Idiotic and Feeble-minded Persons* (1877): 29–35.

[31] Ray, *A Treatise on the Medical Jurisprudence of Insanity*, 72–95.

[32] Ibid., 73–4.

[33] Redfield, *The Law of Wills*, 51.

[34] Ibid., 50.

[35] James Trent, Jr., *Inventing the Feeble Mind: A History of Mental Retardation in the United States* (Berkeley and London: University of California Press, 1994), 6.

grouping mentally disabled individuals appeared stable, the difficulty lay in determining individuals' abilities. The category also expanded; by the last quarter of the nineteenth century, the diagnosis of "moral idiocy" gained currency. Idiocy explicitly became conflated with uncontrollable immoral behavior, a subtext that had existed for decades, but did not become fully articulated until the last decades of the century.

Throughout the nineteenth century, intellectually disabled people living in communities demonstrated a wide range of ability and dependency, ranging from requiring complete care to participating in economic and social networks. One Kentucky land dispute shows how one man eventually declared a legal idiot worked and traded for years in his local community.[36] In 1845, John Boyd's guardian sought to nullify a contract in which Boyd had traded land for slaves on the ground that Boyd was an idiot. The contract had been negotiated years before the county court declared Boyd an idiot. By upholding the contract in the appeal, the Court of Appeals recognized Boyd's behavior as an act of free will premised on rational self-interest. In much of the time between the initial trade and the legal dispute, Boyd held property and profited from working with his father.[37] The community recognized Boyd as mentally impaired; however, his perceived developmental disabilities did not prevent him from participating in legal and economic interactions in his own name.

Idiocy was a fluid category informed by communal knowledge, economic considerations, and medical perspectives. During the first half of the nineteenth century, the Kentucky legislature left it to the community to determine who was legally an idiot for the purposes of exercising legal independence. The legislature suspected that people occasionally declared nondisabled family members idiots in order to receive state treasury support for their maintenance, noting in a statutory preamble that because of "undue and illegal execution of the existing laws in relation to lunatics and idiots, many persons, who are not idiots, are supported out of the public treasury."[38] The legislature, chronically lacking resources, may have been trying to conserve funds. An 1831 statute called for a writ of *de idiola inquirendo* in which twelve local men heard evidence to decide

[36] Penny L. Richards, "'Beside her Sat her Idiot Child': Families and Developmental Disability in Mid-Nineteenth Century America," in Steven Noll and James Trent, Jr., eds., *Mental Retardation in America: A Historical Reader* (New York: New York University Press, 2004), 65–79.

[37] *Hopson v. Boyd*, 45 Ky. 296 (1845).

[38] 1831 Ky. Acts, Title 95 § 2, "An Act to Amend the Law in Relation to Idiots and Lunatics."

whether or not to assign legal idiocy or lunacy in individual cases.[39] Such laws meant that jurors and witnesses in local communities gave meaning to legal language through individual cases heard over time, making legal idiocy or lunacy changeable and the attendant denial of rights uncertain. Also, local relatives might work to legally define someone as mentally incompetent due to a limited ability to support him or herself. Communal knowledge and economic conditions set the parameters for idiocy and lunacy, which then were inflected into legal doctrine determining rights and disabilities.

The Bullitt trial occurred when public displays of extraordinary bodies, billed as freak shows, dime museums, and ostensibly "scientific exhibits," had begun touring regularly throughout the United States.[40] In 1833, Chang and Eng, the famous Siamese twins, appeared in Cincinnati just across the Ohio River from Kentucky.[41] In another touring freak show contemporary to the Bullitt trial, two mentally disabled microcephalic siblings were dressed in stylized garb and presented as "Wild Australian Children."[42] The popular press reported regularly on physical disfigurements, presenting them as scientific curiosities. In 1879, *The South Kentuckian* reported on the "Two-Headed Girls," considered "far more wonderful than the Siamese twins."[43] In 1884, the hugely popular "Buffalo Bill's Wild West Show," which included the savage Indians' "attack on Settler cabin," stopped in Louisville to great fanfare.[44] Such displays, disabilities scholar Rosemary Garland Thomson explains, "structured a cultural ritual that seized upon any deviation from the typical, embellishing and intensifying it to produce a human spectacle whose every somatic feature was laden with significance before the gaping spectator."[45] Residents of Louisville and other urban areas were regularly exposed to performances that highlighted physical difference. Often, as with the Wild West show and the "Wild Australian Children," these shows used racial or physical difference to emphasize inferiority.

39 Ibid.

40 Robert Bogdan, *Freak Show: Presenting Human Oddities for Amusement and Profit* (Chicago: University of Chicago Press, 1988).

41 "The Siamese Twins – Chang and Eng," *Cincinnati Mirror and Western Gazette of Literature, Science and the Arts*, February 2, 1833.

42 Bogdan, *Freak Show*, 120.

43 "Two Headed Girls," *The South Kentuckian* (Hopkinsville), May 20, 1879.

44 "Buffalo Bill's," *The Times: Louisville*, November 6, 1884.

45 Rosemary Garland Thomson, "From Wonder to Error – A Genealogy of Freak Discourse in Modernity," in Rosemary Garland Thomson, ed. *Freakery: Cultural Spectacles of the Extraordinary Body* (New York: New York University Press, 1996), 4.

Polly Bullitt's will case, *Howard v. Coke* (1847), illustrates how challengers' lawyers used vivid descriptions of Bullitt's body to create courtroom spectacle depicting deformity and brutishness. Trials, like freak shows and scientific exhibits, created narratives that emphasized difference. According to the Bullitt family's personal correspondence, the trial was well attended, offering a voyeuristic peek at the social disorder caused by Bullitt's deviant body. The *Louisville Daily Journal* described the audience as "so great ... that hundreds of others were unable to get into the court room."[46] Courtrooms, like the "museums" or "scientific displays" showcasing freaks, served as ritualized sites for presenting deviant bodies. More, however, was at stake in these legal rituals. As opposed to a day's entertainment at a dime museum, such trials often involved people known to the community whose property and personal reputations were at stake. Lawyers, witnesses, and medical experts infused their testimonies with cultural images that gave meaning to physical differences. Trials were much more than sites for the disinterested application of law and justice, becoming theatrical performances in which justice was negotiated and decided.[47] As testators were never present, witnesses and lawyers recreated them through descriptions, images, and the stories they told.

In *Howard v. Coke*, the challengers' lawyers seized upon the meanings assigned to deviant bodies by asking for descriptions of Bullitt's physical "countenance." Witnesses went into great detail, adding commentary as to how they perceived her outward physical appearance. Martha Pope, who lived near Bullitt during childhood, described Bullitt's body as "low and fleshy, and her countenance was dull, stupid and idiotic. She hung her head down and looked up under her brows. She had a large mouth and was very homely."[48] Another witness who saw Bullitt shortly before her death called her "a mass of deformity."[49] Witnesses described Polly Bullitt's voracious eating habits, crying fits, and high temper. Estelle Blancagniel, a student at Nazareth, remembered Bullitt as "very easily excited and cried whenever anything was done to her. She was in the

[46] *Louisville Daily Journal*, May 8, 1849.

[47] For a discussion of courtrooms as sites of cultural spectacle, see Ariela Gross, *Double Character: Slavery and Mastery in the Antebellum Southern Courtroom* (Princeton: Princeton University Press, 2000); Katherine Fisher Taylor, *In the Theatre of Criminal Justice: The Palais de Justice in Second Empire Paris* (Princeton: Princeton University Press, 1993).

[48] "Deposition of Mrs. Martha Pope," *Howard v. Churchill* (1845–1846), Box 29, FL 264, BFP, FHS.

[49] "Deposition of Mrs. Catherine Dailey," *Howard v. Churchill* (1845–1846), Box 30, FL 268, BFP, FHS.

habit of crying out just like a child & would never wipe the tears from her eyes but permitted them to run over her face." Blancagniel described Polly's "appetite as ravenous & like a child was always craving something and when eating was filthy."[50] These descriptions conveyed the witnesses' revulsion at Bullitt's disorderly body. Referring to Bullitt as a child reinforced the perception of Bullitt's dependency. Her inability to control her body defined Bullitt as animalistic, atavistic, and incapable of higher emotion or mental function.

Witnesses describing Bullitt incorporated deeply gendered ideas about her appearance and her performance of domestic tasks. Parents and teachers trained girls of Bullitt's social class in etiquette and genteel manners. The challengers' lawyers asked witnesses whether Polly could "perform on any musical instrument, or sew and knit," and at what age girls usually learned these tasks.[51] The ability to gracefully perform these tasks projected a seemingly natural image of elite white womanhood. The ideals of gender and class appropriate behavior, expressed through controlled and regulated physical movements, informed how people perceived mental capacity and identified abnormality.

Polly Bullitt's appearance affected her participation in rituals of courtship and socializing that formed social and economic networks and reaffirmed appropriate gender relations. Witnesses were asked if they had met with Bullitt "in Society, at any Ball, or at any party?" The challengers contended that Bullitt's physical differences and repugnant behavior excluded her from society events.[52] Bullitt's half sister Helen Martin acknowledged that Polly's inability to perform according to social manners further served to isolate her from her peers. Martin did not "think Polly the worst kind of idiot," but conceded that she "considered her entirely unfit for society, and that it would only be exposing her to ridicule."[53] Martin's comment reveals a complex method of social regulation based on adhering to agreed upon manners and performing elaborate gendered behavioral rituals. Polly Bullitt's physical differences and her lack of bodily control made her an object of derision. By

[50] "Deposition of Miss Estelle Blancagniel," *Howard v. Churchill* (1845–1846), Box 30, FL 269, BFP, FHS.

[51] "Interrogatories for Plaintiffs No. 1," *Howard v. Churchill &c* (November 7, 1845), Box 28, FL 251, BFP, FHS.

[52] Ibid.

[53] "Deposition of Mrs. Helen Martin," *Howard v. Churchill* (1845–1846), Box 31, FL 280, BFP, FHS.

portraying Bullitt as incapable of class appropriate feminine behavior, the challengers argued that she lacked the mental capacity to distribute her property.

The Guthries' attorneys defending the will argued that the challengers exaggerated Polly Bullitt's physical and mental impairments. They elicited descriptions of her ability to meet social expectations. By depicting Bullitt as having an ordinary body and performing feminine tasks, they argued she was no more or less capable than any other woman. Ann Rudd remembered that Bullitt "behaved with as much propriety as any young lady could" and "she was neat in her dress and personal appearance as much so as any young lady."[54] Rudd compared Bullitt to her peers, finding her within the range of acceptable appearances for women. Therefore, the defense argued, Bullitt could make necessary distinctions among her kin and close friends. Her feelings of gratitude and affection led her to make a just distribution of her property.

Henry Clay's closing argument focused on Polly's inability to physically perform the gendered role of a wealthy, unmarried Southern woman. In a letter to John C. Bullitt, his sister Susan described accounts of Henry Clay's final speech to the jury. Susan Bullitt did not attend the trial herself as she believed her appearance "would not look very well" to the broader community.[55] According to Bullitt, Clay repeatedly called attention to Polly's wealth and class standing, against which he superimposed evidence that she had not ever been courted. Clay implied that her physical unattractiveness and disgusting comportment prevented a suitable marriage. Susan Bullitt recounted how Clay noted that he had

> Never heard of Polly Bullitt's having a beau. He supposed there were fortune hunters in Louisville as in every place he had ever seen. And yet a young lady of fortune, of family, in whose veins flowed some of the best blood in Kentucky (and his opponents said of most exquisite form) had never been courted![56]

The parenthetical commentary noting the opponents' argument that Polly had an "exquisite form" ridiculed Clay's legal adversaries by calling attention to Polly Bullitt's body. For Henry Clay and Susan Bullitt, Polly's physical differences provided reason to render her unmarriageable in spite of wealth and family reputation.

[54] "Deposition of Ann H. Rudd," *Howard v. Churchill* (1845–1846), No Box, FL 256A, BFP, FHS.

[55] Susan Peachy Bullitt to John C. Bullitt, May 1849, No Box, FL 162, BFP, FHS.

[56] Ibid.

The high profile of the *Howard v. Coke* trial revealed another aspect of how inheritance litigation was enmeshed in the social relations of the surrounding community. In spite of the many witnesses and medical experts, and the time and expense spent by both sides, the outcome of *Howard v. Coke* illustrates some of the difficulties in interpreting jury verdicts. The jury hung, supposedly with nine men voting against the will and three men for the will. Henry Clay's closing arguments and the newspaper coverage suggest that factors other than the strength of the evidence influenced each juror. According to Susan Bullitt, during his closing remarks Henry Clay suggested that the trial was nothing but a performance; the trial's outcome had already been decided through the back channels of local social networks. Bullitt described Clay as saying that it was "rumored in the street that this would be a hung jury … but I believe you all to be honorable and honest men." Clay said that a hung jury (which would leave the will standing) would "leave a stain on your fair proud city," and implored the jury to decide according to the evidence.[57]

The hung jury verdict and accompanying insinuations that it had been a fixed trial created a minor scandal in Louisville and in the *Louisville Daily Journal*. The *Journal*'s night editor printed the names of the nine jurors voting against the will and the three jurors favoring it, noting that "it is understood that one of the latter would have gone with the majority if the two others had done so."[58] A day later the editor apologized, saying that such a publishing practice was "wrong in principle."[59] This public disclosure brought to light the kinds of manipulations and intrigues that went far beyond legal rules and courtroom testimony in determining jury verdicts. It points to the operation of a legal culture in which legal institutions and deliberations were influenced by and embedded in sociopolitical relations.[60] The honor of the jurors, first impugned by Clay, was then discussed in the local paper. Juror John A. Miller, who voted in favor of the will, asked the paper to print that he was not the juror "willing to go with the majority" if the others also did so.[61] The broader community understood and participated in a legal culture grounded in the conceptions of honor and public reputation yet vulnerable to malfeasance.

[57] Ibid.

[58] *Louisville Daily Journal*, May 9, 1849.

[59] Ibid., May 10, 1849.

[60] For a discussion of "legal culture," see Lawrence Friedman, "Legal Culture and Social Development," *Law and Society* 4 no. 1 (August 1969): 29–44; Ariela Gross, "Beyond Black and White: Cultural Approaches to Race and Slavery," *Columbia Law Review* 101 (2001): 640–90.

[61] *Louisville Daily Journal*, May 9, 1849.

The Bullitt case was not an exception; other will contestants used physical impairment as a proxy for mental impairment. In *Bush v. Lisle* (1889), the challengers to Frank M. Lisle's will conflated images of physical monstrosity with moral turpitude and mental insanity.[62] Frank (F. M.) Lisle died in 1879 and left his substantial wealth almost entirely to his sister Minerva Bush and her family. Lisle had acquired his wealth through gambling, running a faro bank (card game), and shady business dealings. During the last decade of his life, Lisle suffered from end-stage (tertiary) syphilis, which caused paralysis and blindness, and he lived with Bush, who nursed him until his death. John Brax (J. B.) Lisle, F. M.'s brother, contested the will on the grounds of F. M. Lisle's mental unsoundness and the undue influence exerted by Minerva Bush. The county case ended in three hung juries before a fourth Clark County jury overturned the will. Minerva Bush appealed to the Court of Appeals and Judge C. J. Lewis upheld the validity of the will and ordered it to probate on the basis of lack of evidence of insanity or undue influence.

Graphic physical descriptions linked to allegations of Lisle's wickedness and immorality were central to the challengers' case. Lisle had contracted syphilis during the Mexican-American War. The contestants' lawyers dramatically described how during Lisle's last years the disease had horribly disfigured him. They described a

> photograph of his life, physical condition and surroundings and habits. [The] loathsome disease had so permeated his system as to cause the loss of hair and whiskers; the loss of his teeth; the loss of eyesight; the loss of control of locomotion ... it had also drawn his mouth to one side; and had so affected the muscles of his throat as to cause a foul saliva to constantly flow from his mouth, which he could not expectorate ... in addition he was pale and bloodless.[63]

Describing a "photograph" of Lisle's life emphasized the visual repulsiveness of his body to the jury. The brief then highlighted that "his constant companion in such solitude, was a crippled and horribly distorted young man."[64] Using images of physical monstrosity and degeneracy, the lawyers linked F. M. Lisle to moral abasement, pointing out that his

> Constant and daily practice was ... calling Christ a "damned old bald-headed Son of a bitch." He taught his poor crippled and distorted companion to swear likewise; he [Lisle] would ... amuse himself by calling upon him, with his stuttering tongue, to curse and blaspheme the only source from which had there

[62] *Bush v. Lisle*, 89 Ky. 393 (1889).

[63] "Brief for Appellees," *Bush v. Lisle* (1889), Case 19613, Box 839, KCAR, KDLA.

[64] Ibid.

been any "light of reason" left, he could have expected any relief.[65] (underlining theirs)

These descriptions portrayed a debased man who threatened to spread his moral contagion to another susceptible disabled person. Lisle could control neither his "stuttering tongue," his body, or his irrational conduct. Lisle became a spectacle designed to create revulsion and moral outrage in the judges. By linking his physical impairment to his overall immorality, the challengers created an image of a dependent, uncontrollable body that mirrored a dependent and uncontrollable mind. Lisle's body and conduct threatened an orderly society based on self-government. Implicit in the challengers' arguments was that to uphold Lisle's will was to advocate immorality by accepting Lisle as a citizen who had the requisite self-determination to transmit property.

The challengers' attorneys argued that Minerva and her husband Robert Bush's control over Lisle's body inhibited Lisle from distributing his estate according to his free will. Testimony focused on Lisle's dependency on Minerva Bush for care and pain relief. The Bush family dispensed morphine to alleviate the agonizing neurological effects caused by Lisle's affliction. The challengers translated the dependency created by the drug into a dependency on the family who administered the drug. Although he never met Lisle, Samuel Willis, a local doctor testified:

> [S]yphilis itself degraded the moral sense. Was a frequent cause of insanity and in his judgement the loss of hair, drawing of the mouth, impairment of taste, loss of use of lower limbs is conclusive evidence.... And that to a person so affected you add the habitual use of morphine the will power would be utterly destroyed and the person would be like a child in the hands of the family with whom he lived and from or through whom he received his morphine.[66]

Again, disease and physical impairment were linked to moral debasement, this time compounded by Lisle's multiple dependencies on morphine and his caregivers. The challengers presented the issue as one of protecting testamentary freedom. The image of a child occurred frequently throughout the trial to emphasize irrationality and dependency. Depicting Lisle as a "blind; paralyzed; habitual morphine eater, who was thus confined, as helpless as a child," C. F. Ronston, the contestants' lawyer, vividly portrayed Lisle's final public declaration – his will – as an act representative of years of physical, psychological, and mental coercion. To illustrate, he

[65] Ibid.

[66] "Testimony of Samuel Willis," Transcript, *Bush v. Lisle*, 89 Ky. 393 (1889), Case 19613, Box 839, KCAR, KDLA.

emphasized Robert Bush's physical control of the testator's body at the moment of signing the will. Ronston described how Robert Bush held "the paper for him to sign but as well holding the body of the testator and hand to sign."[67] This degree of physical dependency presented legal problems; courts and jurists sought to guard disabled and dependent testators from being coerced mentally and physically into signing wills.

*Bush v. Lisle* is one of several cases in which the challengers drew attention to the testator's inability to physically attest to the will. Signing the will was a symbolic moment in which the physical act gave meaning to the expression of free will represented in the testator's final words. In an 1860 Floyd County case (concluded at the county level), the heirs-at-law quizzed Moses Wells, a witness to the will, about testator William Webb's physical ability to attest to the will. Asked whether he had to hold the old man up to make his mark, Wells replied, "He held the top of the pen and I made the mark.... He had not good use of himself."[68] Wells was not a beneficiary, but the challengers attempted to demonstrate undue influence or impure motives by emphasizing that another person controlled the testator's body.

This act of physical assistance happened with some regularity. Jurist Isaac Redfield confirmed the validity of such wills by arguing that when a testator is "unable from illness and has his hand guided in making his mark, it is a sufficient signature."[69] Still, the courtroom imagery was powerful. Another person holding the body of the testator or guiding his or her hand suggested that this moment was compromised. Challengers argued that though the means of obtaining the signature may have been valid, the free will of the testator was in doubt, as the long history of past physical dependency revealed. The Court of Appeals was less likely than juries to use the potential correlation between physical impairment and mental unsoundness if it believed the testamentary gifts were appropriate.

The cases contesting the wills of Alsey Howard, Polly Bullitt, and Frank Lisle demonstrate the consistency with which physical difference served as a proxy for insanity in the grammar of capacity. In these three cases, however, the testators were under age sixty when they died. In the majority of cases in which the plaintiffs alleged that physical impairments reflected mental infirmities, the testators were considered

67 "Testimony of CF Ronston," Transcript, *Bush v. Lisle*, 89 Ky. 393 (1889), Case 19613, Box 839, KCAR, KDLA.

68 *William Webb's Heirs v. William Webb's Devisee* (1860), Case 827, Box 5, Floyd County Circuit Court Civil Case Files, KDLA.

69 Redfield, *The Law of Wills*, 175.

very old. Physical impairment described as brought on by advanced age more commonly ordered the grammar of capacity. Testators' references to their "infirm bodies" but strong minds were widespread. Of the Harrison and Warren County will sample, 30.9 percent (149 wills) make mention of some kind of infirmity or disability. The standard opening to a will, "I [testator's name], being of sound body and mind ...," led some testators to deliberately qualify the statement. Archibald Casey wrote his will on April 15, 1825, declaring that he was "weak in body and nearly ready to drop into the grave but retaining my usual vigor of mind."[70] Casey's will was probated three months later, in July 1825. This testamentary ritual of describing weak bodies but clear minds continued through the end of the nineteenth century. In 1890, testator Samuel Murrell described himself as ninety-eight years old and "very infirm. I have not been able to stand alone for several years or walk a step." Murrell died within two months of writing his will.[71] These reassurances were more than rhetorical flourish or formulaic legal language; many testators thought death was imminent and wanted to reassure probate judges that they wrote their wills with the proper rational deliberations. The proximity of their wills' creation to the probate dates suggests that often they were right.

In the nineteenth century, people understood the human life cycle much differently than in the twentieth century, when life expectancy increased dramatically.[72] In the early nineteenth century, few people survived past their sixth decade. According to 1870 census data, about 3 percent of the population was sixty-five years old or older.[73] Many people succumbed to chronic diseases like tuberculosis. Kentuckians regularly experienced outbreaks of fevers, smallpox, cholera, and influenza, diseases that caused more deaths among the oldest and youngest populations. Accidents, poor nutrition, and ineffective, unavailable, or even harmful medical care added to high mortality rates. Not until the first decades of the twentieth century did the number of people surviving past age sixty-five significantly

[70] "Will of Archibald Casey" (1825), Harrison County Will Book B, Harrison County Court Records, KDLA.

[71] "Will of Samuel Murrell" (1890), Warren County Will Book 5, Warren County Court Clerk Records, KDLA.

[72] David Hackett Fischer, *Growing Old in America* (New York: Oxford University Press, 1977); Thomas R. Cole, *The Journey of Life: A Cultural History of Aging in America* (New York: Cambridge University Press, 1992).

[73] Andrew Achenbaum, "The Obsolescence of Old Age in America, 1865–1940," *The Journal of Social History* 8 no. 1 (Fall 1974): 52.

increase. In 1840, 23.8 percent of the population would survive past age seventy; by 1900, that number had increased to 41 percent.[74]

Perceptions of aging changed throughout the nineteenth century. From the eighteenth century to the first decades of the nineteenth century, prosperous white men in their old age received veneration in church governance and in local and national politics. At the General Convention of the Protestant Episcopal Church in 1826, one participant described the presiding bishop as a "venerable figure ... now on the verge of fourscore years, as the light fell upon his mild but aged features."[75] Images in popular literature associated old age generally with wisdom and respect. Depending on sex, race, and socioeconomic status, aging did not always inspire the same gravitas. Old women and aging poor people often experienced contempt, ridicule, and isolation.[76] Elderly slaves unable to work were sometimes provided only basic shelter and meager food when no longer able to perform productive labor.

By 1820, old age began to lose its positive associations, replaced with what historian David Hackett Fischer has labeled a "cult of youth."[77] Aging and bodily degeneration grew subject to contempt and ridicule. Although elderly people may have been treated with solicitousness, especially when they controlled financial resources, often their younger counterparts treated them with patronizing condescension. In an 1837 letter to the editor of the *Southern Literary Messenger*, one writer lamented that "among the changes ... in society, there is nothing, Mr. Editor, which strikes an old man more forcibly than the diminished deference which is paid to age.... Even the most humble ... found always in their scanty locks, and tottering frame, the best assurances of kindness and sympathy."[78] Popular depictions continued to portray old men and women living out their last years quietly sitting next to a fireplace in their children's homes. These images often emphasized youth as the time of social authority and old age as a time of isolation and inactivity. One author advised that men "in health and vigor" should strive to "the worthiest actions, either in their public or private stations, so they may

74 "Appendix–Table V, 'Length of Life in America, 1652–1960, Survival from Birth to Old Age,'" in David Hackett Fischer, *Growing Old in America* (New York: Oxford University Press, 1977).

75 N.A., "General Convention," *Gospel Messenger and Southern Episcopal Register* 3 no. 36 (December 1826): 374.

76 Fischer, *Growing Old in America.*

77 Ibid.

78 "Letter to Editor," *Southern Literary Messenger* 3 (December 1837): 743.

have something agreeable to feed on when they are old."[79] A woman writing in 1861 as elderly "Aunt Alice" in the *Saturday Evening Post* asked, "Must we now fold our hands and sit in silence in the old rooms where, of so many years we were so constantly required?"[80] She rejected the idea, but her question demonstrates the fears and realities of isolation for aging individuals.

Probate and court records indicate that since the first New England settlements, some parents retained property until their death. Other parents allowed their children (usually sons) to live on or farm land while they retained title. Occasionally, fathers deeded land or wealth to their daughters on their marriage or after reaching adulthood. Adult children may have resented aging parents who retained their wealth and property, particularly in regions with land scarcity. Children and grandchildren perceived land retention among older generations as an obstacle to their own marital and financial independence. In Puritan New England, accused witches were often older, female, and held land coveted by younger generations.[81] Some Kentucky testators appeared aware of the difficulties their children faced in establishing independence, especially after land was no longer widely available except through purchase. Probated wills reveal that testators mentioned land or wealth previously lent or deeded to children as part of their overall estate distribution.[82] Testator Dumas Jones directed his executor to divide his estate to account for the "improvements" made by his son "who by my consent has settled on the North east corner of my farm."[83] Jones like many testators kept a careful accounting of advancements he had made to all his children. Testator Nancy Devin recorded that she had "advanced to my daughter Nancy C. French (now deceased) and to her children, more than it is possible for me to bequeath to my other heirs." Devin then left her estate to her remaining children, disinheriting her daughter Nancy's children, as an act

[79] William Temple, "Thoughts on Old Age," *Virginia Historical Register and Literary Companion* 5 no. 1 (1852): 49.

[80] Aunt Alice, "Old Age is Honorable," *Saturday Evening Post*, March 23, 1861.

[81] Carol F. Karlsen, *Devil in the Shape of a Woman: Witchcraft in Colonial New England* (New York: Vintage Books, 1987)

[82] Glendyne R. Wergland discusses similar testamentary patterns in Massachusetts. See Glendyne R. Wergland, "Women, Men, Property, and Inheritance: Gendered Testamentary Customs in Western Massachusetts, 1800–1860. Or, Diligent Wives, Dutiful Daughters, Prodigal Sons, Westward Migration, Reciprocity, and Rewards for Virtue, Considered" (January 1, 2001), PhD dissertation, University of Massachusetts, 2001.

[83] "Will of Dumas Jones" (1831), Harrison County Will Book B, Harrison County Court Records, KDLA.

of "justice to my other children and heirs."[84] These kinds of interfamilial property transfers allowed younger generations to survive or to begin their own families by leaving the parental household and striking out with some property.

In some testamentary capacity cases, the bitterness and vitriol resonated in the courtroom from heirs-at-law who believed the testator had denied them long awaited inheritances that might propel them to financial independence or social mobility. For example, in 1865, when he was sixty-five years old, Edmund Munday's persistent kidney disease rendered him increasingly impaired. Munday rented his farm to his son Rueben, who had just returned from the Union army. Rueben and Munday often quarreled over horses and farming arrangements. A year later in 1866, Munday disinherited Reuben, leaving his estate to three other children. Reuben's lawyers described Munday's will as an "unjust disposition in an old and decayed man" who was "extremely *irratable* [*sic*] *and morose*."[85] Arguing that Munday had legitimate reasons for disinheriting Rueben, the beneficiaries' lawyers referred to Munday as "old and venerable," reminding the court that children "despise your advice and when you make a will and discriminate against them they will come into court and declare an insane aversion towards them."[86] Both arguments accounted for aging and physical decline. In one, the aging process was worthy of veneration and deference; in the other, it produced irritability and insanity.

Early in the century, Kentucky judges protected testamentary freedom from zealous family members who, believing themselves slighted, argued that advanced age brought physical and mental decline in the testator. In 1815, the Court of Appeals rebuffed a challenge by testator William Harper's son-in-law, holding that too high a standard of capacity would exclude testators "who had passed the meridian of life; whose faculty of memory and vigor of mind had begun, with the decline of personal strength and activity, to lose some of their more vivid energies."[87] The court admitted difficulty in determining when physical impairment due to age-related decline resulted in mental impairment sufficient to destroy free will. Testator Frances M'Daniel suffered a stroke when he was about

[84] "Will of Nancy Devin" (1893) Warren County Will Book 5, Warren County Court Clerk Records, KDLA.

[85] "Brief for Appellees," *Spears v. Sales* (1867), Case 1251, Box 45, KCAR, KDLA.

[86] "Brief for Appellants submitted by HC McLeod," *Spears v. Sales* (1867), Case 1251, Box 45, KCAR, KDLA.

[87] *In re Harper's Will*, 4 Bibb 244 (1815).

sixty years old, leading the challengers to argue that "his mind appeared to be as much affected by paralysis, as his body ... that his tongue and limbs were very much paralyzed, but his greatest suffering was in his head."[88] The court acknowledged the possibility of devastating cerebral and physical effects, but wavered on establishing a direct link between paralyzed, infirm bodies and mental impairment. "How, or to what extent a paralysis of the corporeal, operates on the intellectual man," the court hedged, "no speculation can ever explain."[89] Judge Robertson's decision upholding the will strengthened the court's authority, allowing future judges greater latitude in interpreting the facts of the case.

Beneficiaries who remained with aging parents or relatives, often through grueling years of caregiving, argued that their sacrifices of time and money entitled them to make special claims on testators' wealth.[90] The court looked favorably on children who cared for aged testators. Returning to Alsey Howard's case, *In re Howard* (1827), Judge Logan mentioned that although deformed, Alsey Howard's affections were not "benumbed." He referred to Howard's testamentary recognition of her mother, who had "nursed her from infancy to old age." Howard's brother, the challenger, resided in Tennessee and appeared only after his sister's death. Bibb believed that Howard's sentiments toward her mother's efforts were "proof ... of memory, of reason and of social affections and moral sense." Bibb emphasized the moral economy of testation and familial obligation by equating Howard's testamentary gifts to her mother with "social affections and moral sense."

Judges took this moral economy into account when ruling on testators' capacity. Testator Rachel Higdon died at eighty-five years old with a small estate valued at $300. She left most of it to her son, Thomas, "for the love and natural affection I have for my son Thomas Higdon & his attention & services which he has rendered me."[91] A Nelson County Court judge ruled Higdon was "incompetent" and Thomas Higdon appealed. Agreeing with the lower court judge that Higdon was "impaired," with "perceptibly decayed" faculties, the Court of Appeals judges assessed the

[88] *In re M'Daniel's Will*, 25 Ky. 331 (1829).

[89] Ibid.

[90] For a discussion of the emotional toll women experienced as they cared for family members, see Emily K. Abel, "Family Caregiving in the Nineteenth Century: Emily Hawley Gillespie and Sarah Gillespie, 1858–1888," *Bulletin of the History of Medicine* 68 no. 4 (1994): 573–99.

[91] "Will of Rachel Higdon" (1831), Nelson County Will Book G, Nelson County Court Records, KDLA.

worthiness of the heirs.[92] Chief Justice Robertson upheld the will, noting that Higdon had lived with Thomas and that he was "more kind and attentive to her, than any of the other children."

Frank Lisle's will dispute illustrates the lengths to which the Court of Appeals would go to sanction wills that validated informal relational caretaking networks. The court upheld Frank Lisle's will in spite of his advanced syphilis and reputation for blasphemy, immorality, and general cantankerousness, partially because it saw his will as a "just and equitable disposition of his property."[93] Lisle had made offers to his brother Brax and cousin Rufus Lisle to exchange his estate for care. Eventually, he moved in with Minerva Bush. As his condition advanced, no one else seemed willing or able to care for Lisle. H. Taylor, a family friend testified, "I wouldn't keep anyone at all in that fix unless he was a relation to me."[94] Minerva Bush and her family were morally deserving. After describing Lisle as "totally blind, unable to walk," with "offensive matter" escaping from his mouth, the court commended Minerva's care for him as "the most assiduous, careful and affectionate nursing and attention."[95]

Like other social relations, the economy of caregiving was embedded in gender relations. Testator William C. Knight sought to make arrangements in the eventuality of his wife or daughter's disability. He delegated the authority to dispose of the estate to his friend and executors rather than to either of his female beneficiaries, devising that if either "should be affilicted [*sic*] with a long and protracted spell of sickness that is likely to terminate fatally in that event I ... authorize my executors and my friend AJ Newton in their discretion to mortgage or sell one half of the lot willed above to procure money or comfort."[96] When disabled and aged people received daily care from family members, it was usually from women whose unpaid household labor was considered part of their marital duties and consonant with their natural predisposition. In 1889, Minerva Bush testified that she took care of her brother Frank Lisle by making "his bed and did knitting and sewing for him. I made his bed because he said that when I made it he did not fall out."[97] In *Ridgway v. Hall* (1871), Samuel

92 Nelson County Order Book A (1830–1834), Nelson County Court Records, KDLA.

93 *Bush v. Lisle*, 12 S.W. 762 (1889), 764.

94 "Testimony of H. Taylor," Transcript, *Bush v. Lisle*, 89 Ky. 393 (1889), Case 19613, Box 839, KCAR, KDLA.

95 *Bush v. Lisle*, 12 S.W. 762 (1889).

96 "Will of William Knight" (1871), Warren County Will Book D, 111, Warren County Court Clerk Records, KDLA.

97 "Testimony of Minerva Bush," Transcript, *Bush v. Lisle*, 89 Ky. 393 (1889), Case 19613, Box 839, KCAR, KDLA.

Ridgway disinherited the "orphan children" of his deceased son in favor of his daughter, Malinda Hall, who had nursed him, worked on his farm, and ministered to his sick slaves. The contestants argued that Ridgway's weak mental state allowed Hall to unduly influence him to disinherit his grandchildren. Although Hall assumed a familiar female role as a caregiver, she also assumed a masculine role as the household authority.

Testimony in *Ridgeway v. Hall* also revealed how racial ideology influenced caregiving and testation. When white people nursed African Americans or vice versa, these relationships acquired different cultural and economic valences. The proponents of the will argued that Hall had been an obedient daughter and was a particularly worthy beneficiary. She had gone beyond expected duties by taking care of Ridgway's sick slaves, a task described as a particularly odious burden. Ridgway's neighbor, Lucy Ann Magruder, testified that Hall "waited on him & his wife & the negroes when sick," declaring that nursing slaves was a "disagreeable" task. In Hall's place, Magruder would not "do what she [Hall] had to do for the farm and Negroes."[98] Magruder never commented on whether Hall's nursing duties to her mother and father also were offensive. Her silence could be read to imply that, although a sacrifice, it was expected that daughters would take care of aging parents and disabled family members. Another witness, F. S. Sewell, concurred that when the slaves became sick in 1862, "I would not have waited on them as she did for the Negroes ... at that particular time."[99] When asked about his reference to a "particular time," Sewell answered, "I believe the Negroes would be free." If the slaves would be freed, Sewell saw no reason for heroic care, as Malinda Hall would lose part of her inheritance once the slaves were freed. In Sewell and Magruder's view, the obligation to take care of household members was determined according to race and grounded in the economic relations of slavery.

When African Americans nursed white people, no reciprocal expectations of testamentary gifts existed. For those who could afford it, testators or their families sometimes hired African Americans to assist in nursing duties. Their tasks were no less onerous than those performed by white family members, and these relationships sometimes lasted for years. In *Bush v. Lisle* (1889), Orrin Bates, described as "a colored boy," testified

[98] "Testimony of Lucy Ann Magruder," Transcript, *Ridgway v. Hall* (1871), Case 4387, KCAR, KDLA.

[99] "Testimony of FS Sewell," Transcript, *Ridgway v. Hall* (1871), Case 4387, KCAR, KDLA.

that he "cooked, worked on the farm and waited on Mr. Lisle" for five years. Bates slept in Lisle's room and was at Lisle's beck and call to supply morphine, food, or read the newspapers to Lisle. He received nothing.

White testators rarely left property to African American beneficiaries after emancipation in 1866. White caregivers staked a claim of testamentary reward based on their compassion and the socially understood but not statutorily encoded obligations of testators. Black caregivers received only the meager wages testators and their families paid them. The notion of leaving property to an African American caregiver rarely occurred to testators or challengers to wills. The obligations of caregiving were racialized. The 1881 dispute between Anne Cooke's paramour, James Ross, and her sister, Jane Weaver, turned on the tensions between her obligations to blood relations and her obligations to her white caregiver. Testimony made clear that while Anne Cooke suffered from her final illness, James Ross and Minerva Cox, "a woman of color," took care of her. Weaver had spent little time visiting or nursing Cooke. Summarizing the evidence, a brief supporting the will stated that "Ross patiently tenderly and constantly nursed her. There was no other person except the woman Minerva Cox to render her assistance."[100] Anne Cooke and the Court of Appeals judges recognized Ross's claims; Cooke had left most of her estate to him and the court upheld the will. Neither Cox nor Ross had a blood relation to Cooke, although she and Ross had a sexual relationship. Still, Cooke and Ross suffered moral opprobrium because their sexual relationship occurred outside the bounds of marriage and Cooke was known as a brothel keeper. During the trial, no one claimed that Minerva Cox was unreasonably ignored in the testamentary distribution.

After 1866, in the few instances when testators made interracial gifts, they frequently mentioned caregiving. Testator James Young left a one-fourteenth share of his estate to Mary, a "col girl," for her "services rendered me in my old age."[101] Overwhelmingly, though, after 1866, the disputes between caregiving beneficiaries and heirs-at-law occurred within the boundaries of whiteness. The idea that African Americans served white bodies without acknowledgment remained firmly fixed in inheritance practices. While either race could nurse ailing whites, only white family members expected to receive public recognition and reward through a will.

[100] "Brief for Appellant," *Ross v. Weaver* (1881), Case 13247, Box 527, KCAR, KDLA.

[101] "Will of James Young" (1872), Warren County Will Book 4, Warren County Court Clerk Records, KDLA.

In testamentary capacity cases, images of monstrosity, functional impairment, and physical deviance suffused testimonies and opinions. Testamentary gifts publicly reinforced the expectation that kin would take care of physically disabled people. In challenges, witnesses, contestants' lawyers, and judges emphasized physical difference as indicative of mental unsoundness. Disability and impairment were forms of evidence presented in trials, drawn from a wider social discourse that devalued disabled bodies. This connection, however, was not firmly fixed. The point of contention in these cases was particularity; whether this particular testator's physical body housed an unsound mind. Polly Bullitt's body, in her appearance and gestures, differed from the other students at Nazareth Female Academy, where she had spent much of her life. We will never know what Bullitt's intellectual capabilities were; we can explore how historical actors stigmatized Bullitt's physically uncontrollable body as a signifier of mental incapacity. What the challengers lawyers chose to focus on in their interrogatories – the combination of her physical appearance and functional abilities deeply informed by gender ideologies – reveals that the challengers chose a strategy in which they disregarded the rhetoric of natural obligations to her bloodline relatives, arguing instead that Bullitt appeared monstrous and subhuman, incapable of legally disposing of her property. Rather than making an affirmative argument for themselves as worthy heirs, they excluded Bullitt as uncontrollable and brutish.

In *Bush v. Lisle*, the challengers used Lisle's venereal disease and its visibility as evidence of an immoral, profligate character whose will was unworthy of legal approval. In other cases, the testators' advanced age or functional impairments signaled dependency and mental unsoundness. Often, in a concurrent line of legal reasoning, one or both parties of litigants articulated special claims on testators' estates, as they had sacrificed time and money to nurse often vexatious relatives who required exhausting care. Those that had special claims however, were defined first by race and then by blood relation. Nursing, especially when testators were physically immobile, also opened caregivers to allegations of undue influence. By controlling testators' bodies, they controlled their minds. At a time when social services did not exist, the Court of Appeals strove to balance the claims of disinherited bloodline relatives against caregivers, fracturing the doctrine supporting "the natural objects" of the testators' bounty.

# 5

# A Special Power

## *Women's Testamentary Capacity*

In 1879, Robert Johnson asked his wife, Mildred, to relinquish her dower interest in a portion of his land on which he wished to build a whiskey distillery.[1] Mildred feared that the distillery venture would be "disastrous and wreck his fortune, leaving her and her then infant children without support."[2] In exchange for consenting to the distillery deal, Mildred insisted Robert deed to her a sizable lot in Lexington, Kentucky. As Mildred predicted, Robert eventually lost the distillery investment, but she retained the Lexington lot. Over the next thirteen years, at Mildred's instigation, Robert conveyed almost all of his estate to her, which was valued at two hundred thousand dollars and included "one of the handsomest homes in the city of Lexington." Robert was not rewarded for his largesse. Before Mildred died in 1894, she wrote a will disinheriting Robert and leaving the estate to their children, entreating them to "never let your father want at any time of life." Robert sued to overturn the will, claiming his wife was "dead to all sense of justice ... [and] ignorant of all moral obligation."[3] Robert contended that for years, Mildred

[1] Dower was a portion, usually one-third, of the marital estate set aside after the death of a husband for the widow's support. Widows did not own this land but had a "life-interest" in it. They had only a life-interest in dower lands and could not sell or waste them. Under certain circumstances, a wife had to assent formally to any sale her husband made of dowable property.

[2] "Brief for Appellants," in *Johnson's Admr., & c, v. Robert F. Johnson*, Case 26822, Box 1159, Kentucky Court of Appeals Records (hereafter KCAR), Kentucky Department for Libraries and Archives, Frankfort, Kentucky (hereafter KDLA).

[3] "Brief for Appellee," in *Johnson's Admr., & c, v. Robert F. Johnson*, Case 26822, Box 1159, KCAR, KDLA.

manipulated him to renounce his property rights, which he did for the sake of domestic peace. As Mildred's "disordered brain" weakened from disease, their daughters unduly influenced Mildred to disinherit him. After her death, their children ejected Robert from his former estate, turning him "penniless and homeless into the street."[4]

After a mistrial, a second local jury overturned the will. The Court of Appeals judges concurred on appeal, reproving the daughters, whose "offensive impertinence" led Mildred to "aggravate and embitter her mind against her husband." Noting Robert's "unexampled generosity," the court expressed repugnance at Mildred's "unflagging pertinacity." As the judges saw it, Robert was a henpecked husband who "asked in return only those evidences of affection which the wife owes the husband," although they conceded that Robert was a weak household head with "little or no firmness of purpose."[5] By overturning the will, the court returned to Robert his financial independence and punished his daughters' "unfilial conduct." This decision probably came as little surprise to anyone following the Court of Appeal's jurisprudence on women's testamentary capacity; the court consistently reinforced a doctrine of marital unity that protected husbands' inheritance prerogatives over the household estate, often at the expense of their wives' wishes.

The Johnson trial illustrates the convergence of two lines of capacity jurisprudence, which resulted in legal double jeopardy for women until the Kentucky legislature passed comprehensive reform legislation in 1893. Before Robert's conveyances, Mildred lacked legal capacity to affect the division of the marital estate after she or Robert died. As a married woman, Mildred inhabited a legal nether world, subsumed by the doctrine of coverture within Robert's legal identity in which he was a fully constituted, rights-bearing individual. For Mildred to have the legal capacity to will property, Robert had to transfer title into the equivalent of a legal holding pen, a fictive device called a separate estate. Mildred then could will whatever was in this separate estate. When the seemingly inevitable disputes arose in the Johnson household after Mildred's death, Robert did not question the legality of Mildred's maneuverings, which granted her the legal capacity to write a will. He had a more potent weapon, derived from the social meanings of the very actions that secured Mildred's legal capacity. He challenged her mental capacity. While Mildred had surmounted one obstacle to securing her testamentary

[4] Ibid.

[5] *Johnson's Adm'r. v. Johnson*, 20 Ky. L. Rptr. 138 (1898).

wishes, she was stymied in the end by another, from which she could not defend herself.

## THE DOUBLENESS OF WOMEN'S LEGAL SUBORDINATION: COVERTURE AND CAPACITY

None of this conflict over women, inheritance, and independence was particularly new. In a study of the seventeenth-century Puritan witchcraft trials, historian Carol Karlsen argues that witchcraft accusations against women sometimes functioned to restore to male heirs property that had passed to female heirs or beneficiaries. Statistically, these women were much more vulnerable to witchcraft accusations than non-property-holding women or men. They were "aberrations in a society with an inheritance system designed to keep property in the hands of men."[6] Law changed, absorbing modern values: rather than using seventeenth-century accusations of demonic possession, disinherited heirs-at-law in the nineteenth century mobilized the grammar of capacity to undermine women's assertions of testamentary power. Relatively few property-holding women actually needed to be accused of witchcraft or found mentally unsound for the social and legal message to be clear. The gendered nature of the accusations – that property-holding women were less legitimate, even suspicious – normalized restrictions on them and challenged their assertions of authority. By the turn of the nineteenth century, women's ability to control property remained fraught with difficulty, as it had been for centuries.[7]

Rather than gaining individual rights and greater access to property as their male counterparts did after the Revolution, American women inherited the common law legacy of coverture, which stripped them of almost all legal autonomy during marriage under the guise of their own best interests. As early nineteenth-century American legal authority James Kent noted, women's legal disabilities originated from "an indissoluble connection, by which she is *placed under the power and protection* of her husband."[8] The Kentucky Court of Appeals adopted a view of coverture similar to that expressed in Samuel Toller's treatise, *The Law of*

[6] Carol F. Karlsen, *Devil in the Shape of a Woman: Witchcraft in Colonial New England* (New York: Vintage Books, 1987).

[7] Ariela A. Dubler, "In the Shadow of Marriage: Single Women and the Legal Construction of the Family and the State," *Yale Law Journal* 112 (2003): 1645–51.

[8] James Kent, *Commentaries on American Law: Volume 2* (New York: O. Halsted, 1827), 127, italics mine.

*Executors and Administrators*, which it cited authoritatively and often in the first decades of the court's existence. In 1811 in *Crostwaight v. Hutchinson*, the court drew on Toller's definition, explaining, "In legal contemplation, the very existence of the wife is merged in that of the husband. So completely is she identified with him, that for all civil purposes she is deemed to have no will of her own."[9] Even widowhood did not always bring full legal independence. Widows could not will property from the marital estate unless their husbands made specific designations in their wills. Husbands often limited their widows' control through encumbrances or restrictions on what they could do with property. Additionally, women at common law could not waste the estate by significantly altering it in order to ensure its preservation for their husbands' heirs.

From the earliest cases dealing with women's legal capacity, the Court of Appeals and county judges evinced punctilious concern with formalist readings of law and doctrine, eliminating almost completely any alternative interpretations rooted in legal localism, which so heavily informed mental capacity jurisprudence. Between legislative recalcitrance to change married women's status, the Court of Appeals's rigid interpretation of statutory language, and judges' skepticism toward equity principles, Kentucky stands out as imposing particularly onerous burdens on women. One historian has observed that in terms of controlling property, married women found the "avenues for judicial relief narrower in Kentucky than in other states, the disabilities more significant."[10] The legislature waited until 1893 to pass a comprehensive married women's property act, known as the Weissinger Act. Before it, women were caught in a muddle of piecemeal legislation and restrictive case law, vulnerable to the vicissitudes of their husbands' economic decisions.

Before the Weissinger Act, Kentucky women found expansive access to property limited, but not impossible. Exceptions to wives' state of legal suspended animation did exist, particularly for women with the economic and legal resources to sidestep coverture's restrictions. Although treatise

[9] *Crostwaight v. Hutchinson* (1811), 408; Toller's definition of coverture for the purposes of executing a will is "In contemplation of the law, a complete unity of person subsists between husband and wife. As long as the relationship continues, they are regarded as one individual. The very existence of the wife is suspended during the coverture or entirely merged, or incorporated in that of the husband." Samuel Toller, *The Law of Executors and Administrators, Second Edition* (London: A. Strahan, 1806), 212.

[10] Martha Carson, "Kentucky Married Women's Property Act: An Early Appeal for Justice," *Border States: Journal of the Kentucky-Tennessee American Studies Association* 5 (1985): 23; Paul Fuller, *Laura Clay and the Woman's Rights Movement* (Lexington: University of Kentucky, 1975), 39.

writers and jurists may have refused to divide a theoretically unitary household sovereign (based in an old principle rooted in kingship), some women took advantage of statutory and equity interventions that fragmented their husbands' nearly absolute authority over most household property. Separate estates first emerged in early modern England through a body of law known as equity, litigated in separate courts called chancery courts.[11] With its basis in the king's power to ensure justice, equity offered legal options or remedies that addressed issues of fairness and justice for civil disputes (not criminal) ignored by the rigid precedential reliance of the common law. States in the new American republic developed parallel bodies of common and equity law, shorn of their monarchical roots. These bodies were not insulated from each other.

Theoretically, equity rules forbade a result contrary to common law. In Kentucky as in many other states during the nineteenth century, county or circuit court judges sat as equity chancellors and also oversaw common law litigation.[12] In practice, many Kentucky common law jurists shared with their counterparts in other states hostility toward equity jurisprudence. Judges, jurists, and litigants dickered over the definition, reach, and wisdom of separate estates in equity since their earliest use in American law.[13]

For fathers concerned about the profligate habits of future sons-in-law, equity rules allowed them to cordon off property from their daughters' intended husbands' legal control and keep it in their familial bloodline. As Elizabeth Cady Stanton noted, fathers called for protection from "dissipated, thriftless sons-in-law" since colonial New York was governed by a transplanted Dutch aristocracy.[14] A manager or trustee, rather than the

[11] On the development of separate estates in England, see Amy Louise Erickson, *Women and Property in Early Modern England* (London: Routledge, 1993), 102–55.

[12] Louisville, however, was a notable exception because it had its own Court of Chancery dedicated exclusively to equity issues. A few other states had separate equity courts and benches. On the development of equity in the United States, see Stanley Katz, "The Politics of Law in Colonial America: Controversies over Chancery Courts and Equity Law in the Eighteenth Century," *Perspectives in American History* V (1971): 485–518; Gary L. McDowell, *Equity and the Constitution: The Supreme Court, Equitable Relief and Public Policy* (Chicago: University of Chicago Press, 1982).

[13] Richard B. Chused, "Late Nineteenth Century Married Women's Property Law: Reception of the Early Married Women's Property Acts by Courts and Legislatures," *The American Journal of Legal History* 29 no. 1 (January 1985): 3; Norma Basch, "Equity vs. Equality: Emerging Concepts of Women's Political Status in the Age of Jackson," *Journal of the Early Republic* 3 no. 3 (Autumn 1983): 297–318.

[14] Theodore Stanton and Harriot Stanton Blatch, eds., *Elizabeth Cady Stanton As Revealed in Her Letters, Diary, and Reminiscences, Vol. 1* (New York: Harper & Row, 1922), 150.

woman, held the title for the estate and would use it for the woman's best interests and, more important, protect it from her husband's control.[15] Depending on the grant of the estate, the married woman could direct the manager to use or will the estate as she wished. Occasionally, husbands would set up separate estates for their wives in the event they died first. Depending on the language of the separate estate grant, it could then be free from any subsequent control even if the wife remarried.

Seeking more control over household inheritance decisions and wealth management, a few women sought to cut this Gordian knot of statutory law and equity practices by engaging formal legal structures through informal elusions. Mildred Johnson importuned her husband through pleading, inveighing, and, as some familiar with the case might say, pestering him to grant her legal land titles, at which point she gained substantial control of the family's economic future. The trial transcript indicates Mildred Johnson did everything she could to secure legal right to will the property. She went through the process of becoming a *feme sole* (same status as an unmarried woman) sometime after 1880 and then carefully tended her separate estate.[16] In a similar case, testator Johanna Umpfenbach attempted to create a separate estate for her earnings as a seamstress through a separate bank account free from her husband's control so she could support her young niece.[17] Other women who considered remarriage wanted separate estates to assure that children from their first marriage would inherit their property rather than risk their disinheritance by their second husbands. These cases were not legal rarities; they occurred again and again, as what actually happened in families diverged from its expression in statutory and case law.

Women did write wills and deed property throughout the nineteenth century. Some were single or acquired property after their husbands' deaths. Others had separate estates. Sometimes husbands granted their wives testamentary power in their wills over part or all of the estate. Significant property possession (indicated by an estate valuable enough

[15] Marylynn Salmon, *Women and the Law of Property in Early America* (Chapel Hill: University of North Carolina Press, 1986), 81–119; Suzanne Lebsock, *The Free Women of Petersburg: Status and Culture in a Southern Town, 1784–1860* (New York: W.W. Norton & Co., 1984), 55–66; Lawrence M. Friedman, *Dead Hands: A Social History of Wills, Trusts and Inheritance Law* (Stanford: Stanford University Press, 2009), 101–2.

[16] "Brief for Appellants," *Johnson's Admr., & c, v. Robert F. Johnson*, Case 26822, Box 1159, KCAR, KDLA.

[17] *Wehle v. Umpfenbach*, 15 Ky. L. Rptr. 346 (1893); Reva B. Siegel, "The Modernization of Marital Status Law: Adjudicating Wives' Rights to Earnings, 1860–1930," *Georgetown Law Journal* 82 (1995): 2127–211.

TABLE 5.1. *Decedents by Sex in Harrison County*

| | Female Intestate | Male Intestate | Female Testate | Male Testate | Total # of Estates Sampled |
|---|---|---|---|---|---|
| 1795–1851 # of estates probated | 9 | 61 | 3 | 49 | 122 |
| 1795–1851 % of estates probated | 7.3% | 50% | 2.4% | 40.1% | 122 |
| 1852–1905 # of estates probated | 39 | 113 | 23 | 63 | 238 |
| 1852–1905 % of estates probated | 16.3% | 47.4% | 9.6% | 26.4% | 238 |

*Note*: The sample is n = 1/10. The Decedent Index does not include the years in which each estate was probated. Therefore it is difficult to know how many female wills were written after 1894 when restrictions on married women's legal capacity to testate were removed. Decedent's sex was determined by name or excluded from sample. Determination of testate or intestate was determined by whether the clerk indicated an administrator (intestate) to the estate or an executor (testate). I then randomly cross-referenced the testate estates against the will books to make sure that a recorded will existed and check the clerk's accuracy.
*Source*: Harrison County Court Decedents Estate Index, 1795–1905, Harrison County Court Clerk Records, KDLA.

to probate) and testation by women increased dramatically after the mid-century. Table 5.1 indicates that the number of women dying with property increased substantially in the last half of the nineteenth century. Of total estates probated, the number of women writing wills tripled during the last half of the century. The percentage of female testators rose while the percentage of women dying intestate diminished after 1852. It is impossible to know what percentage of all women's estates had enough property to go through the probate process because accurate death statistics were not kept.

Table 5.2 shows how sex ratios look when considered only among people who died testate. When broken down over ten year increments, the percentage of female testators tends over time to rise, although it dipped during two decades, from 1831 to 1840 and from 1871 to 1880. As Table 5.3 shows, when the testators are separated out by county and divided by the will books in which the wills appeared, this dip disappears. The percentage of female testators more than doubled

TABLE 5.2. *Testation by Sex over Time*

| | Male Testators | Percent of Male Testators (%) | Female Testators | Percent of Female Testators (%) | Total Testators |
|---|---|---|---|---|---|
| 1818–1830 | 36 | 81.8 | 8 | 18.2 | 44 |
| 1831–1840 | 53 | 96.4 | 2 | 3.6 | 55 |
| 1841–1850 | 56 | 91.8 | 5 | 8.2 | 61 |
| 1851–1860 | 51 | 79.7 | 13 | 20.3 | 64 |
| 1861–1870 | 28 | 69.3 | 13 | 31.7 | 41 |
| 1871–1880 | 64 | 88.9 | 8 | 11.1 | 72 |
| 1881–1890 | 55 | 67.9 | 26 | 32.1 | 81 |
| 1891–1900 | 32 | 59.3 | 22 | 40.7 | 54 |
| 1818–1900 | 375 | 79.4 | 97 | 20.6 | 472 |
| 1818–1850 | 145 | 91.7 | 15 | 9.3 | 160 |
| 1851–1900 | 230 | 73.8 | 82 | 26.2 | 312 |

TABLE 5.3. *Testation by Sex in Each County*

| | Warren County 1827–1862 Will Book D | Warren County 1862–1889 Will Book 4 | Warren County 1890–1898 Will Book 5 | Harrison County 1818–1853 Will Books B–F | Harrison County 1853–1882 Will Books G–K | Harrison County 1882–1897 Will Book L |
|---|---|---|---|---|---|---|
| Total | 89 | 96 | 47 | 104 | 81 | 62 |
| Male | 79 | 74 | 30 | 93 | 60 | 44 |
| Testate | (88.7%) | (77.1%) | (63.8%) | (89.5%) | (74.1%) | (71%) |
| Female | 10 | 22 | 17 | 11 | 21 | 18 |
| Testate | (11.2%) | (22.9%) | (36.2%) | (10.5%) | (25.9%) | (29%) |

in the second half of the century as noted in the last two rows of Table 5.2. By the end of the century, the percentage of female testators almost tripled from its earliest levels. This increase suggests that Kentucky social changes – if not statutory changes – spurred female testation even as the judiciary guarded husbands' authority through preserving marital unity.

Male kin sometimes abrogated coverture restrictions by using their wills to grant women testamentary control over property. Gradually over the nineteenth century, more male testators sought to grant female beneficiaries testamentary power through their wills. Table 5.4 shows husbands increasingly devising land to their wives in fee simple, which would

TABLE 5.4. *Husbands' Devises of Fee Simple Property to Their Wives*

| Decade Will was Written | Some Property in Fee Simple | No Property in Fee Simple | % of Wills with a Fee Simple Gift |
|---|---|---|---|
| 1821–1830 | 5 | 22 | 22. |
| 1831–1840 | 11 | 34 | 32.3 |
| 1841–1850 | 17 | 39 | 43.6 |
| 1851–1860 | 18 | 26 | 69.2 |
| 1861–1870 | 5 | 23 | 21.7 |
| 1871–1880 | 17 | 47 | 36.1 |
| 1881–1890 | 14 | 28 | 50 |
| 1891–1900 | 9 | 11 | 81.8 |

include a testamentary right.[18] The percentage of husbands making fee simple gifts dropped rather dramatically after 1860 but climbed to over 81 percent by 1900. The dip after 1861 may be a result of statistical anomaly in the small sample size or possibly reflect the dislocation caused by the Civil War or the retrenchment of gender roles in marriage.[19] If this trend after the Civil War held true in other states or counties, it would beg historians' scrutiny.

The rise in fee simple gifts prior to 1860 coincides with other probate analyses.[20] In Kentucky, however, judicial and legislative attitudes did not reflect or support these changes in testamentary behavior. Rather, the legislature waited another forty-one years (1893) after their original limited grant of testamentary power in 1852 to pass meaningful protections for married women's testamentary rights.

## ASSENT AND DESCENT: SEEKING EQUALITY IN EQUITY COURTS

For many women, choosing a husband may have been the most important decision they made. Marriage most often meant years of childbearing

[18] When husbands granted their wives estates in fee simple, it did not necessarily create a separate estate. If the wife were to remarry, she would have to create a separate estate in order to devise the property or her new husband's marital rights would attach.

[19] On the centrality of marriage after the Civil War, see Laura F. Edwards, *Gendered Strife and Confusion: The Political Culture of Reconstruction* (Urbana: University of Illinois Press, 1997).

[20] Richard H. Chused, "Married Women's Property Law: 1800–1850," *Georgetown Law Review* 71 (1983): 1359–425; Lebsock, *The Free Women of Petersburg*.

and hard physical work, often with little recognition for their efforts. Married women were subject to the whims of their husbands' dispositions. If their husbands were violent, drunkards, or simply poor businessmen, wives had limited options to protect themselves and their children. They could call upon family, friends, or other respectable community members to intervene on their behalf. In extreme cases, they could petition the courts or the legislature for relief, separation, or, even more rarely, divorce.[21] As Laura Edwards has shown in the Carolinas, in local legal cultures, some women's claims garnered support when miscreant husbands pushed their families to the point of desperation or disturbed the public peace.[22] Most often, though, husbands stood on firm legal and customary ground when they asserted their marital rights, particularly over property.

While equity law theoretically offered respite from coverture, the path to exercising those rights was riddled with legal hazards, especially if a will challenge went to the appellate court. The spirit of equity law may have offered opportunities to married women, but appellate-level courts often narrowly interpreted equity mandates against the common law default.[23] In 1830, Judge Robertson of the Court of Appeals noted that under common law the "legal unity of husband and wife" passed control of wives' property to their husbands, "yet modern adjudications in equity have established, to a limited extent, the doctrine of the civil law which recognizes the separate existence and proprietary rights of married women."[24] Still, the court doubted the wisdom or expansiveness of married women's equity rights. Judge Robertson continued:

> But this, comparatively new, and constructive equity of married women, should [never] be enforced against opposing rights, unless it can be made out clearly and satisfactorily. In the language of Lord Macclesfield, "as it (is) against *common right*, that the wife should have a separate property from the husband, (they being

[21] The Kentucky legislature empowered the circuit courts to grant divorce in 1809. Statute cited in *A Digest of the Statute Law of Kentucky, Being a Collection of All the Acts of the General Assembly of a Public and Permanent Nature from the Commencement of Government to May Session 1823* (Frankfort: Kendall and Russell, 1823), Ch. LX § 1, 432.

[22] Laura F. Edwards, *The People and Their Peace: Legal Culture and the Transformation of Inequality in the Post-Revolutionary South* (Chapel Hill: University of North Carolina Press, 2009); esp. chapter four, "Bread from Chaff," 100–33; "Law, Domestic Violence, and the Limits of Patriarchal Authority in the Antebellum South," *The Journal of Southern History* 65 no. 4 (1999): 733–70.

[23] Salmon, *Women and the Law of Property*, 120.

[24] *Long's Administrator v. White's Administrators and Heirs*, 28 Ky. 226 (1830).

both in law, but as one person,) *so all reasonable intendments and presumptions (should be) admitted against the wife.*[25]

At the appellate level, judges tested agreements for technical language rather than overall intent. They rarely considered whether or not a community consensus had developed in which these wills were accepted as the product of testamentary power granted by husbands.[26]

The Court of Appeals judges saw the paramount need to maintain legal unity of the marital couple unless unequivocal evidence of intent to grant wives testamentary power and proper documentation existed. In *In re Yates* (1834), Mrs. Yates's husband challenged her will on the grounds of lack of mental and legal capacity. The Court of Appeals quickly dismissed the mental unsoundness charge, noting that the will's draftsmen and subscribing witnesses were men of "respectability, intelligence." They deferred to the local knowledge and reputations of the men present at the moment of testation. On the more technical legal issue of whether Mrs. Yates had a separate estate, the Court of Appeals judge refused to defer to county court judges, calling them "illy qualified" to determine the validity of separate estates because these principles constituted "some of the most abstruse and difficult learning of the law."[27] The court held that Mrs. Yates's will included property not specifically included in the separate estate, which the husband had legal right to administer.[28] In the Yates will dispute, localism prevailed in terms of mental capacity; its power foundered when the claim turned on legal capacity.

This technical emphasis that emerged in interpreting equity law meant that wives rarely found refuge from highly formalized requirements to establish the consent of the male kin who granted the testamentary power to the married woman. Judges brooked little ambiguity when ascertaining the reach of the married woman's right, particularly if a husband was transferring his own power to his wife. In the dispute over Yates's will, Judge Nicholas admitted that through "exceptions" a married woman such as Yates (who had a separate estate) could make a will. Although the court acceded that Yates may have had a right to dispose of her estate, it emphasized the restrictions imposed by coverture. Nicholas interpreted

[25] Ibid. Italics in original.

[26] On the "subordination" of substantive equity principles to legal formalism, see Morton Horwitz, *Transformation of American Law, 1870–1960: The Crisis in Legal Orthodoxy* (New York: Oxford University Press, 1977), 17. For a different view, see Lawrence M. Friedman, *A History of American Law* (New York: Simon and Schuster, 1973), 346.

[27] *In re Yates Will*, 32 Ky. 215 (1834).

[28] Ibid. at 218.

equity agreements as "limited."[29] Any acknowledgment of Yates's testamentary right "should not extend to deprive her husband" any portion of her estate not specifically included in the trust.[30] Court of Appeals judges, when interpreting equity law dealing with married women's estates, presumed and protected the husbands' marital rights. Equity may have appeared to offer women remedies to the inflexibility of coverture, but the very concept of equitable fairness rested on legal scaffolding that limited women's prerogatives.

Although this legal scaffolding appeared to limit women's economic participation, in small towns and rural areas across Kentucky married women bought and sold goods, traded, bartered, and made economic decisions without their husbands' explicit approval of every transaction. The merchants and customers with whom these women did business and their husbands accepted them as independent actors in their business dealings. If no dispute emerged from the deal, then for the purposes of the individuals involved, it was valid. Once these transactions were disputed in courtrooms they became subject to all sorts of legal strictures. As early as 1818, the court nullified a deed made by Mrs. Black days before she remarried in which she transferred property from her first marriage to her children, unbeknownst to her second husband. The court found that her silence about the deed "constituted a fraud on his marital rights, and a court of equity ought not, under such circumstances, to interpose for the purpose of enforcing a claim founded upon the deed."[31] In this case, Judge Bibb of the Court of Appeals was well within the equity tradition in negating the claims of her children because of the equity maxims that held that "he that hath committed iniquity shall not have equity."[32] Black's attempt to secure her property to her children was construed as fraud on her second husband because under common law coverture, he had every expectation that the property would become his. For those disputing contracts executed by married women, the ideological artifice of coverture often provided a path to a favorable verdict.[33] In *Uhrig v. Horstman and Sons* (1871), the court scoffed at the legitimacy of implied

[29] *In re Yates Will*, 32 Ky. 215 (1834).

[30] Ibid.

[31] *Black v. Jones*, 8 Ky. 312 (1818).

[32] On this and other equity maxims, see Richard Francis and William Walter Hening, *Maxims of Equity: First American Edition* (Richmond: Shepard and Pollard, Printers, 1823), 7.

[33] *Johnston and Wife v. Jones*, 51 Ky. 326 (1851); *Burch and Wife v. Breckinridge*, 55 Ky. 482 (1855).

consent inferred from community members' willingness to deal with married women as *feme soles*, an exception made by other state courts.[34] Mrs. Uhrig had conducted business for years with her husband's informal consent. Clearly both Uhrigs and the vendors with whom Mrs. Uhrig dealt believed that she acted as a *feme sole*. The court found to the contrary because the Uhrigs had never solemnized her status before a chancellor. It asserted that in some states, women became *feme soles* "if the husband permits his wife after marriage to carry on business on her sole and separate account [without a formal agreement, but] There is no case in Kentucky in which the doctrine has been carried to that extent."[35]

In cases involving women's legal testamentary capacity, the Court of Appeals emphasized formal procedure, sometimes contradicting acts ordinary people accepted as doing the legal work of establishing women's legal capacity. Timing, even more so than evidence of intent, mattered in terms of the attachment of capacity. Viewing legal capacity as contingent for women, judges scrutinized the chronology of events and the precision of legal language. Under equity rules, a husband could renounce his control of his wife's property by consenting to her will. This principle did not challenge marital unity or the hierarchy of governance in the household. It firmly recognized husbands' authority and discretion. According to legal authorities, a husband could revoke his consent at any time during his wife's life, but once the will was probated, he "was not at liberty to retract his assent."[36] Still, Kentucky jurists' strict construction and judicial attitudes wary of dissolving marital unity benefited husbands who had second thoughts.

In 1850, Mrs. Bussing (first name not in the record) wrote a will with the consent of her husband, John, in which she left most of her estate to him. She manumitted a slave, George, effective at the time of her husband's death. She died shortly thereafter. A little less than a year after the will was probated, John Bussing found himself in debt and moved to overturn the will and revoke George's future manumission. When John

[34] See, for example, *Morgan v. Elam*, 12 Tenn. 374 (1833); *Van Winkle v. Schoonmaker*, 15 N.J. Eq. 384 (1862); *Webster v. M'Ginnis* 5 Binn. (Penn.) 235 (1812); *Pond v. Carpenter* 12 Minn. 430 (1867). Jurist Joseph Story identified the conditions of consent as a legal muddle in his treatise on conflicting laws. Joseph Story, *Commentaries on the Conflict of Laws, Foreign and Domestic in Regard to Contracts, Rights and Remedies, and Especially in Regard to Marriages, Divorces, Wills Succession, and Judgments* (Boston: Billard, Gray and Company, 1834), 135–49.

[35] *Uhrig v. Horstman and Sons*, 71 Ky. 172 at 175.

[36] Edward Vaughn Williams, *A Treatise of the Law of Executors and Administrators*, Vol. 1 (Philadelphia: R.H. Small Law Bookseller, 1849).

Bussing challenged his wife's will, he was no stranger to the Garrard County courtroom. The traces he left in the legal record suggest a man with an ornery disposition, prone to debt, and adept at creative legal strategies to mitigate his financial woes. His name appeared several times in the Garrard County Court Order Books, in litigation twice in 1837, and again in 1839, 1842, and 1853. In 1839, Bussing took John Cleaveland to court, alleging that Cleaveland had slandered him by calling him a "damned thief," thereby "intending to injure the plaintiffs good name and reputation."[37] He was called into court over a debt in 1853.[38] When John Bussing chose to challenge his wife's will in 1851, Garrard County court records suggest that John Bussing had had plenty of experience with the local justice system. Even if he did not know the specific rules governing inheritance and married women's testation, John Bussing knew how to find a lawyer and bring a claim.

Mrs. Bussing's will had emancipated George at John Bussing's death. Perhaps John Bussing sought to overturn the manumission in order to make George sellable. According to the 1850 Kentucky slave census, John Bussing's household had four slaves.[39] Two slaves were women aged sixty-five and thirty-seven. The other two slaves were men aged fourteen and twenty-eight. The census does not list slave names, so it is difficult to know which description might have referred to George. If George was either male slave, he would have been a valuable asset to Bussing. Under the will, his imminent freedom upon Bussing's death negated his saleable value. John Bussing's lawyers argued that he never gave his written consent to his wife, only his oral consent, which they acknowledged. The Court of Appeals judge, pondering the legal force of a verbal assent, rhetorically asked when a husband's consent validated his wife's will. Citing several legal treatises, he decided oral consent would authorize only married women's wills that transmitted personal property. The opinion pointed out that slaves were real property rather than personal property in terms of testation under Kentucky statutory code. Devising real property required "some appropriate instrument of writing."[40] Therefore,

[37] *John Bussing v. John Cleaveland* (1839), Case 134, Box 6, Bundle 23, Garrard County Circuit Court Case Files, KDLA.

[38] *Chas K. McCoy's Adm. v. John Bussing* (1853), Case 3703, Bundle 112, Garrard County Circuit Court Case Files, KDLA.

[39] Population Schedules of the Seventh Census of the United States, 1850. Slave Schedule, Garrard County, Reel 225, KDLA.

[40] *George v. Bussing*, 54 Ky. 558 (1855).

the judges reasoned, the oral consent had no force, George's manumission was invalid, and he became the unencumbered property of John Bussing.

The decision in *George v. Bussing* (1855) had two implications. It made manumissions by married women more difficult by requiring a written legal document that created a separate estate or formally documented the husband's consent. It placed control over manumissions and slave transfers more firmly in white men's hands by negating one route through which married women could make dispositions. The Court of Appeals also more generally limited married women's ability to devise valuable real property (land and slaves) even with their husbands' oral consent. The court contended that oral consent to bequeath personal property "is no more than a waiver of his rights as her administrator" and not an eschewal of marital rights. By defining Bussing as an estate administrator for the purposes of distributing personal property rather than a husband, the court avoided eroding marital unity, instead linking the validity of oral consent to the legal position of the administrator. As the court noted, "her will, made even with the husband's consent, only operates to pass such things as do not belong to the husband, but which he would have a right to after her death only as her administrator."[41] Even when wives obtained their husbands' consent, wills that did not properly implement recondite equity agreements were vulnerable to challenges from the husband or his heirs.

In Kentucky, court judges continued to give husbands broad latitude to define consent. Judges generally assumed that husbands would circumscribe their wives' testamentary power unless explicit language indicated contrary intentions. In 1877, the court heard *Bell v. Rogers*, a case in which, on her deathbed, Lydia Bell wrote a note in which she forgave a debt her mother, Elizabeth Rogers, owed her.[42] When Bell's husband, John, entered the room, Lydia Bell told him she had cancelled the debt. John Bell said nothing. After Lydia Bell's death, John Bell sued to claim Rogers's debt. The question before the court turned on how oral consent was defined. The court found that:

> Common humanity forbade the husband to deny, in open and express terms, his consent to an act which she desired to consummate, however much he may have disapproved it.... The law does not require a man to protect his legal rights

[41] Ibid.

[42] *Bell v. Rogers* 9 Ky. Op. 292 (1877).

by wounding the feelings and embittering the last moments of a dying wife. His silence under the circumstances was inconsistent with the supposed consent, and if it evidenced anything it was his disapproval of the gift.[43]

A specific vision of marital roles informed the judicial reasoning in *Bell v. Rogers*. By construing Bell's silence as "disapproval of the gift," the court argued that Bell appeared as a generous, respectful husband. According to the court's interpretation, Bell's authority as a husband required a positive unequivocal verbal assent, in spite of his knowledge of the written note to the contrary. The judges' interpretation allowed Bell to appear in apparent compliance of his wife's dying wishes in front of the others present. The court's jurisprudence on husbands' consent probably appeared contradictory to the casual legal observer. In one case, the husband's oral consent was not sufficient to validate a will if he later changed his mind. In another case, the husband's silence was more than enough to invalidate a testamentary gift. Married women wishing to choose their own beneficiaries became strung up on the legal barbs surrounding and protecting legal patriarchy.

## A SPECIAL POWER TO THAT EFFECT: LIMITED STATUTORY RIGHTS

Kentucky's General Assembly added married women's property acts incrementally beginning in 1846, resulting in decades of confusing litigation. The General Assembly's first statute protected slave and real property women brought to their marriages from their husbands' creditors.[44] This sort of statutory intervention was common across the antebellum South, but did little to change prevailing ideas about women's ordained social and domestic roles.[45] Instead, after devastating financial panics, legislatures passed these early acts to protect families by insulating married women's property from their husbands' creditors. As dismayed Kentucky woman's rights activist Josephine K. Henry observed in 1889, a woman left the marriage altar "not even the legal possessor of the clothes she has on her back. She cannot make a will, and if the husband dies one week

[43] Ibid. Statutory enactments in 1868 gave wives the ability to "alienate" their debts with their husbands' consent.

[44] Acts, Ch. 368 §. 1–3 (1846).

[45] Chused, "Married Women's Property Law: 1800–1850," 1359–425; See also Kathleen Sullivan, *Constitutional Context: Women and Rights Discourse in Nineteenth Century America* (Baltimore: Johns Hopkins University Press, 2007).

after the marriage ... the wife's money goes to his nearest male relative, unless he generously wills the defenseless wife her own estate."[46]

Kentucky's Revised Statutes of 1852 granted married women limited rights to will property without their husbands' express consent but required complicated prenuptial agreements. The 1852 Statutory Code stated that "a married woman may by will dispose of any estate secured to her separate by deed or devise, or in the exercise of a special power to that effect."[47] This statute granted only what equity had theoretically provided. It meant married women could write wills as long as they owned property in a separate estate that explicitly granted them the right to will it. Other states had more liberal laws; by 1849, New York granted married women the right to will property as if they were unmarried.[48] Although the Kentucky statute did not grant new rights, it did legally validate the premise that married women might have divergent interests in distributing their estates.

After the 1852 statutory changes, the judiciary acted as a brake on married women's exercise of their new special power. Eliza Ford wrote a will leaving her slaves, personal property, and realty to her relatives and excluding her second husband, Charles Ford, from her estate.[49] Eliza Ford had acquired the property, slaves, and realty under an 1846 will from her first husband, Theophilus Walker. Specifically granting Eliza Ford the testamentary power to will personalty and slaves, Walker's will noted that the realty would be passed to "her heirs." His will lacked a separate clause explicitly granting testamentary control over the realty. Charles Ford contested Eliza Ford's will, arguing she did not have the legal right to will any property by virtue of her status as a married woman.

The case initially went before a Harrison County judge rather than a jury. The lower court judge did not rule on Eliza Ford's testamentary capacity based on Walker's will. Instead, he ruled to protect her second husband's potential property rights by holding that, after nineteen years, it was impossible to know if Eliza Ford still possessed any of the

[46] Josephine K. Henry, *Married Women's Property Rights under Kentucky Laws: An Appeal for Justice* (Versailles, Ky., 1889), quoted in Carson, "The Kentucky Married Women's Property Act," 21.

[47] Revised Statutes of Kentucky of 1852, Ch. 106 § 4.

[48] Property was often distinguished by whether it was realty, which included land, buildings, improvements, and slaves, or personalty (personal property), which referred to personal goods, household items, leases, cash, and stocks. For a judicial ruling on the New York law, see *Waters v. Cullen*, 2 Bradf. Sur. 354.

[49] *Ford's Executor v. Ford*, 63 Ky. 418 (1866).

same slaves or items from her first husband's estate.[50] Thus, Eliza Ford's dispositions potentially could impinge on Charles Ford's marital property rights by allowing her to will property not specifically covered in Walker's will. No proof existed that she still had held the specific property mentioned in Walker's will, making the issue of her capacity to will that property moot.

On appeal by Eliza Ford's family, the Court of Appeals took up the question of her capacity to will the property from Walker's estate. The court's decision both protected and limited married women's testamentary power. The decision overturned the lower court's ruling concerning the personalty and the slaves, noting that Theophilus Walker's will expressly conferred the power to will personal property and slaves. That disposition remained legitimate. The devise involving real estate gave the Court of Appeals an opportunity to interpret the statutory clause that referred to married women's devises under the exercise of a "special power." The court had the opportunity to enlarge married women's legal right by defining Walker's reference to "her heirs" as an exercise of the special power acknowledging her testamentary power over the realty. At the very least, the court could have interpreted the clause as creating a separate estate that reserved the property for her bloodline descendants, instead of a grant of full testamentary power, which Eliza Ford assumed she had. The court chose instead to nullify that clause, holding that the legislature did nothing more than reaffirm existing common law principles in the 1852 statutory code. In the court's words:

> On common law principles this is indisputable, and the Kentucky statute declaring that "a married woman may, by will, dispose of any estate secured to her separate use by deed or devise, or in the exercise of a special power to that effect," is not a restrictive qualification, but only a declaratory recognition of the common law doctrine. "Special power" means nothing more nor less than express power applied to the special property devised.[51]

While granting some protection to explicit grants of power made by another male, the court also weakened the power of the statute and strengthened the rights of husbands. In *Ford v. Ford*, both the local and Court of Appeals court judges moved to protect male prerogative and limit female property rights using different reasoning. The lower court

[50] Transcript, *Ford's Executor v. Ford* (1866), Case 299, Box 9, KCAR, KDLA.
[51] *Ford's Executor v. Ford*, 63 Ky. 418 (1866).

judge acted to prevent the potential subversion of Charles Ford's property rights, while the Court of Appeals sought to prevent a wider subversion of husbands' customary common law rights in their wives' property.

In succeeding years, the Court of Appeals judges continued to guard husbands' claims against wives who had other ideas about inheritance practices.[52] In 1868, the Kentucky General Assembly granted married women the statutory power they theoretically enjoyed under equity rules but limited it to real property.[53] The statute did represent a small but significant gain by eliminating the need for a trustee of the separate estate and giving married women direct control over their real property. After 1866, the Kentucky legislature haphazardly drafted new statutes and modified old ones to accommodate the new legal landscape most notably altered by the emancipation of slaves. This legislation included revisions to the laws governing marriage, in part to address issues of legitimizing freed people's children and to assure the creation of black households in which freedmen would be responsible for their dependents.[54] In 1866, the Kentucky legislature passed a law that classified all "negroes and mulattos" who had lived together as husband and wife as married regardless of whether they registered their relationship at the county clerk's office. In the same section, the legislature also allowed a married woman to formally petition to become a *feme sole*, or trade as an unmarried woman, but only through an exacting and formal legal process in which her husband had to consent.[55] And again, in spite of the legislative reform, the meaning and extent of consent became judicial fodder for narrowing statutory gains.

When Mary E. Shreve married her second husband, James Harbeson, in 1866, she brought with her a considerable estate she had inherited from her first husband, L. L. Shreve. James Harbeson, whatever his charms may have been, was not an astute businessman, demonstrating "improvidence" with the wealth he gained from Mary and now controlled. Fortunately, the couple decided to address the "just apprehensions ... entertained by both himself and his wife as to the safety of the estate in his hands" and jointly signed a deed in which they agreed that

[52] Lebsock, *The Free Women of Petersburg*. As Lebsock observes, "separate estate was a means of keeping property in the family when times were hard and families stood to lose everything because of the husband's indebtedness," xvi.

[53] Acts of the Kentucky General Assembly, 1867–8, Vol. 1, 5 § 1.

[54] Laura F. Edwards, "'The Marriage Covenant Is at the Foundation of All Our Rights': The Politics of Slave Marriages in North Carolina after Emancipation," *Law and History Review* 14 no. 1 (Spring 1996): 81–124.

[55] 1873 Kentucky Acts, Ch. 52 Art. 2 § 6, citing Kentucky Revised Statutes, Ch. 47 § 16(2) (1866), passed February 14, 1866.

"in consideration of the fact that the property hereinafter conveyed was devised to the said Mary E. by the will of her late husband, L. L. Shreve ... that her rights and interests therein should be protected." The deed specifically allowed her to "use, sell, or exchange, or to re-invest *or otherwise dispose of the whole or any part of said property and effects*, and the proceeds thereof, in any manner she may think proper."[56] Like Mildred Johnson, Mary Harbeson obtained the authority to act as a *feme sole*, which also required her husband's consent. The marriage was short; Mary died in 1870 after what witnesses described as living "harmoniously" with her husband. She wrote a will in which she bequeathed most of the property to her infant son by Harbeson. Her widower must have had second thoughts about his "apprehensions" at managing the property. He challenged her legal capacity to write the will.

The case turned on how the judges interpreted the language in the deed. On appeal from the Louisville Chancery Court, after much discussion of the deed's language and existing statutory law, the judges asked first whether the deed created a separate estate. They preserved any remnant of James Harbeson's marital right, ruling that the deed evinced "no words of entire exclusion of his marital rights of certain and definite technical import." Of course, it is impossible to know if James Harbeson thought he was acceding testamentary power to Mary when he signed the contract. He may have thought she would outlive him or may not have even considered the testamentary implications of the deed's language. Clearly, Mary Harbeson believed or at least hoped she had testamentary power. She most likely hoped to protect her infant son from his father's imprudence.

Nationally, early women's rights advocates recognized the burden the legal confusion over consent imposed. This sort of statutory and judge-made legal restrictiveness led women's rights activists to call for sweeping changes to the spirit and letter of property law. One woman petitioning the Massachusetts state legislature in 1850 called for the elimination of husbands' testamentary consent, observing irately, "Should a woman make her will without her husband's consent in writing, it is of no use.... In many cases she is as competent, and sadly to be pitied if not in many cases more so."[57] Kentucky courts continued to demur to

[56] *Harris v. Harbeson* (1873), 72 Ky. 397 at 399, italics mine.

[57] "Mary Upton Ferrin's Address to the Judiciary Committee of the Massachusetts Legislature, 1850," in Elizabeth Cady Stanton, Susan B. Anthony, and Matilda Joslyn Gage, eds., *History of Woman Suffrage, vol. 1: 1848–1861* (New York: Fowler and Wells, Publishers, 1881), 212.

these perceived injustices. In *Daniel's Devisees v. Daniel* (1871), the court demanded "language unequivocally manifesting" Polly Daniel's first husband's wishes that Daniel could dispose of the property if she remarried. Otherwise, Judge Lindsay implied, if Daniel's first husband even had contemplated that his wife might remarry after his death, he certainly did not mean to continue her testamentary independence. Furthermore, Lindsay questioned the legal validity of Polly Daniel's attempt to secure her estate to herself prior to her second marriage. The 1852 statute granting women testamentary power over separate estates did not "embrace" separate estates "created by the act of the *feme* herself," even if it occurred previous to the second marriage.[58] By not recognizing female legal independence between marriages, like the decision in *Ford v. Ford* (1866), female testators' ability to will property was determined according to how the court interpreted the first husband's grant of power against the claims of the second husband's marital right. Polly Daniel's intentions and her decisive action to protect her estate meant little. Subsequent court decisions reflect continuing concern for protecting husbands' authority over their wives' property when married women attempted to circumvent these restrictive laws.

In the late 1880s, Johanna Umpfenbach, evidently aware of the restrictive laws governing married women's property dispositions, had several deeds and bank notes placed in her name by her debtors and her employers in an effort to create a separate estate. Although in 1873, the Kentucky legislature granted married women's earnings protection from their husbands' creditors and allowed employers to pay wages directly to married women, it did not prevent husbands from controlling their wives' wages or grant wives the right to bequeath their earnings without a separate estate.[59] The legislature did not grant married women the unimpeded statutory right to their own earnings until 1900.[60]

Umpfenbach wrote a will leaving this property to her sister Augusta Heinz and other relatives. She disinherited her husband, Christopher Umpfenbach. He challenged the will on the grounds that his wife's personalty vested in him under coverture, and that she had not created a separate estate. Jefferson County Court of Common Pleas judge Emmet

[58] *Daniel's Devisees v. Daniel*, 5 Ky. Op. 670 (1871).

[59] "An Act of the Benefit of Married Women in this Commonwealth," Ch. 52 § 1, approved April 11, 1873.

[60] Lowell Harrison and James C. Klotter, *A New History of Kentucky* (Lexington: University Press of Kentucky, 1997), 287.

Field held for Christopher Umpfenbach, and the beneficiaries appealed.[61] The Court of Appeals affirmed Field's decision, ruling that a third person or her husband did not secure the separate estate to her. Instead, during the marriage Johanna Umpfenbach secured the deeds to herself, deliberately circumventing her husband's marital rights and subverting the legal order.

Johanna Umpfenbach's beneficiaries based their defense of the will on two assertions: that her estate consisted of wealth she had earned through her work as a seamstress and that Johanna Umpfenbach did secure a separate estate. Heinz's attorneys called several witnesses who testified that Umpfenbach had done sewing every week for twenty-one years and continually invested her wages. Bankers and real estate agents then testified about her requests to have notes specifically made in her name.[62] Her attorney James S. Pirtle testified that she had consulted him on how to arrange her estate for "the purpose of enabling her to make a will."[63] In doing so, Umpfenbach both upheld and challenged late nineteenth-century legal and social structures.

Johanna Umpfenbach upheld the cultural ideologies of middle-class Victorian America in several ways. She "kept house" for her husband for twenty-five years, performing work ideologically linked to wifely duty.[64] Although she earned wages, she sewed – labor traditionally associated with domesticity and considered women's work. She valued her family members and wished to nurture their education. One provision in the will designated a gift "to my young friend and step-granddaughter Blanch Kahlert to be used in completing her musical education," demonstrating that although she had no children, she acted upon maternal feelings and valued educational duties associated with women.[65]

Her strategies for securing a separate estate demonstrate that Johanna Umpfenbach also rejected the social and legal ideologies that placed her wages under her husband's control. She attempted to create her own legal identity and express her wishes concerning her family through her will. No indication in the record suggests that Johanna Umpfenbach had in

[61] *Umpfenbach v. Wehle* (1891), Case 32137, Box 370, Jefferson County Court of Common Pleas Records, KDLA.

[62] Transcript, *Wehle v. Umpfenbach* (1893), Case 22454, Box 982, KCAR, KDLA.

[63] "Testimony of James Pirtle," Transcript, *Wehle v. Umpfenbach* (1893), Case 22454, Box 982, KCAR, KDLA.

[64] "Testimony of Christopher Umpfenbach," Transcript, *Wehle v. Umpfenbach* (1893), Case 22454, Box 982, KCAR, KDLA.

[65] "Will of Johanna Umpfenbach," Transcript, *Wehle v. Umpfenbach* (1893), Case 22454, Box 982, KCAR, KDLA.

mind launching an explicit political or legal challenge to male prerogative as did, for example, woman suffragists of the time. Instead, it appears that she attempted to arrange for her side of the family, fearing that if her husband outlived her he would not. The Court of Appeals interpreted her strategies much differently.

Judge Pryor of the Court of Appeals expressed great indignation at Johanna Umpfenbach's legal maneuvering. The court focused its ire, as Pryor put it, on Umpfenbach's attempt "to divest him [Charles Umpfenbach] of his marital right." The court ignored the testimony concerning Johanna Umpfenbach's years of work as a wage-earning seamstress. As the court would do seven years later with Robert Johnson's claim against Mildred Johnson's will, the judge portrayed the wife as scheming and intent on defrauding her unsuspecting husband. Pryor noted the "estate ... created by his daily labor has been disposed of by her without his knowledge."[66] Pryor castigated Johanna Umpfenbach, holding that even if

> the wife had accumulated this property during the existence of the marital relation, she had no right to convert it into a separate estate without the consent of the husband, so as to enable her to deprive him of his marital rights. Such was never contemplated by the framers of the statute empowering a married woman to make a will, and the facts of this case indicate very plainly the necessity for such a construction, and afford ample reason for restricting the exercise of such power by a feme covert.[67]

The court directed its displeasure at Johanna Umpfenbach's attempt to subvert the customary social and familial structures that placed the male household head as the independent authority on financial matters. The challengers pointed to the will's threatening dispositions and the social disorder implicit in such an exercise of legal power. In this case, the threat was not to whom she bequeathed her property, but her attempt to upset the natural and legal order by circumventing her husband's power and then excluding him from her estate.

In Kentucky, inheritance law defined women through their relationships to men, especially through marriage. Eliza Ford and Polly Daniel's testamentary rights were negotiated through either their deceased first husbands' wills or through their second husbands' claims to marital privileges. The Court of Appeals protected Christopher Umpfenbach's marital privileges against his wife's deliberate incursions. In these cases, in the

[66] *Wehle v. Umpfenbach*, 15 Ky. L. Rptr. 346, (1893).
[67] Ibid.

face of contradictory evidence, the trial and appellate courts reinforced the social and cultural ideologies that cast the husband as the engine of household wealth production and the wife as nonproductive and ancillary. As these cases demonstrate, when married women asserted their wishes through testamentary dispositions, the courts generally refused to reconcile those claims with the centuries-old doctrine of marital unity.

When women's rights activists began to seek independence in the mid-nineteenth century, drawing on the language of individual rights, control over property constituted an important front. Women's rights activists in Kentucky struggled, as did national organizations, with the same internal tensions over directing efforts exclusively toward suffrage or toward a much broader agenda that included legal, political, and educational equality. Kentucky was home to the first suffrage organization in the former slave states, the Kentucky Woman Suffrage Association, founded in 1881. In 1888, working with prominent national suffragist Lucy Stone, Kentuckian Laura Clay (daughter of fiery abolitionist Cassius Clay) oversaw a merger with the Kentucky Equal Rights Association (KERA), which advocated for a much broader agenda.[68] Clay, who served as president from 1888 to 1912, urged the Kentucky General Assembly to reconsider overturning married women's legal disabilities. She saw clearly that rights activists had to address the seemingly inveterate arguments about women's innate lack of capacity. Averring that dependency created the conditions for mental weakness, she pointed out that if women "owe men obligations greater than men's reciprocal obligations to them, they [women] must assume a weak mental and moral attitude, bringing its attendant evils upon the whole of society."[69] Clay's argument turned the basis for legal patriarchy on its head by linking women's weakness to artificial legal restraints rather than innate weakness.

The delegates at the 1891 constitutional convention refused to add married women's property rights to the state constitution in spite of heavy lobbying by women's rights activists. Finally, on May 16, 1893, the Kentucky legislature passed a married woman's property act. Kentucky legislators granted married women testamentary capacity and other, albeit limited property rights, an act Josephine Henry proclaimed a "a victory over fossilized ignorance, selfishness and tyranny."[70] In May 1894, Kentucky

[68] Fuller, *Laura Clay and the Woman's Rights Movement*, 40.

[69] Quoted from *Louisville Courier Journal* in *The Weekly News and Courier* (S.C.), March 25, 1896.

[70] 1894 Ky. Acts, Ch. 76 § 37; Josephine Henry, quoted in Fuller, *Laura Clay and the Woman's Rights Movement*, 47.

state legislator Rozel Weissinger, author of the act, observed that critics of the married women's property laws "predict disastrous social results" because the laws would threaten the "'sacredness of home' that the man is 'head of the family.'"[71] Weissinger correctly identified how women exercising property rights potentially usurped male authority. Inheritance practices, loaded with economic and symbolic meanings, served as a crucial site in the ability of men to govern households and maintain justice and order. When women appeared as testators, they did not mediate their testamentary desires through a man; instead, they established a direct relationship with state concerning the validity of their probate. Still, from 1894 until 1942, married women had to obtain their husbands' signature to sell or mortgage property, demonstrating the longevity of Kentucky lawmakers and jurists' commitment to husbands' authority over wives' decisions about property.

## THE GENERAL APTITUDE OF THE SEX: WOMEN AND MENTAL CAPACITY

At first glance, this jurisprudence defining legal capacity appears tangentially related to jurisprudence governing the determination of mental capacity. These two kinds of capacity were mutually constitutive however; for women, the architecture of legal capacity structured assumptions about mental capacity in a way that it did not for men. Weissinger, speaking to the Woman's Club of Louisville in 1894, concluded by asking if the married woman "shall not have an equal right with man to use her faculties after her own choice, or that she shall be denied the right of property?"[72] When Weissinger connected faculties to property rights, he identified the intimate association between testators using their mental faculties – their capacity – and pursuing freedom through property rights. Women's inferior legal status reflected a generalized perception of inferior mental capacity, particularly concerning their ability to understand the masculine world of business and the values and uses of property. Exercising testamentary freedom implicated debates beyond those over women's innate abilities; testamentary freedom, like other more politicized issues such as suffrage and citizenship, involved questions about

[71] Rozel Weissinger, "The Husband and Wife Statute of 1894: An Address before the Woman's Club of Louisville Ky., Delivered May 15, 1894," N.P. Rare Pamphlet Collection, FHS.

[72] Ibid.

who could participate in society as a fully constituted, self-determining human being.

When local people testified about women's mental capacity, they did so in a matrix of gendered values through which they understood rationality. In the context of legal localism, the testimonies of ordinary people brought these to the courtroom. The persistence of local values and judgments about sex appropriate behavior sometimes subjected female testators to more withering scrutiny at the local level than it did at the appellate level. Jurists, local community members, and the popular press consistently expressed doubts about women's ability to control property or exercise political authority. Similar attitudes about women's business aptitude appeared throughout will disputes. As one journalist noted in a local Kentucky paper in 1879, "few men are inclined to grant women the credit of having any business tact or of doing business."[73] Few argued that all women were inherently incapable of managing property. Rather, many believed that most women lacked the necessary aptitude to responsibly control it.

Women's influence on voting was also a suspect intrusion into the realm of male authority.[74] In an 1879 appeal against female suffrage, *The South Kentuckian*'s editor ranted, "God forbid that the day will ever come when our mothers, sisters, wives and daughters, will be found in the profane and vulgar rabble around the polls, elbowing their way through a crowd of greasy negroes, or white men as rude and filthy."[75] The editor identified women only through their familial relationships with men. His appeal to male heads-of-households rested on the imagery of their female dependents' abasement by allowing them in the profane, mixed-race, and often dangerous world of public politics. Kentucky's most influential nineteenth-century journalist, Henry Watterson, the politically powerful editor of the *Louisville Courier Journal*, agreed that "Crazy Janes" did not belong at the polls. Watterson used an imputation of mental unsoundness – "crazy" – to describe female suffragists. He saw the very exercise of public political power as a transgression of the prevailing gender regime, referring to "These he-women [who] are

[73] "A Business Woman," *The South Kentuckian*, February 18, 1879.

[74] For a discussion of the relationship between women's familial roles and struggles for equal citizenship, see Reva B. Siegel, "She the People: The Nineteenth Amendment, Sex Equality, Federalism, and the Family," *Harvard Law Review* 115 (February 2002): 947–1046.

[75] "Miss Susan B. Anthony," *The South Kentuckian*, October 28, 1879.

themselves essentially masculine."[76] Politically conscious women sacrificed their femininity because the political world was not a feminine space. Women's intercession into politics degraded the political process and feminine virtues. This attitude was inflected into at least one will dispute. When testator John Wills appeared to value women's political perspectives, it provided evidence of his lack of mental capacity. In *Wills v. Locknane* (1873), witness A. L. Haggard testified that he believed John Wills was incompetent to do business. To illustrate, Haggard described how as a local candidate, when he tried to solicit Wills's vote, Wills "referred me to his womans fold and said they could do me more good."[77] Whether Haggard believed Wills was mentally unsound because he valued women's political perspectives or because Wills gave up his household and political authority matters little. Haggard cited Wills's delegation of political authority to women to support his opinion that Wills lacked mental capacity.

Judges drew on these characterizations of women's acumen, infusing legal proceedings with these gender biases formally and informally. As Louisville Chancery Judge S. S. Nicholas told the jury in Polly Bullitt's 1846 will case, aside from questions of Bullitt's alleged idiocy, "the general aptitude of the sex [female] for the management of property is so small that it would not do to make that the criterion of capacity for making a will."[78] These comments prefaced his instructions to the jury, designed to give legal laymen a reference point for understanding the abstract legal standard. Nicholas began with an "illustration" designed to explain the mental capacity required to "judiciously manage" property. Nicholas recalled "the best house servant I ever knew." He located the slave in terms of innate racial capacities: "His mental inferiority to the other house servants who had been raised with the whites was obvious enough, but I do not know that it would have been apparent among slaves at a Negro quarter on a farm." After acknowledging that this man "had the mental capacity to dispose of it [property] by will – though no one could

[76] "The Most Momentous Question of Modern Times," *Louisville Courier Journal*, August 24, 1913. Reprinted in Arthur Krock, ed., *The Editorials of Henry Watterson, Compiled with an Introduction and Notes by Arthur Krock* (New York: George H. Doran Co., 1923).

[77] "Testimony of AL Haggard," *Wills v. Locknane* (1873), Case 5843, Box 229, KCAR, KDLA.

[78] Judge S.S. Nicholas, "Charge to the Jury, May 2, 1846," Box 28, FL 255, *Howard v. Churchill*, BFP, FHS.

pretend that he was capable of trafficking with or judiciously managing it," Nicholas then turned to women's ability to control property:

> The whole female part of our society – whatever may be your partiality for the sex, whatever degree of your chivalrous feeling … you must in candor admit that the capacity of most of our females for trafficking with & managing property, consists pretty much in the capacity to select an agent or friend to do it for them.[79]

These doubts were based on women's capacity as women; the assumption of rationality that attached to white men did not apply to women.[80]

The duality historians have identified in Victorian ideological perceptions of women as either chaste, obedient dependents or depraved temptresses saturated inheritance disputes. As historians have emphasized, this duality was ideological. Lived experience revealed much different conduct. Still, these ideas were culturally powerful. Challengers often called attention to female testators' sexual or marital behavior. For example, in his closing argument in Polly Bullitt's will case, Henry Clay's discussion of Bullitt's lack of a beau suggested that young women who did not participate in courtship rituals evinced their deviance.[81] In *Sarah v. Miller* (1864), unmarried testator Jane Miller's avoidance of men also came under scrutiny (discussed in Chapter 2). The language used to describe Miller's relationships with men emphasized her rejection of them. Other trial participants either derided or felt it necessary to justify Miller's status as an unmarried woman and her apparent lack of interest in courtship and marriage. Attorney for Miller's beneficiaries C. D. Bradley justified disinheriting Miller's brother Isaac because years previously Isaac withheld money "at the very period girls like to dress." Bradley asked, "Who knows what prospects of marriage and requited love were wholly blighted" by Isaac's "mean selfishness?"[82] One witness believed her unmarried status indicated derangement. H. B. Hunchson reasoned "that a woman that does not want to marry is deranged."[83] For the Trigg County community, Miller's unmarried status at the very least

79 Ibid.

80 Yvonne Pitts, "Disability, Scientific Authority, and Women's Political Participation in the Turn of the Twentieth Century United States," *Journal of Women's History* 24 no. 2 (Summer 2012): 37–61.

81 Clay's speech recorded in a letter by Polly Bullitt's relative. Susan Peachy Bullitt to John C. Bullitt, May 1849, No Box, FL 162, BFP, FHS.

82 "Brief for Appellants," *Sarah v. Miller* (1864), Case 74, Box 3, KCAR, KDLA.

83 "Testimony of HB Hunchson," quoted in "Brief for Appellants," *Sarah v. Miller* (1864), Case 74, Box 3, KCAR, KDLA.

needed justification; it also could serve as evidence of mental unsoundness. Indeed, in these trials, marriage signified women's social value and acceptance of the natural order of familial relations. While not marrying could signal deviance, female testators' alleged sexual licentiousness almost always indicated mental unsoundness. Testator Eliza Atkinson personified the traits that identified sexually deviant female testators. After her husband's death in 1857, Atkinson refused to live the life of a gentry widow within her husband's kin network. Instead, acquaintances characterized her as a hard-drinking, sexually active woman who dressed flamboyantly and acted outrageously. Atkinson died in 1868, leaving her estate to William Grayson, whose family had taken care of her during her last years. Atkinson had inherited a sizeable estate from her husband, Amos Atkinson. She wrote a will, following the familiar practice of devising to her caregivers. As one witness recalled, Atkinson stated that if Colonel Grayson's family would "have the trouble of taking care of her," she thought "it would be right for them to have the property."[84] Atkinson changed her will at least once as she moved from residence to residence to reward the family who provided for her as she became increasingly sick. After Eliza Atkinson died, Amos Atkinson's son-in-law Frank Pecantet and his children (Amos's grandchildren) from Amos's first marriage contested the will.[85]

The contestants had no blood or legal relation to Eliza Atkinson other than they were her deceased husband Amos Atkinson's heirs-at-law. At least two witnesses did not see Eliza Atkinson as a legitimate testator, opining that the property should go to Pecantet and his family. Family friend and physician J. L. Dismukes testified that he "could never see why she had such an insane aversion to Pecantet the Son-in-law to her husband and the natural heir to her estate. This alone would have told me that her affections and emotional nature were at fault."[86] Even though Atkinson left her property to her caregivers, another witness believed she – and her estate – should have remained within her deceased husband's kin network. J. Campbell, former circuit court judge and lawyer for Amos Atkinson, advised her "as she was a lonely woman there by herself and Pecantet had married the only child of Amos Atkinson, she had better make an arrangement for Pecantet and his family to come and

[84] "Testimony of ES Adams," Transcript, *Pecantet v. Grayson* (1872), Case 5727, Box 225, KCAR, KDLA.

[85] Eliza Atkinson was Amos Atkinson's second wife. They had no children together.

[86] "Testimony of Dr. JL Dismukes," Transcript, *Pecantet v. Grayson* (1872), Case 5727, Box 225, KCAR, KDLA.

live there and take care of her giving her decent, comfortable support."[87] Campbell's counsel suggests the durability of the idea that the property was never really hers. Instead, it should descend through her husband's bloodline. Such reasoning reflected the persistence of patrilineal customs influencing inheritance practices. Even though Amos Atkinson was dead, Eliza Atkinson was expected to remain in continuing dependency under the paternal gaze of his son-in-law. According to the challengers, Atkinson, by accident of survival, merely held Amos's estate for her life, much like dower property, which widows held for maintenance until it descended to their husbands' heirs or beneficiaries.

Physician witnesses attributed Atkinson's behavior to an underlying mental condition caused by "a disease peculiar to her sex," as the court put it.[88] As noted in Chapter 3, in testamentary capacity challenges, physicians medicalized aberrant gendered behavior by diagnosing such behavior as physiologically based and quantifiable conditions. Dismukes admitted he did not know "what was the idiopathic cause of her derangement, but I think some of the exciting causes were *alcoholic stimuli, opium and Nymphomania*."[89] The diagnosis of nymphomania medicalized Atkinson's sexual desire as an uncontrollable manifestation of insanity. The challengers constructed a declension narrative in which after Amos Atkinson's death, Eliza Atkinson became morally dissipated and insane. During her marriage, witnesses described Atkinson as "genial, social and quite an intelligent woman," although she had a "strong disposition" toward intoxicants.[90] Still, while Amos Atkinson lived, neighbors believed that he "no doubt, operated as a restraint upon her." Once Amos Atkinson died, as James Husbands, a family friend, testified, Eliza "threw off all the restrain and prudence that her husband had been able to exercise over her."[91] As another neighbor remembered, Atkinson

> began to dress more extravagantly, bought a new wig with long black gloss curls which she wore in girlish disarray, hanging and clustering about her neck and shoulders. Put on short sleeved and low necked dresses. Procured a full set

[87] "Testimony of J. Campbell," Transcript, *Pecantet v. Grayson* (1872), Case 5727, Box 225, KCAR, KDLA.

[88] *Pecantet v. Grayson*, 6 Ky. Op. 80 (1871).

[89] "Testimony of Dr. JL Dismukes," Transcript, *Pecantet v. Grayson* (1872), Case 5727, Box 225, KCAR, KDLA. Underlining in transcript.

[90] "Testimony of James B. Husbands," Transcript, *Pecantet v. Grayson* (1872), Case 5727, Box 225, KCAR, KDLA.

[91] Ibid.

of artificial teeth and purchased and wore a gold watch and chain and a large amount of gew-gaws and fancy jewelry.[92]

Several other witnesses found Atkinson's clothing choices and adornment evidence of insanity. Her changes in dress seemed particularly to incite their wrath and disparagement because neighbors perceived her as making these choices in order to attract sexual attention.

The imputations of insanity brought by Atkinson's choice of apparel occurred in a context in which single women beyond young adulthood were expected to maintain modesty in speech, manner, and dress. National magazines including *Godey's Lady's Book* frequently published stories describing proper dress and decorum for widows. The *Lexington Weekly Press* counseled that "old maids are modest. They think their youth is over and their beauty gone."[93] Witness J. B. Husbands expressed disgust at Atkinson for "los[ing] sight of those rules of modesty sacred to a lady."[94] Atkinson, adorned in "gew-gaws" with her hair in "girlish disarray," hardly conformed to the sentimentalized image of a "civilized" Victorian widow historians have identified in self-help books and prescriptive literature.[95] Atkinson's undisguised sexual desires and unconventional behavior patterns spurred local indignation. Albritton derided Atkinson because she "seemed to be exceedingly anxious to procure another husband."[96] J. Campbell agreed that "on the subject of making a will, and getting a husband, she was a Monomaniac," but was unsure if Atkinson's insanity was caused by "ardent spirits" or "age."

The Court of Appeals, following copious testimony, derided Atkinson as an "incompetent" woman who "upwards of sixty years of age, dressed in as fashionable and gaudy colors as any of the young ladies of the neighboring town, made love to the young men, and conducted herself in such an unbecoming, and frequently indecent manner."[97] Atkinson's disregard for sexual and behavioral conventions provided enough evidence to overturn her will, despite her conformity to other socially and legally favored testation practices. Eliza Atkinson's trial offers a counterpoint to

92 "Testimony of TC Albritton," Transcript, *Pecantet v. Grayson* (1872), Case 5727, Box 225, KCAR, KDLA.

93 "Comfort for Old Maids," *Lexington Weekly Press*, January 19, 1881.

94 "Testimony of James B. Husbands," Transcript, *Pecantet v. Grayson* (1872), Case 5727, Box 225, KCAR, KDLA.

95 Thomas R. Cole, *The Journey of Life: A Cultural History of Aging in America* (New York: Cambridge University Press, 1992).

96 "Testimony of TC Albritton," Transcript, *Pecantet v. Grayson* (1872), Case 5727, Box 225, KCAR, KDLA.

97 *Pecantet v. Grayson*, 6 Ky. Op. 80 (1872).

the trial over Frank Lisle's will described in Chapter 3. That case shared many similarities with Atkinson's. Both testators suffered from failing health, appeared morally depraved, frequently used intoxicants, and were allegedly verbally abusive and profane. In Eliza Atkinson's trial, the local jury upheld the will. The jury did the opposite in Lisle's trial, finding him lacking mental capacity and unduly influenced by his caretakers. The Court of Appeals reversed both verdicts, overturning Atkinson's will and upholding Lisle's.

The telling distinction in these appellate decisions reflects the court's concern with maintaining male independence, central to its broader concern with marital unity, reflected in women's legal capacity cases. In Lisle's case, the court rejected any imputation of dependency, finding that none "of the devisees acquired such dominion or influence over him as deprived him of the power to dispose of his estate in accordance with his own wishes."[98] In Atkinson's case, her assertions of testamentary independence led the court to find her incompetent. The judges reasoned she was "seventy years of age, weak, unhealthy ... and whilst some of her passions evidencing a failing, or ruined intellect had subsided, still the inordinate desire to give and dispose of her imaginary wealth seems never to have left her."[99] The trait that mattered most to the Court of Appeals and affirmed Lisle's will – independence – damned Atkinson's. Reducing the outcome of these two cases to the sex of the testator would be gross oversimplification. Comparing these cases demonstrates the appellate judiciary's ongoing preoccupation with preserving male independence and distrust of the same trait in women.

Sexual independence and desire in widowed male testators was understandable, and reaffirmed one male testator's virility. The challengers' lawyers in *Broaddus v. Broaddus* (1874) noted that shortly after his first wife's death, George Broaddus remarried "a maid of 36 summers, stout, vigorous & luscious – full of muscle and blood. He was a man of strong passions & was doubtless hunting just such a woman."[100] Broaddus "passions" were not representative of mental unsoundness in this case; rather, it was the venality of his second wife. The comparison of depictions of sexuality not only reveals the double standard long identified by historians, but links gendered standards of sexuality to sanity and property

[98] *Bush v. Lisle*, 89 Ky. 393 at 401.

[99] *Pecantet v. Grayson*, 6 Ky. Op. 80 at 83.

[100] "Brief for Heirs," *Broaddus' Devisees v. Broaddus' Heirs* (1874), Case 6767, Box 266, KCAR, KDLA.

rights. Regulation of inheritance practices worked to contain female sexuality within a narrow range of virtuous standards.

Regulating sexuality extended beyond criminal law and vice enforcement into a complex system of rewards and impediments shot through property law. In *Ross v. Weaver* (1881), testator Anne Cooke's reputation for sexual immorality and as a brothel keeper supported claims to overturn her will. Cooke, who witnesses testified "kept a house of prostitution," disinherited her sister and left her estate to her sexual partner, James Ross. Like Eliza Atkinson and Jane Miller, Cooke's unmarried status figured prominently in the community members' understandings of sanity and naturalness. The challengers attacked Ross's and Cooke's characters by describing several arguments between them. Drawing on images of carnality and greed, they portrayed Ross as "lazing around Ann Cooke's house to gratify his lusts and get her property."[101] Had Cooke and Ross socially and legally legitimized their relationship through marriage, Weaver would have had much more difficulty in bringing suit against the will. Such a disposition by Cooke to her husband would have been considered natural. Their attorneys argued that it did not matter how "low and degraded a person may become when he or she comes to die their affections will turn to those of their own blood ... and not unduly influenced, will leave to those of their own blood what property they may have, in preference to strangers of blood. It is unnatural to do otherwise."[102]

Although Ross and Cooke had lived together for five years, the brief emphasized blood over choice, portraying Ross "as an entire stranger ... [of] blood" compared to Cooke's "sister who under law is entitled to it is virtually left without anything."[103] This argument exposed the sexual economy in the grammar of capacity. It positioned blood relatives as natural heirs, regardless of affectionate ties to the testator. To choose otherwise, particularly in favor of an unsanctioned sexual relationship, was equated with unnaturalness, immorality, and violation of natural hierarchies. Clearly, the challengers put the relationship between Cooke and Ross on trial as much as they did Cooke's sanity. Witness and local doctor L. C. Porter testified Cooke was insane because he believed it was a "bad will."[104] Juryman Robert Heard was overheard saying he believed

101 "Appellees' Brief," *Ross v. Weaver* (1881), Case 13247, Box 527, KCAR, KDLA.

102 Ibid.

103 Ibid.

104 "Testimony of Dr. LC Porter," Transcript, *Ross v. Weaver* (1881), Case 13247, Box 527, KCAR, KDLA.

her estate "ought to go to her relations."[105] Weaver's attorneys used the language of moral indignation at Cooke and Ross's conduct to insist upon an appropriate punishment by overturning the will and restoring the natural order.

To defend the will, Ross's attorneys invoked a different strand of the grammar of capacity by equating duty with entitlement. They argued that Cooke had a duty to Ross that trumped bloodline claims because Cooke's sister Jane Weaver had not fulfilled her familial obligations. Ross conscientiously nursed Cooke when her sister failed to visit or care for her. Ross's attorneys attacked Jane Weaver as callously ignoring her dying sister. They argued Cooke believed Weaver "cared no more for her than a dog."[106] By failing to fulfill her natural obligations to her sister, Weaver relinquished the strong claims to Cooke's estate based in blood. On the other hand, Cooke owed Ross a debt for his caregiving, a point Ross's attorney labeled an "appreciation of his services." Her will reflected her acknowledgment of her obligations, and therefore was the product of a sane mind. Ross's lawyers' strategy did not work at the local level. The Warren County jury stripped Cooke of her testamentary freedom and sent a strong message to the community that Ross would not be rewarded for his conduct. Although the Court of Appeals overturned the decision, the local jury had firmly set the local boundaries of sane and appropriate behavior for unmarried women.

Within marriage too, litigants scrutinized the sexual behavior of female testators. In *Johnson v. Johnson* (1898), the case with which this chapter began, witnesses debated the sexual conduct of both Mildred and Robert Johnson. Like other testamentary capacity cases, the circumstances surrounding the dispute reveal a troubled and conflicted family. As the lawyers defending the will admitted, their marriage "had not been happy."[107] The proponents of the will argued that Mildred Johnson wrested control of her husband's property to "save for her children something from the wreck of the estate of her improvident husband."[108] This defense of Mildred Johnson's sanity depicted Johnson as a concerned mother seeking to provide for her children. Like testator Johanna Umpfenbach, who

105 "Testimony of Robert Heard," Transcript, *Ross v. Weaver* (1881), Case 13247, Box 527, KCAR, KDLA.

106 "Testimony of Minerva Cox," Transcript, *Ross v. Weaver* (1881), Case 13247, Box 527, KCAR, KDLA.

107 "Brief for Appellants," *Johnson's Admr., & c, v. Robert F. Johnson*, Case 26822, Box 1159, KCAR, KDLA.

108 Ibid.

sought to provide for her niece's education, such concerns rested squarely within social expectations for married women.

Other evidence suggested Mildred Johnson failed to perform her sexual obligations to her husband. Mildred had refused to occupy the marital bed on several occasions. Their daughter Blanche Daley testified that on her wedding day, her father (Robert) threatened to "disgrace all of you this day unless your mother comes to my bed." Daley recalled that her mother responded that to prevent "disgrace" on her daughter's wedding night, "Robert, I will be in your bed tonight."[109] Robert denied this incident in his cross-examination. While Daley most likely recalled this incident to reveal her father's brutishness, other incidents came to light that the court interpreted much differently. After Mildred Johnson had acquired deeds to their Lexington property, she left Robert for her daughter's home in Detroit. Robert Johnson testified that after her return to Lexington, Mildred "never came back to my bed any more."[110] Two narratives emerged, one in which Mildred was the long-suffering wife at the hands of her brutish husband. In the other narrative, Robert, in spite of his kindness and entreaties, was denied his conjugal right. This event illustrated a broader pattern of behavior in which Mildred Johnson had refused to provide Robert with the affections and services expected of a wife.

Judge Burnham, who wrote for the Court of Appeals, chose to defend the marriage ideal against incursions such as those presented by Mildred Johnson.

> Having succeeded, by every species of artifice and persuasion, in devesting [*sic*] her husband of all his property ... she gave open expression to her contempt and aversion for him, which had been ... tempered by her selfishness and greed to get possession of his property. She refused any longer to recognize him as her husband, or to remain in the same house with him, and left his residence in the fall of 1892.[111]

Much of Burnham's narration of the Johnson's marriage focused on Mildred's misbehavior. Burnham depicted with abhorrence Mildred's "contempt" and "greed," although he admitted in the opinion that evidence proved Robert was "deficient in will power." When the will's

109 "Testimony of Blanche Daley," Transcript, *Johnson's Admr., & c, v. Robert F. Johnson*, Case 26822, Box 1159, KCAR, KDLA.

110 "Testimony of Robert Johnson," Transcript, *Johnson's Admr., & c, v. Robert F. Johnson*, Case 26822, Box 1159, KCAR, KDLA.

111 *Johnson's Adm'r v. Johnson,* 20 Ky. L. Rptr. 138 (1898).

proponents suggested Robert failed to live up to the obligations of marriage due to alleged infidelity, the court treated these accusations much differently than Mildred's avoidance of her sexual obligations.

The beneficiaries tried to make an issue out of Robert's alleged peccadilloes, but the court accommodated the sexual double standard. Blanche Daley (the Johnsons' daughter) testified that a neighbor suggested that "your father is too intimate with Mrs. Grigsby."[112] Mr. Bickers, a business associate of Robert Johnson's, remembered that another daughter, Moiselle Johnson, threatened to "publish that diary of his," which detailed the infidelity and would "drive her father out of town."[113] The Court of Appeals treated Johnson's alleged infidelity as ancillary. In doing so, its reasoning remained consistent with Kentucky divorce laws, which until 1894 granted divorce for adultery only if the wife was the offender.[114] According to the court, Mildred Johnson had no reciprocal claim on the sexual integrity of her husband's body. Instead, the court blamed the Johnsons' disobedient and obstreperous daughters for the marital rift, noting that Moiselle Johnson took her father's diary

> seeing that it contained something that was calculated to exasperate and anger her mother towards him, immediately took it and showed it to her. Another daughter, having heard idle gossip to the effect that her father had been intimate with another woman, hastened to her mother to repeat this scandal, also. The only motive apparent for this unfilial conduct of these devisees in this constant abuse of their father … was to poison their mother's mind against appellee to such an extent as would make forgiveness and reconciliation impossible, and destroy the last vestige of memory on her part of his generosity and kindness to her, and to unduly influence her to his prejudice in the disposition of her property.[115]

The court refused to take seriously the possibility that Robert Johnson had violated his marital obligations. Instead, the judges expressed ire that the Johnson daughters would repeat the rumors to their mother. This pretermission implicitly sanctioned husbands and fathers' prerogatives and reinforced submission from their dependents.

Clearly, the Johnson case – indeed, most testamentary disputes – placed local juries, community members, and the Court of Appeals in the unenviable position of mediating family disputes. These cases brought

112 "Testimony of Blanche Daley," Transcript, *Johnson's Admr., & c, v. Robert F. Johnson*, Case 26822, Box 1159, KCAR, KDLA.

113 "Testimony of Mr. Bickers," Transcript, *Johnson's Admr., & c, v. Robert F. Johnson*, Case 26822, Box 1159, KCAR, KDLA.

114 Harrison and Klotter, *A New History of Kentucky*, 287.

115 *Johnson's Adm'r v. Johnson*, 20 Ky. L. Rptr. 138 (1898).

into public discussion the most intimate details of day-to-day life. In this process, witnesses and lawyers chose which details they believed would most likely convince a local jury of the worthiness of their positions. In cases involving women's testamentary capacity, these details most often involved adherence to rigid standards of feminine dependency. Of course, these cases also reveal that this docility and dependency were not the lived experiences of these women. Female testators and female beneficiaries conducted business, engaged in sanctioned and unsanctioned sexual relationships, made and broke promises, and made decisions within a range of options. Still, the ability to marshal evidence based on a standard of feminine behavior and sexual continence that became conflated with sanity reveals the power of the grammar of capacity.

Women's wills were vulnerable to two kinds of testamentary capacity challenges, based on their marital status or their mental capacity. Ordinary people and legal elites expressed doubts about women's capacity for making even rudimentary decisions about property distribution, even as women made politic, rational decisions about property. Insanity and rationality, refracted through naturalized ideals of proper familial relations, were deeply gendered. In spite of reformist changes toward emancipating women's legal capacity from coverture, methods of restricting their freedom remained, accommodating evolving gender ideology. Separate states, initially formed according to equity law, were subject ultimately to the interpretation of the Court of Appeals. The ongoing hostility, combined with equity's byzantine rules, kept the overall percentage of women using it relatively low. Women needed the resources to create and manage the separate estate, a task made more complicated by the evolving case law and strict documentation separate estates required. In these cases and others, appellate jurists consistently muted women's property claims they and their beneficiaries sought to have confirmed in legal proceedings.

Writing a will, with its link to the material and symbolic reproduction of the family, remained a battleground in Kentucky's conflicts over the appropriate forms of household governance. The standard of capacity itself was based on an assumed masculine right to independence and to conduct business. The meanings of sanity and insanity differed for men and women according to how people understood the gendered constellations of moral and appropriate behavior associated with each sex and race. Likewise, the same behavioral ideals shaped how the community perceived the worthiness of the chosen heir, particularly when disinherited bloodline family seemed worthy. To disinherit a deserving family member in favor of an heir considered by witnesses as debauched surely indicated insanity. Focusing on gender appropriate behavior allowed juries and testifying witnesses to condemn testators' or heirs' behavior by using ideals that while not practiced by everyone, were affirmed through law and dominant social values. Such testimony established the parameters of sanity and reinforced gender appropriate behavior and proper family relationships within the crucial institution of the household.

# Epilogue

Let's choose executors and talk of wills:
And yet not so, for what can we bequeath
Save our deposed bodies to the ground?
– William Shakespeare, *Richard II*, Act Three, Scene Two

"The right of the testator to make a will according to his own wishes is jealously guarded by the courts regardless of a court's view of the justice of a chosen disposition," pronounced Kentucky Court of Appeals Chief Judge Charles B. Lester in 1992.[1] Lester's comment appeared in *Wallace v. Scott*, a testamentary capacity case over the validity of Ardeen Boston's will. Boston had willed the lifetime use of her estate to Bill Scott, with whom she had had lived for the past six years. When Scott died, the estate passed to the Methodist Home of Kentucky. Boston's two children, her disinherited heirs-at-law, challenged the lower court's refusal to grant them a trial, arguing that Boston lacked mental capacity and was unduly influenced by Scott. The disinherited heirs invoked a modern grammar of capacity to argue against the will, some of which would have resonated with their nineteenth-century counterparts. They cited Boston's medical problems and Valium use, which they argued had left her mentally impaired. This charge echoes the debates over the effects of chronic disease and laudanum on nineteenth-century testator Eliza Atkinson.[2]

[1] *Wallace v. Scott*, 844 S.W. 2d 439 (1992) cited from *New v. Creamer*, 275 S.W.2d 918 (1955) at 920. In 1975, the Kentucky legislature amended the state constitution to add the Kentucky Supreme Court. The Court of Appeals became an intermediary appellate court.

[2] *Pecantet v. Grayson*, 6 Ky. Op. 80 (1872).

Boston's children claimed the will was "unnatural" because Scott, lacking the legitimacy conferred by a legal relationship such as marriage, inherited rather than her bloodline kin. Such allegations would likely come as no surprise to James Ross, testator Anne Cooke's paramour and beneficiary in her 1881 will dispute.

In *Wallace v. Scott* (1992), the Court of Appeals applied a capacity test cited in a 1989 decision: "First, did the testator know the natural objects of his bounty, and his obligations to them. Second, could he make a rational survey of his estate. Third, did he dispose of that estate according to a fixed plan of his own."[3] Indeed, this test was strikingly similar in language to the one the court applied in the dispute over Walter Shropshire's will more than 160 years before in 1830. The court noted that Shropshire "pretermitt[ed]" several heirs-at-law and held that the law voided wills in which the testator had not "a sound memory, nor sufficient mind, or a mind in a proper state for disposing of his estate 'with reason,' or according to any fixed judgment, or settled purpose of his own."[4] These similarities remind us of the enduring power of "capacity" and inheritance practices to shape the contours of property rights, moral obligations, and family.

Despite the similarities in language, Walter Shropshire's will dispute in 1830 occurred on a vastly different legal and social landscape from that of *Wallace v. Scott* (1992). Before the American Revolution, inheritance law, recondite and vexing, had preserved familial status and power by yoking inherited property to blood through intestacy law, primogeniture, and entailment. In the early American republic, inheritance by blood was more troublesome. The nation had just rejected rule by descent through the king's bloodline, embracing instead rule by consent of the governed. Yet bloodline descent (the default absent a will) still determined the transmission of private property, the foundation of American liberty. American inheritance law, with its minimal requirements for writing a will, seemed to accommodate both of these impulses, descent and consent. The centuries-old tradition of descent continued, while those able to give consent – those possessing capacity – had the right to determine property distribution through a will. The ability to testate, however, was defined by a latticework of legal, cultural, and medical values. Testators had to possess capacity, a concept laden with formalist legal meaning *and*

[3] The decision cited the test used in *Fischer v. Heckerman*, 772 S.W. 2d. 642 (1989), decided three years before *Wallace v. Scott* (1992).

[4] *Shropshire v. Reno*, 28 Ky. 91 (1830).

with competing communal values about sanity and free will. Capacity underwrote all wills. When disinherited heirs-at-law challenged wills on a capacity ground, the ensuing trials made visible abiding conflicts that had riven an American society founded in the conflicting values of material acquisition, free will, and communitarianism.

For centuries, writing a will has been one of the rituals undertaken in the contemplation of impending mortality. It was an intensely personal, meaningful, and momentous act for testators and their families. Benjamin Rush advised young doctors who might find themselves at their patients' deathbeds, "never to suffer a patient to die who has a right, and is in a condition, to make a will."[5] At the same time, wills and their subsequent trajectories as legal instruments of property conveyance were public, technical, and abstract. Inheritance, for all its social, cultural, and familial implications, was about property transmission between generations. As such, the changing mandates of property law influenced its development: easy alienability, systemization, clarity, and eventually a rejection of legal identity based on status and community relations in favor of one based in abstracted individual rights. State-level lawmakers and judges worked to develop a body of property law that would encourage a stable yet expansive market economy. In a world in which some people were also property, a status determined by race, the legal system also endorsed and protected white supremacy. On the local level, property could be a vehicle for expressing all sorts of social and cultural messages, integral elements in the litigation and outcomes of these cases. When people litigated over property, they shaped structures and values at the core of American society.

Legitimate bloodline family was at the center of inheritance practices. As recently as 1989, litigants in a rent-control dispute in New York argued that the definition of family was found by looking to inheritance, "with this State's intestacy laws." The court rejected that definition, finding instead that family "should not rest on fictitious legal distinctions or genetic history, but instead should find its foundation in the reality of family life."[6] Kentucky testators Jeremiah Minor and his "black family" and James Ross probably would have agreed with this definition. The depiction of family as a bedrock social institution by litigants and jurists emphasizes that families required (and were given) careful tending through legal oversight.

[5] Benjamin Rush, "Lecture XVI: On the Study of Medical Jurisprudence (1810)."

[6] *Braschi v. Stahl Associates*, 74 N.Y.2d 201 (1989) at 211.

The judicial surveillance of family through inheritance litigation reveals the instability of legal concepts like capacity and the permeation of applied law with individuals' lived experiences. Perhaps most contested by litigants, lawyers, and jurists were the words that defined family members' "natural" obligations to each other. The legal descriptive "natural" in "natural objects of their bounty" converged with communal beliefs, creating networks of claims and social obligations between generations of legitimate family members. The obligations that inhered in affective relationships between testators and their beneficiaries received greater scrutiny when not legally legitimized. Although testators' "natural" obligations ostensibly were defined by blood and law, they were affected by other factors such as the behavior and local reputation of the beneficiaries and heirs, regardless of their legal or blood relation to the testators.

Viewing property through the testamentary capacity requirement speaks to the tenacity of legal localism. Local knowledge often provided the best barometer to judge sanity and insanity, a principle confirmed after jurists and medical experts' mid-century attempts to impose scientific theories on judicial processes. Determining mental capacity required ascertaining that which was ultimately ascertainable – the interiority of the testator's mind. It relied heavily on local infusions of evidence to fill in the qualitative meaning of the sterile legal tests devised by jurists. State law did gain increasing authority, but localized law as an important determinant of mental capacity never fully disappeared in the nineteenth century. At the same time, communal knowledge did not monopolize judicial definitions of testamentary capacity at any time in the nineteenth century. The grammar of capacity provided a scientific and moral vocabulary through which medical experts combined moral judgments with medical empiricism, masking diagnoses in a seemingly objective scientific nomenclature. The process of defining legal capacity became systematized at the state level early on, in part because it drew on complex equity rules and common law doctrines elaborated in a coherent body of treatise and case law.

The early rationalization of the jurisprudence of legal capacity had the most consequences for women who wished to write wills. Women had disposed of property since the Founding in spite of lawmakers' reservations about their ability to write just, responsible wills. The grammar of capacity rather than the language of individual rights mediated women's claims to property. Both categories – capacity and individual rights – rested on ideas about women's ability to rationally consent and ultimately to exercise the responsibilities of self-government. In Kentucky, the gendered cultural assumptions and concern with systemization resulted in narrow, formalized interpretation of women's legal capacity. It limited women's access to property, which consolidated wealth among white male property holders, and it preserved the legal and social fiction of marital unity under male household authority.

With the right of testation came authority, but not as an overtly coercive mechanism that legally compelled certain behaviors. Rather, this sort of authority resembled what historians of foreign relations deem "soft power." Its force came from testators creating incentives for particular actions. It was insinuative or, as some heirs and beneficiaries might have seen it, insidious. The penalty came from being disinherited and that threat hung over heirs and beneficiaries for the life of the testator. With some testamentary gifts conditional on ongoing behavior, this power continued even after testators shed their mortal coils.

Inheritance practices also served as a crucial site of power from which men governed their households. When women wrote wills they did not mediate their testamentary desires through a man; instead, they established a direct relationship with the state, their beneficiaries, and their heirs. In local probate courts, a complex picture emerges, with women seeking to work around statutory law and customary practices that frustrated their testamentary ambitions. From the mid-nineteenth century to the turn of the twentieth century, testamentary capacity cases reveal struggles between women determined to assert authority over their own property and judicial attempts to preserve male authority in households.[7] This jurisprudence illuminates some of the legal contradictions in the gradual, often grudging shift from a legal regime grounded in coverture and legal dependency to one in which women slowly gained legal independence and with it, authority over property and family. Anxieties about gender and racial order saturated will disputes, but only occasionally as explicit justifications for overturning wills. Instead, these values emerged within the grammar of capacity as judges and juries instilled cultural meanings into legal prose. The grammar of capacity's usefulness extended beyond its ability to inculcate cultural values into property law. It was flexible, accommodating statutory changes.

[7] On ways in which constitutional and legal interpretations have been used to slow reform or transform reform-minded legislation into the status quo, see Reva Siegal, "Why Equal Protection No Longer Protects: The Evolving Forms of Status-Enforcing State Action," *Stanford Law Review* 49 (1997): 1111–48.

In 1879, Kentucky Court of Appeals Judge Martin Cofer ruminated on the challenges of inheritance law. Courts had to "lay down a rule … and must bear in mind that hard cases make shipwreck of the law." Cofer believed that the risk of shipwreck was compounded by the perennial, perhaps irreconcilable, tensions in inheritance law that mediated the "strongest passions of human nature – love and animosity."[8] Cofer was correct; will disputes crisscrossed a variety of legal and cultural terrains: ordinary people's understandings of family, insanity, and justice, medical experts and evolving science, and the independence claims of women's rights activists, to name only three. The history of testamentary capacity disputes presents an opportunity to rethink the complicated interplay between law and social norms. Witnesses related morality tales of moral degeneration, physical impairment, and aging, alongside narratives of justice redeemed, unconditional love, and sacrifice. They demarcated normative behavior within families through monitoring property distribution while simultaneously reinforcing and challenging white supremacy, patriarchal authority, and other hierarchies of power. Such contradictions defy easy categorization of law as a tool of entrenched elites or law as an engine of social change. They remind us that law is an expression of human fallibility.

[8] *Mercer's Admin v. Macklin*, 77 Ky. 434 (1879) at 443.

# Bibliography

## Archival Collections by Repository


*Filson Historical Society, Louisville, Kentucky*

- Bullitt Family Papers
- Diary of Lemuel Porter
- Green Family Papers
- Rare Book and Pamphlet Collection
- Yandell Family Papers

*Kentucky Department for Libraries and Archives, Frankfort, Kentucky*

- Court of Appeals Records, 1864–1911
- Floyd County Circuit Court Civil Case Files, 1855–1865
- Garrard County Circuit Court Case Files, 1830–1860
- Harrison County Court Clerk Records, 1795–1905
- Henderson County Court Clerk Records, 1840–1850
- Jefferson County Court of Common Pleas Files, 1830–1894
- Kentucky State Slave Census, 1850 and 1860
- Madison County Court Clerk Records, 1840–1860
- Nelson County Court Records, 1831–1835
- Scott County Court Records, 1843–1850
- State Auditor's Reports, 1820–1880
- Trigg County Court Clerk Records, 1851–1865
- Warren County Court Clerk Records, 1827–1898
- Woodford County Court Clerk Records, 1834–1838

## Primary Sources

### *Published Statutes, Digests, and Government Reports*


Decisions of the Kentucky Court of Appeals in *Kentucky Law Reporter* and *Kentucky State Reports.*

*Private Institution for the Education of Feeble-Minded Youth Twenty-Fifth Biennial Report.* (Barre, MA: Charles Rogers, 1898). Report. www.disabilitymuseum.org/lib/docs/1707.htm?page=3. Accessed January 20, 2006.

Reports Communicated to Both Branches of the Legislature of Kentucky at the December Session, 1845 (Auditor's Report), Legislative Document No. 10 (Frankfort, KY: A.G. Hodges, 1845).

Statutes and Acts of the Kentucky General Assembly, 1794–1910.

U.S. Department of the Interior, Census Office. Kentucky Slave Census for 1850. Population Schedules of the Seventh Census of the United States, 1850.

U.S. Department of the Interior, Census Office, Tenth Census, 1880. "Report on the Defective, Dependent, and Delinquent Classes of the Population of the United States," Government Printing Office, 1888.


### *Published Primary Sources*


No Author. "Definition of Insanity – Nature of Disease." *The American Journal of Insanity* 1 no. 2 (1844): 99–16.

No Author. "Startling Facts from the Census." *The American Journal of Insanity* 8 no. 2 (October 1852): 153–5.

Allen, James Lane. *The Choir Invisible.* New York: The Macmillan Co., 1898.

*The Reign of Law: A Tale of the Kentucky Hemp Fields.* New York: The Macmillan Co., 1900.

Anonymous. "An Enquiry Concerning the Duty of Christian Heads of Families Toward their Black Servants," *The Almoner* (Lexington, Ky.) 1 no. 6 (May 1815).

Aunt Alice (pseud.). "Old Age is Honorable," *Saturday Evening Post.* March 23, 1861.

Beck, Theodric Romyn. *Elements of Medical Jurisprudence* 2nd ed. London: W. Lewis, 1825; Ray, Treatise on the Medical Jurisprudence of Insanity (1838).

Blackstone, William. *Commentaries on the Laws of England, Book the Second.* Oxford: Clarendon Press, 1775.

Caldwell, Charles M. "A Succinct View of the Influence of Mental Cultivation on the Destinies of Louisville, An Introductory Lecture Delivered at the Opening of the Louisville Medical Institute." *Louisville Journal of Medicine and Surgery* (1838).

Carroll, Alfred L. "The Plea of Insanity," in *Papers Read before the Medico-Legal Society of New York.* Third series, 1875–1878. Revised edition. New York: The Medico-Legal Journal Association, 1886.

Cartwright, Samuel A. "Report on the Diseases and Physical Particularities of the Negro." *The New Orleans Medical and Surgical Journal* 7 (1851): 692–713.

Chipley, William S. "In the Court of Appeals, State of Kentucky: Smith vs. Commonwealth." *American Journal of Insanity* 23 no. 1 (July 1866): 1–45.

Conklin, W. J. "The Medical Expert," *The Ohio Medical and Surgical Journal* (April 1878): 127–47.

Cook, George M. "Mental Hygiene," *The American Journal of Insanity* 15 no. 3 (January 1859): 272–82.

Douglass, Frederick. *Narrative of the Life of Frederick Douglass, An American Slave.* 1845. Reprint, New York: Dover Publications, 1995.

Francis, Richard and William Walter Hening. *Maxims of Equity: First American Edition.* Richmond: Shepard and Pollard, 1823.

Gaskell, G. A. *Gaskell's Compendium of Forms, Educational, Social, Legal and Commercial.* Chicago: Standard Publishing, 1889.

Grissom, Eugene. "True and False Experts," *The American Journal of Insanity* 35 (July 1878): 1–36.

Hammond, William A. M.D., "Opinion Relative to the Testamentary Capacity of the Late James C. Johnston, of Chowan County, North Carolina," in *Insanity in its Medico-Legal Relations.* New York: Voorhis and Co, second edition, 1875. Original date, 1867.

Harper, William. "Slavery in the Light of Social Ethics." In *Cotton is King and Proslavery Arguments.* Edited by E. N. Elliott. Augusta: Pritchard, Abbott & Loomis, 1860.

Hastings Hamilton, Frank. "Medical Expert Testimony." *Popular Science Monthly* 26 no. 37 (1885): 603–11.

Howe, Samuel Gridley. "A Selection from 'Report Made to the Legislature of Massachusetts'" (1848). In *Mental Retardation in America: A Historical Reader.* Edited by Noll Steven and James Trent, Jr. New York: New York University Press, 2004.

Jarvis, Edward. "On the Supposed Increase of Insanity," *The American Journal of Insanity* 8 no. 4 (April 1852): 333–64.

"Insanity among the Colored Population of the Free States." *The American Journal of Insanity* 8 no. 3 (January 1852): 268–82.

"What Shall We Do With Our Insane?" *The Western Journal of Medicine and Science* 5 no. 2 (February 1842): 81–126.

Lee, Charles A. "A Medico-Legal Opinion Relative to the Sanity of Carlton Gates." In *Papers Read Before the Medico-Legal Society of New York.* First series. Third edition. New York: The Medico-Legal Journal Association, 1889: 204–34.

"Letter to Editor," *Southern Literary Messenger* 3 (December 1837).

Locke, John. *Second Treatise of Government.* 1690. Edited by C. B. McPherson. Hackett Publishing Company, Indianapolis and Cambridge, 1980.

Maudsley, Henry. *Body and Will, Being an Essay Concerning Will in its Metaphysical, Physiological, and Pathological Aspects.* New York: D. Appleton and Co., 1884.

O'Dea, James J. "The Sphere, Rights and Obligations of Medical Experts." In *Papers Read before the Medico-Legal Society of New York.* First series, Third edition. New York: The Medico-Legal Journal Association, 1889: 402–43.

Ordroneaux, John. "The Proper Status of the Insane and Feebleminded." In *Papers Read before the Medico-Legal Society of New York*. Third series, 1875–1878. Revised edition. New York: The Medico-Legal Journal Association, 1886.

Paine, Thomas. *Common Sense* in *Common Sense, The Rights of Man, and Other Essential Writings*. Edited with an introduction by Sidney Hook. New York: Penguin Books, 1984.

Patterson, Edward. "Monomania as Affecting Testamentary Capacity." In *Papers Read before the Medico-Legal Society of New York*. Third series, 1875–1878. Revised edition. New York: The Medico-Legal Journal Association, 1886.

Pennington, James C. "The Fugitive Blacksmith; or Events in the History of James C. Pennington." In *I was Born a Slave: An Anthology of Classic Slave Narratives, Volume Two* 1849–1866. Edited by Yuval Taylor. Chicago: Lawrence Hill Books, 1999.

"Proceedings of the Association: Twentieth Annual Meeting of the Association of Medical Superintendents of American Institutions for the Insane." *The American Journal of Insanity* 23 no. 1 (July 1866): 75–145.

Ray, Isaac. "American Legislation on Lunacy." *American Journal of Insanity* 21 no. 1 (1864): 21–63.

"Hints to the Medical Witness in Questions of Insanity." *American Journal of Insanity* 8 no. 1 (July 1851): 53–67.

"Testamentary Capacity." In *Papers Read before the Medico-Legal Society of New York*, Third series, 1875–1878. Revised edition. New York: The Medico-Legal Journal Association, 1886.

*A Treatise on the Medical Jurisprudence of Insanity*. Boston: Little and Brown, 1838.

Read, Harlan Eugene. *The Abolition of Inheritance*. New York: Macmillan, 1918.

Redfield, Isaac. *The Law of Wills, Embracing the Making and Construction of Wills; The Jurisprudence of Insanity; The Effect of Extrinsic Evidence; The Creation and Construction of Trusts, So Far As Applicable to Wills, with Forms and Instructions for Preparing Wills* Part I, 2nd edition. Boston: Little Brown and Co, 1866.

"Reports of American Insanity." *The American Journal of Insanity* 21 no. 4 (April 1865): 567–8.

"Review of *The Law of Wills* by Isaac Redfield." *The American Journal of Insanity* 21 no. 3 (January 1865): 406–7.

Roberts, W. Lewis. "Property Rights of Married Women in Kentucky," *Kentucky Law Journal* 11 (November 1922): 1–9.

Rush, Benjamin. "Lecture XVI: On the Study of Medical Jurisprudence," in *Sixteen Introductory Lectures, to Courses of Lectures upon the Institutes and Practice of Medicine*. Philadelphia, 1811. Transcribed at U.S. National Library of Medicine Online. http://collections.nlm.nih.gov/muradora/objectView!getDataStreamContent.action?pid=nlm:nlmuid-2569048R-bk&dsid=OCR&mimeType=text/plain. Accessed June 28, 2012.

Skidmore, Thomas. *The Rights of Man to Property: Being a Proposition to Make It Equal Among the Adults of the Present Generation, and to Provide For Its*

*Equal Transmission to Every Individual of Each Succeeding Generation on Arriving at the Age of Maturity*. Ming, 1829.

Stewart, J. Q. A. "The Industrial Department of the Kentucky Institution for the Education and Training of Feebleminded Children." *Proceedings of the Association of Medical Officers of American Institutions for Idiotic and Feeble-Minded Persons* (1882): 236–9.

Stokes, William H. "On a Court of Medical Experts in Cases of Insanity." *The American Journal of Insanity* 10 no. 2 (October 1853): 112–22.

Story, Joseph. *Commentaries on the Conflict of Laws, Foreign and Domestic in Regard to Contracts, Rights and Remedies, and Especially in Regard to Marriages, Divorces, Wills Succession, and Judgments*. Boston: Billard, Gray and Company, 1834.

Temple, William. "Thoughts on Old Age." *Virginia Historical Register and Literary Companion* 5 no. 1 (1852).

Watterson, Henry. "The South at Christmas." In *The Editorials of Henry Watterson, Compiled with an Introduction and Notes by Arthur Krock*. New York: George H. Doran Co., 1923.

Wilbur, H. B. "The Classifications of Idiocy." *Proceedings of the Association of Medical Officers of American Institutions for Idiotic and Feeble-minded Persons* (1877): 29–35.

Williams, Edward Vaughn. *A Treatise of the Law of Executors and Administrators*. Philadelphia: R.H. Small Law Bookseller, 1849.

Williams, Henry Smith. "Social Relations of the Insane." *North American Review* 157 (November 1893): 611–22.

Weissinger, Rozel. "The Husband and Wife Statute of 1894: An Address before the Woman's Club of Louisville Ky., Delivered May 15, 1894. N.P. N.D. Rare Pamphlet Collection, Filson Historical Society, Louisville, Ky.

## Newspapers

Cincinnati Mirror and Western Gazette of Literature, Science and the Arts
Lexington Weekly Press
Louisville Courier Journal
Louisville Daily Journal
Louisville Weekly Journal
The Louisville Times
New York Times
The South Kentuckian
Southern Literary Messenger

## PhD Dissertations

Bennett, Charles Raymond. "All Things to All People: The American Colonization Society in Kentucky, 1829–1860," PhD dissertation. University of Kentucky, 1980.

Shreck, Kimberly A. "Splitting Heirs: Gender, Race and the Properties of Unreconstructed Households," PhD dissertation. University of Missouri – Columbia, 2004.

Wergland, Glendyne R. "Women, Men, Property, and Inheritance: Gendered Testamentary Customs in Western Massachusetts, 1800–1860, Or Diligent Wives, Dutiful Daughters, Prodigal Sons, Westward Migration, Reciprocity, and Rewards for Virtue, Considered." PhD dissertation. University of Massachusetts, 2001.

White, Ronald. "A Dialogue on Madness: Eastern State Lunatic Asylum and Mental Health Policies in Kentucky, 1824–1883. PhD dissertation. University of Kentucky, 1984.

**Secondary Sources**

Abel, Emily K. "Family Caregiving in the Nineteenth Century." Emily Hawley Gillespie and Sarah Gillespie, 1858–1888." *Bulletin of the History of Medicine* 68 no. 4 (1994): 573–99.

Achenbaum, Andrew. "The Obsolescence of Old Age in America, 1865–1940." *The Journal of Social History* 8 no. 1 (Fall 1974): 48–62.

Alexander, Gregory S. *Commodity and Propriety: Competing Visions of Property in American Legal Thought, 1776–1970*. Chicago and London: University of Chicago Press, 1997.

"Dead Hand and the Law of Trusts in the Nineteenth Century," *Stanford Law Review* 37 no. 5 (May 1985): 1189–266.

Alston, Lee J. and Morton Owen Shapiro. "Inheritance across Colonies: Causes and Consequences." *The Journal of Economic History* 44 no. 2 (June 1984): 277–87.

Aron, Stephen. *How the West Was Lost: The Transformation of Kentucky from Daniel Boone to Henry Clay*. Baltimore, MD: Johns Hopkins University Press, 1996.

Arpey, Andrew W. *The William Freeman Murder Trial: Insanity, Politics and Race*. Syracuse: Syracuse University Press, 2003.

Astor, Aaron. *Rebels on the Border: Civil War, Emancipation and the Reconstruction of Kentucky and Missouri*. Baton Rouge: Louisiana State University Press, 2012.

Ayers, Edward L. *The Promise of the New South: Life after Reconstruction*. New York: Oxford University Press, 1992.

Bainbridge, William Sims. "Religious Insanity in America: The Official Nineteenth Century Theory," *Sociological Analysis* 45 no. 3 (Autumn 1984): 226.

Baird, Nancy Disher. *David Wendel Yandell: Physician of Old Louisville*. Lexington: University Press of Kentucky, 1978.

Ball, Edward. *Slaves in the Family*. New York: Farrar, Straus and Giroux, 1998.

Banner, Stuart. *American Property: A History of How, Why, and What We Own*. Cambridge: Harvard University Press, 2011.

Bardaglio, Peter. *Reconstructing the Household: Families, Sex and the Law in the Nineteenth Century South*. Chapel Hill: University of North Carolina Press, 1995.

Baron, Jane B. "Property and 'No Property,'" *Houston Law Review* 42 no. 5 (January 2006): 1425–49.

Barton, Keith C. "Good Cooks and Washers: Slave Hiring, Domestic Labor and the Market in Bourbon County, Kentucky," *Journal of American History* 84 no. 2 (1997): 436–60.

Basch, Norma. "Equity vs. Equality: Emerging Concepts of Women's Political Status in the Age of Jackson," *Journal of the Early Republic* 3 no. 3 (Autumn 1983): 297–318.

Baynton, Douglas C. "Disability and the Justifications of Inequality in American History." In *The New Disability History: American Perspectives*. Edited by Paul K. Longmore and Lauri Umanski, 33–57. New York and London: New York University Press, 2001.

Beam, John Malcolm William. *The Decline of English Feudalism, 1215–1540*. Manchester: Manchester University Press, 1967.

Belkin, Gary S. "Moral Insanity, Science and Religion in Nineteenth Century America: The Gray-Ray Debate," *History of Psychiatry* 7 (1996): 591–613.

Bercaw, Nancy. *Gendered Freedoms: Race, Rights and the Politics of the Household in the Delta, 1861–1875*. Gainesville: University Press of Florida, 2003.

Biancalana, Joseph. *The Fee Tail and Common Recovery in Medieval England*. New York: Cambridge University Press, 2001.

Billingsley, Carolyn Earle. *Communities of Kinship: Antebellum Families and the Settlement of the Cotton Frontier*. Athens: University of Georgia Press, 2004.

Block, Sharon. "Lines of Color, Sex and Service: Comparative Sexual Coercion in Early America." In *Sex, Love, Race: Crossing Boundaries in North American History*. Edited by Martha Hodes, 141–63. New York: New York University Press, 1999.

Blumenthal, Susanna. "The Deviance of the Will: Policing the Bounds of Testamentary Freedom in Nineteenth Century America," *Harvard Law Review* 119 (February 2006): 959–1034.

"Of Mandarins, Legal Consciousness, and the Cultural Turn in US Legal History." *Law and Social Inquiry* 37 no. 1 (Winter 2012): 167–86.

Bogdan, Robert. *Freak Show: Presenting Human Oddities for Amusement and Profit*. Chicago: University of Chicago Press, 1988.

Brewer, Holly. *By Birth or Consent: Children, Law, & the Anglo-American Revolution in Authority*. Chapel Hill: University of North Carolina Press, 2005.

"Entailing Aristocracy in Colonial Virginia: "Ancient Feudal Restraints" and Revolutionary Reform," *The William and Mary Quarterly* 54 no. 2 (April 1997): 307–46.

Brown, Richard C. "The Free Blacks of Boyle County Kentucky, 1850–1860: A Research Note." *Register of the Kentucky Historical Society* 88 (Autumn 1989): 426–38.

Buccafusco, Christopher J. "Spiritualism and Will(s) in the Age of Contract." February 21, 2008. Available at SSRN: http://ssrn.com/abstract=1096367.

Bynum, Victoria E. *Unruly Women: The Politics of Social and Sexual Control in the Old South*. Chapel Hill: University of North Carolina Press, 1992.

Bynum, William F. *Science and the Practice of Medicine in the Nineteenth Century*. New York: Cambridge University Press, 1994.

Carson, Martha. "Kentucky Married Women's Property Act: An Early Appeal for Justice." *Border States: Journal of the Kentucky-Tennessee American Studies Association* 5 (1985): 20–8.

Channing, Steven. *Kentucky: A Bicentennial History*. New York: W.W. Norton & Co., 1977.

Chused, Richard. "Late Nineteenth Century Married Women's Property Law: Reception of the Early Married Women's Property Acts by Courts and Legislatures." *The American Journal of Legal History* 29 no. 1 (January 1985): 3–35.

"Married Women's Property Law: 1800–1850." *Georgetown Law Review* 71 (1983): 1359–425.

"Married Women's Property and Inheritance by Widows in Massachusetts: A Study of Wills Probated between 1800 and 1850." *Berkeley Women's Law Journal* 2 (Fall 1986): 42–88.

Cogan, Jacob Katz. "Note: The Look Within: Property, Capacity, and Suffrage in Nineteenth-Century America." *Yale Law Journal* 107 (November 1997): 473–98.

Cohen, Morris. "Property and Sovereignty." *Cornell Law Quarterly* 13 (1927): 10–14.

Cole, Thomas R. *The Journey of Life: A Cultural History of Aging in America*. New York: Cambridge University Press, 1992.

Cooley, Thomas. *The Ivory Leg in the Ebony Cabinet: Madness, Race, and Gender in Victorian America*. Amherst: University of Massachusetts Press, 2001.

Cott, Nancy. *Public Vows: A History of Marriage and the Nation*. Cambridge: Harvard University Press, 2000.

Coulter, E. Merton. *The Civil War and Readjustment in Kentucky*. Reprint 1966. Chapel Hill: University of North Carolina Press, 1926.

Cummings, Scott and Michael Price. "Race Relations and Public Policy in Louisville: Historical Development of an Urban Underclass." *Journal of Black Studies* 27 (1997): 615–49.

Davis, Adrienne D. "The Private Law of Race and Sex: An Antebellum Perspective," *Stanford Law Review* 51 (January 1999): 221–88.

Davis, Lennard J. *Enforcing Normalcy: Disability, Deafness, and the Body*. New York: Verso Press, 1995.

deFuria Jr, Joseph W. "Testamentary Gifts Resulting from Meretricious Relationships: Undue Influence or Natural Beneficence?" *Notre Dame Law Review* 64 (1989): 200–21.

Digby, Anne. *Madness, Morality and Medicine: A Study of the York Retreat, 1796–1914*. Cambridge: Cambridge University Press, 1985.

Dowbiggin, Ian. *Inheriting Madness: Professionalization and Psychiatric Knowledge in Nineteenth-Century France*. Berkeley: University of California Press, 1991.

Drake, Richard B. *A History of Appalachia*. Lexington: University of Kentucky Press, 2003.

Dubler, Ariela. "In the Shadow of Marriage: Single Women and the Legal Construction of the Family and the State." *Yale Law Journal* 112 (2003): 1645–51.

Dunn, John. "Consent in the Political Theory of John Locke." *The Historical Journal* 10 no. 2 (1967): 153–82.

Edwards, Laura F. *Gendered Strife and Confusion: The Political Culture of Reconstruction*. Urbana: University of Illinois Press, 1997.

"Law, Domestic Violence, and the Limits of Patriarchal Authority in the Antebellum South." *The Journal of Southern History* 65 no. 4 (1999): 733–70.

"'The Marriage Covenant Is at the Foundation of All Our Rights': The Politics of Slave Marriages in North Carolina after Emancipation." *Law and History Review* 14 no. 1 (Spring 1996): 81–124.

*The People and Their Peace: Legal Culture and the Transformation of Inequality in the Post-Revolutionary South*. Chapel Hill: University of North Carolina Press, 2009.

Ely, James W. Jr. *The Guardian of Every Other Right: A Constitutional History of Property Rights*. 2nd edition. New York and Oxford: Oxford University Press, 1998.

"'There Are Few Subjects in Political Economy of Greater Difficulty': The Poor Laws of the Antebellum South." *American Bar Foundation Research Journal* 10 no. 4 (Autumn 1985): 849–79.

Erickson, Amy Louise. *Women and Property in Early Modern England*. London: Routledge, 1993.

Fellows, Mary Louise. "Wills and Trusts: The Kingdom of the Fathers." *Law and Inequality: A Journal of Theory and Practice* 10 no. 1 (December 1991): 137–62.

Fields, Barbara. *Slavery and Freedom on the Middle Ground: Maryland during the Nineteenth Century.* Yale University Press, 1985.

Fischer, David Hackett. *Growing Old in America*. New York: Oxford University Press, 1977.

Flannery, Michael A. "Kentucky History Revisited: The Role of the Civil War in Shaping Kentucky's Collective Consciousness." *The Filson Club History Quarterly* 71 no. 1 (January 1997): 27–51.

Foner, Eric. *Reconstruction: America's Unfinished Revolution, 1863–1877*. New York: Harper and Row, 1988.

*The Story of American Freedom*. New York: W.W. Norton and Co, 1998.

Forbath, William E., Hendrik Hartog, and Martha Minow. "Legal Histories From Below." *Wisconsin Law Review* (July/August 1985): 759–69.

Foucault, Michel. *Madness and Civilization: A History of Insanity in the Age of Reason*. Translated by Richard Howard. New York: Vintage Books, 1965.

Friedman, Lawrence M. *Dead Hands: A Social History of Wills, Trusts and Inheritance Law*. Stanford: Stanford University Press, 2009.

Fuller, Paul E. *Laura Clay and the Woman's Rights Movement*. Lexington: University of Kentucky Press, 1975.

Genovese, Eugene. "'Our Family, White and Black': Family and Household in the Southern Slaveholders' Worldview." In *In Joy and In Sorrow: Women, Family, and Marriage in the Victorian South, 1830–1900*. Edited by Carol Bleser, 69–87. New York: Oxford University Press, 1991.

Gordon, Robert "Critical Legal Histories." *Stanford Law Review*, 36 no. 1/2, Critical Legal Studies Symposium (January 1984): 57–125.

Greenberg, Kenneth S. *Honor & Slavery: Lies, Duels, Noses, Masks, Dressing as a Woman, Gifts, Strangers, Humanitarianism, Death, Slave Rebellions, The Proslavery Argument, Baseball, Hunting and Gambling in the Old South*. Princeton, NJ: Princeton University Press, 1996.

Grob, Gerald N. *From Asylum to Community: Mental Health Policy in Modern America*. Princeton, NJ: Princeton University Press, 1991.

*Edward Jarvis and the Medical World of Nineteenth-Century America*. Knoxville: University of Tennessee Press, 1978.

*Mental Illness and American Society, 1875–1940*. Princeton, NJ: Princeton University Press, 1983.

"Presidential Address: Psychiatry's Holy Grail: The Search for the Mechanisms of Mental Diseases." *Bulletin of the History of Medicine* 72 no. 2 (1998): 189–219.

Groneman, Carol. *Nymphomania: A History*. New York: W.W. Norton, 2000.

Gross, Ariela J. "Beyond Black and White: Cultural Approaches to Race and Slavery." *Columbia Law Review* 101 (April 2001): 640–89.

*Double Character: Slavery and Mastery in the Antebellum Southern Courtroom*. Princeton, NJ: Princeton University Press, 2000.

Grossberg, Michael.*Governing the Hearth: Law and Family in Nineteenth Century America*. Chapel Hill: University of North Carolina Press, 1985.

*A Judgment for Solomon: The d'Hautville Case and Legal Experience in Antebellum America*. New York: Cambridge University Press, 1996.

Hakkonssen, Lisabeth. *Medicine and Morals in the Enlightenment: John Gregory, Thomas Percival and Benjamin Rush*. The Wellcome Series in the History of Medicine, Clio Medica 44. Atlanta: Rodopi, 1997.

Harris, J. William. *Plain Folk and Gentry in a Slave Society: White Liberty and Black Slavery in Augusta's Hinterlands*. New Hampshire: University Press of New England, 1985.

Harris, William C. *Lincoln and the Border States: Preserving the Union*. Lawrence: University Press of Kansas, 2011.

Harrison, Lowell Hayes. *The Civil War in Kentucky*. Lexington: University Press of Kentucky, 2009.

Harrison, Lowell Hayes and James C. Klotter. *A New History of Kentucky*. Lexington: University Press of Kentucky, 1997.

Hartog, Hendrik. "Lawyering, Husbands' Rights and the 'Unwritten Law' in Nineteenth Century America." *Journal of American History* 84 no 1 (1997): 67–96.

*Man and Wife in America: A History*. Cambridge and London: Harvard University Press, 2000.

"Marital Exits and Marital Expectations in Nineteenth Century America." *Georgetown Law Journal* 80 (1991): 109–29.

"Mrs. Packard on Dependency." *Yale Journal of Law and the Humanities* 1 (December 1988): 79–103.

"Snakes in Ireland: A Conversation with Willard Hurst." *Law and History Review*, 12 no. 2. (Autumn 1994): 370–90.

*Someday All of This Will be Yours: A History of Inheritance and Old Age.* Cambridge: Harvard University Press, 2012.

Hindus, Michael. *Prison and Plantation: Crime, Justice, and Authority in Massachusetts and South Carolina, 1767–1878.* Chapel Hill: University of North Carolina Press, 1980.

Hoff, Joan. *Law, Gender, and Injustice: A Legal History of Women.* New York: New York University Press, 1991.

Hodes, Martha. *White Women, Black Men: Illicit Sex in the Nineteenth Century South.* New Haven: Yale University Press, 1997.

Horine, Emmet Field. *Biographical Sketch and Guide to the Writings of Charles Caldwell, M.D.* Brooks, KY: High Acres Press, 1960.

Horwitz, Morton. *The Transformation of American Law, 1780–1860.* Cambridge: Harvard University Press, 1979.

*Transformation of American Law, 1870–1960: The Crisis in Legal Orthodoxy.* New York: Oxford University Press, 1992.

Howard, Victor B. "The Kentucky Press and the Negro Testimony Controversy." *Register of the Kentucky Historical Society* 71 (April 1974): 111–42.

Howington, Arthur F. "'Not in the Condition of a Horse or an Ox': *Ford v. Ford*, the Law of Testamentary Manumission, and the Tennessee Court's Recognition of Slave Humanity." *Tennessee Historical Quarterly* 34 no. 3 (1975): 249–65.

Hughes, John S. "Labeling and Treating Black Mental Illness in Alabama, 1861–1910." *The Journal of Southern History* 58 (August 1993): 435–60.

*In the Law's Darkness: Isaac Ray and the Medical Jurisprudence of Insanity in Nineteenth Century America.* New York: Oceana Publications, 1986.

Ireland, Robert. *The County Courts in Antebellum Kentucky.* Lexington: University Press of Kentucky, 1972.

*The County in Kentucky History.* Lexington: University Press of Kentucky, 1976.

"Insanity and the Unwritten Law." *The American Journal of Legal History* 32 no. 2 (1988).

*Little Kingdoms: The Counties of Kentucky, 1850–1891.* Lexington: University Press of Kentucky, 1977.

Isenberg, Nancy. *Sex and Citizenship in Antebellum America.* Chapel Hill: University of North Carolina Press, 1998.

Jimenez, Mary Ann. *The Changing Faces of Madness: Early American Attitudes and Treatment of the Insane.* University Press of New England, 1987.

Johnson, Walter. *Soul by Soul: Life inside the Antebellum Slave Market.* Cambridge, MA: Harvard University Press, 1999.

Jones, Bernie D. *Mixed Race Inheritance in the Antebellum South.* Athens: University of Georgia Press, 2009.

Jones, Jacqueline. "The Political Economy of Sharecropping Families: Blacks and Poor Whites in the Rural South, 1865–1915." In *In Joy and In Sorrow:*

*Women, Family, and Marriage in the Victorian South, 1830–1900*. Edited by Carol Bleser, 196–215. New York: Oxford University Press, 1991.
Karlsen, Carol F. *Devil in the Shape of a Woman: Witchcraft in Colonial New England*. New York: Vintage Books, 1987.
Katz, Stanley. "The Politics of Law in Colonial America: Controversies over Chancery Courts and Equity Law in the Eighteenth Century." *Perspectives in American History* V (1971): 485–518.
"Republicanism and the Law of Inheritance in the American Revolutionary Era." *Michigan Law Review* 76 no. 1 (1977): 1–29.
Kerber, Linda K. *No Constitutional Right to Be Ladies: Women and the Obligations of Citizenship*. New York: Hill and Wang, 1999.
Klages, Mary. *Woeful Afflictions: Disability and Sentimentality in Victorian America*. Philadelphia: University of Pennsylvania Press, 1999.
Klausen, Jimmy Casas. "Room Enough: America, Natural Liberty, and Consent in Locke's Second Treatise." *Journal of Politics* 69 no. 3 (2007): 760–9.
Klotter, James C. *The Breckinridges of Kentucky*. Lexington: University of Kentucky Press, 1986.
*Kentucky Justice, Southern Honor, and American Manhood: Understanding the Life and Death of Richard Reid*. Baton Rouge: Louisiana State Press, 2003.
Lawrence Susan. "Iowa Physicians: Legitimacy, Institutions, and the Practice of Medicine, Part One: Establishing a Professional Identity, 1833–1886." *The Annals of Iowa* 62 (Spring 2003): 151–200.
Lebsock, Suzanne. *The Free Women of Petersburg: Status and Culture in a Southern Town, 1784–1860*. New York: W.W. Norton & Co., 1984.
Leslie, Kent Anderson. *Woman of Color, Daughter of Privilege: Amanda America Dickson, 1849–1893*. Athens, GA and London: University of Georgia Press, 1995.
Lucas, Marion Brunson. *A History of Blacks in Kentucky from Slavery to Segregation, 1760–1891*. Lexington: University of Kentucky Press, 2003.
Lunbeck, Elizabeth. *The Psychiatric Persuasion: Knowledge, Gender and Power in Modern America*. Princeton, NJ: Princeton University Press, 1995.
Marshall, Anne Elizabeth. *Creating a Confederate Kentucky: The Lost Cause and Civil War Memory in a Border State*. Chapel Hill: University of North Carolina Press, 2010.
McCandless, Peter. *Moonlight, Magnolias and Madness: Insanity in South Carolina from the Colonial Period to the Progressive Era*. Chapel Hill: University of North Carolina Press, 1996.
McCurry, Stephanie. *Masters of Small Worlds: Yeoman Households, Gender Relations, and the Political Culture of the Antebellum South Carolina Low Country*. New York: Oxford University Press, 1995.
McDowell, Gary F. *Equity and the Constitution: The Supreme Court, Equitable Relief and Public Policy*. Chicago: University of Chicago Press, 1982.
Mensel, Robert E. "Right Feeling and Knowing Right: Insanity in Testators and Criminals in Nineteenth Century American Law." *Oklahoma Law Review* 58 (Fall 2005): 397–437.

Mohr, James C. *Doctors and the Law: Medical Jurisprudence in Nineteenth Century America*. New York: Oxford University Press, 1993.

"The Paradoxical Advance and Embattled Retreat of the 'Unsound Mind': Evidence of Insanity and the Adjudication of Wills in Nineteenth Century America." *Historical Reflections* 24 no. 3 (1998): 415–35.

Moss, Kay, ed. *Southern Folk Medicine, 1750–1820*. Columbia: University of South Carolina Press, 1999.

Murphy, Lamar Riley. *Enter the Physician: The Transformation of Domestic Medicine, 1760–1860*. Tuscaloosa: University of Alabama Press, 1991.

Murray, Mary. *The Law of the Father: Patriarchy in the Transition from Feudalism to Capitalism*. London: Routledge Press, 1995.

Murthy, Veena K. "Undue Influence and Gender Stereotypes: Legal Doctrine or Indoctrination?" *Cardozo Women's Law Journal* 4 (1997): 105–35.

Narrett, David E. *Inheritance and Family Life in Colonial New York City*. Ithaca: Cornell University Press, 1992.

Neely, Jeremy. *The Border between Them: Violence and Reconstruction on the Kansas-Missouri Line*. Columbia: University of Missouri Press, 2008.

Niedermeier, Lynn E. *Eliza Calvert Hall: Kentucky Author and Suffragist*. Lexington: University of Kentucky Press, 2007.

Novak, William. "Law, Capitalism, and the Liberal State: The Historical Sociology of James Willard Hurst." *Law and History Review* 18 no. 1 (Spring 2000): 97–145.

Orth, John. "After the Revolution: 'Reform' of the Law of Inheritance," *Law and History Review* 10 no. 1 (Spring 1992): 33–44.

Parsons, Elaine Frantz. *Manhood Lost: Fallen Drunkards and Redeeming Women in the Nineteenth Century United States*. Baltimore, MD: Johns Hopkins University Press, 2003.

Pitts, Yvonne. "Disability, Scientific Authority, and Women's Political Participation in the Turn of the Twentieth Century United States." *Journal of Women's History* 24 no. 2 (Summer 2012): 37–61.

"'I Desire to Give My Black Family Their Freedom': Manumissions, Inheritance, and Visions of Family in Antebellum Kentucky." In *Women Shaping the South: Creating and Confronting Change*. Edited by Angela Boswell and Judith McArthur. Columbia: University of Missouri Press, 2006.

Porter, Ray. *Madness: A Brief History*. New York: Oxford University Press, 2002.

Reid, John Phillip. *Rule of Law: The Jurisprudence of Liberty in the Seventeenth and Eighteenth Centuries*. Dekalb: Northern Illinois University Press, 2004.

Richards, Penny L. "'Beside Her Sat Her Idiot Child': Families and Developmental Disability in Mid-Nineteenth Century America." In *Mental Retardation in America: A Historical Reader*. Edited by Steven Noll and James W. Trent Jr., 65–79. New York: New York University Press, 2004.

Rosenberg, Charles E. and Janet Golden. *Framing Disease: Studies in Cultural History*. New Brunswick, NJ: Rutgers University Press, 1992.

Ross, Brian Alan. "Undue Influence and Gender Inequity." *Women's Rights Law Reporter* 19 (Fall 1997): 97–119.

Rothman, David J. *The Discovery of the Asylum: Social Order and Disorder in the New Republic*. Boston: Little, Brown, 1990.

*The Discovery of the Asylum: Social Order and Disorder in the New Republic*. Boston and Toronto: Little, Brown and Co., 1971.

Rothman, Joshua. *Notorious in the Neighborhood: Sex and Families across the Color Line in Virginia, 1787–1861*. Chapel Hill: University of North Carolina Press, 2003.

Russett, Cynthia Eagle. *Sexual Science: The Victorian Construction of Womanhood*. Cambridge: Harvard University Press, 1989.

Ryan, Mary P. *Cradle of the Middle Class : The Family in Oneida County, New York, 1790–1865*. Cambridge and New York: Cambridge University Press, 1981.

Salmon, Marylynn. *Women and the Law of Property in Early America*. Chapel Hill and London: University of North Carolina Press, 1986.

Scull, Andrew. *Social Order/Mental Disorder: Anglo-American Psychiatry in Historical Perspective*. Berkeley: University of California Press, 1989.

Schafer, Judith. *Becoming Free, Remaining Free: Manumission and Enslavement in New Orleans, 1846–1862*. Baton Rouge: Louisiana State University Press, 2003.

Schweber, Howard. "The 'Science' of Legal Science: The Model of the Natural Sciences in Nineteenth-Century American Legal Education." *Law and History Review* 17 no. 3 (Fall 1999): 421–66.

Shammas, Carole. "English Inheritance Law and Its Transfer to the Colonies." *American Journal of Legal History* 31 no. 3 (April 1987): 145–63.

*A History of Household Government in America*. Charlottesville: University of Virginia Press, 2002.

Shammas, Carole, Marylynn Salmon, and Michel Dahlin. *Inheritance in America from Colonial Times to the Present*. New Brunswick and London: Rutgers University Press, 1987.

Shorter, Edward. *A History of Psychiatry: From the Era of the Asylum to the Age of Prozac*. New York: Wiley, 1997.

Sicherman, Barbara. "The Uses of a Diagnosis: Doctors, Patients, and Neurasthenia." *Journal of the History of Medicine and Allied Sciences* 32 (1977): 33–54.

Siegel, Reva B. "The Modernization of Marital Status Law: Adjudicating Wives' Rights to Earnings, 1860–1930," *Georgetown Law Journal* 82 (1995): 2127–211.

"She the People: The Nineteenth Amendment, Sex Equality, Federalism, and the Family." *Harvard Law Review* 115 (February 2002): 947–1046.

"Why Equal Protection No Longer Protects: The Evolving Forms of Status-Enforcing State Action." *Stanford Law Review* 49 (1997): 1111–48.

Smith-Rosenberg, Carroll. "Discourses of Sexuality and Subjectivity: The New Woman, 1870–1936." in *Hidden From History: Reclaiming the Gay and Lesbian Past*. Edited by Martin Bauml Duberman, Martha Vicinus, and George Chauncey Jr., 264–80. New York: NAL Books, 1989.

"The Hysterical Woman: Sex Roles and Role Conflict in Nineteenth-Century America." In *Disorderly Conduct: Visions of Gender in Victorian America*. New York: Knopf, 1985.

Sommerville, Diane Miller. *Rape and Race in the Nineteenth Century South*. Chapel Hill: University North Carolina Press, 2004.

Spear, Julia Cowan. "Undue Influence in Louisiana: What It Was, What It Is, What It Might Be." *Loyola Law Review* 43 (Fall 1997): 443–74.

Spitko, Gary. "Gone But Not Conforming: Protecting the Abhorrent Testator from Majoritarian Cultural Norms Through Minority-Culture Arbitration." *Case Western Law Review* (Winter 1999): 275–314.

Sprague, Stuart Seely. "The Kentucky Pocket Plantation: Sources and Research Strategies, Mason County as a Case Study." *The Filson Club Quarterly* 71 no. 1 (January 1997): 69–86.

Stanley, Amy Dru. *From Bondage to Contract: Wage Labor, Marriage and the Market in the Age of Emancipation*. New York: Cambridge University Press, 1998.

Stevenson, Brenda. *Life in Black and White: Family and Community in the Slave South*. New York: Oxford University Press, 1996.

Sullivan, Kathleen. *Constitutional Context: Women and Rights Discourse in Nineteenth Century America*. Baltimore, MD: Johns Hopkins University Press, 2007.

Sussman, Marvin B., Judith N. Cates, and David T. Smith. *The Family and Inheritance*. Russell Sage Foundation, New York, 1970.

Tachau, Mary K. Bonsteel. *Federal Courts in the Early Republic: Kentucky, 1789–1816*. Princeton, NJ: Princeton University Press, 1978.

Tallant, Harold B. *Evil Necessity: Slavery and Political Culture in Antebellum Kentucky*. Lexington: University of Kentucky Press, 2003.

Thomson, Rosemarie Garland. *Extraordinary Bodies: Figuring Physical Disability in American Culture and Literature*. New York: Columbia University Press, 1997.

ed. *Freakery: Cultural Spectacles of the Extraordinary Body*. New York: New York University Press, 1996.

Tomlins, Christopher L. *Law, Labor, and Ideology in the Early American Republic*. New York: Cambridge University Press, 1993.

Torrey, Fuller E., and Judy Miller. *The Invisible Plague: The Rise of Mental Illness from 1750 to the Present*. New Brunswick and London: Rutgers University Press, 2001.

Trent, James Jr. *Inventing the Feeble Mind: A History of Mental Retardation in the United States*. Berkeley and London: University of California Press, 1994.

Tushnet, Mark V. *The American Law of Slavery, 1810–1860: Considerations of Humanity and Interest*. Princeton, NJ: Princeton University Press, 1981.

Waldinger, Robert. "The Sleep of Reason: John P. Gray and the Challenge of Moral Insanity." *Journal of the History of Medicine* 34 no. 2 (April 1979): 163–79.

Waldrep, Christopher. "The Impact of Race Law on Kentucky." *The Register of the Kentucky Historical Society* 90 no. 2 (Spring 1992): 165–82.

Warner, John Harley. "The Fall and Rise of Professional Mystery: Epistemology, Authority, and the Emergence of Laboratory Medicine in Nineteenth-Century America." In *The Laboratory Revolution in Medicine*. Edited by Andrew Cunningham and Perry Williams. Cambridge: Cambridge University Press, 1992.

*The Therapeutic Perspective: Medical Practice, Knowledge, and Identity in America, 1820–1885*. Cambridge, MA: Harvard University Press, 1986.

Wecht, Cyril H. "The History of Legal Medicine." *Journal of the American Academy of Psychiatry and the Law* 33 no. 2 (June 2005): 245–51.

Welke, Barbara. *Recasting American Liberty: Gender, Race, Law and the Railroad Revolution*. New York: Cambridge University Press, 2001.

Wendell, Susan. *The Rejected Body: Feminist Philosophical Reflections on Disability*. New York: Routledge, 1996.

White, Ronald. "Custodial Care for the Insane at Eastern State Hospital in Lexington, Kentucky, 1824–1844." *Filson Club Quarterly* 62 (1988): 303–35.

"John Rowan Allen, M.D., and the Early Years of the Psychiatric Profession in Kentucky, 1844–1854." *Filson Club Quarterly* 63 (January 1989): 5–23.

"William Stout Chipley and the Evolution of the Medical Superintendency at the Eastern State Lunatic Asylum, 1855–1869." *Filson Club Quarterly* 69 (April 1995): 140–58.

Wiggins, Sarah Woolfolk. "A Victorian Father: Josiah Gorgas and His Family." In *In Joy and In Sorrow: Women, Family, and Marriage in the Victorian South, 1830–1900*. Edited by Carol Bleser, 233–52. New York: Oxford University Press, 1991.

Wilf, Steven. *Law's Imagined Republic: Popular Politics and Criminal Justice in Revolutionary America*. New York: Cambridge University Press, 2010.

Woodward, Vann C. "Introduction." In *In Joy and In Sorrow: Women, Family, and Marriage in the Victorian South, 1830–1900*. Edited by Carol Bleser. New York: Oxford University Press, 1991.

Worby, Sam. *Law and Kinship in Thirteenth-Century England*. Woodbridge Royal Historical Society: Boydell Press, 2010.

Works Project Administration. *Medicine and its Development in Kentucky*. Louisville, KY: Standard Printing Company, 1940.

Wright, George C. *Life Behind a Veil: Blacks in Louisville Kentucky, 1865–1930*. Baton Rouge: Louisiana State University Press, 1985.

*Racial Violence in Kentucky, 1865–1940: Lynching, Mob Rule and "Legal Lynchings."* Baton Rouge: Louisiana State University Press, 1990.

Wyatt-Brown, Bertram. *Southern Honor: Ethics and Behavior in the Old South*. New York and Oxford: Oxford University Press, 1982.

# Index